ROUTLEDGE LIBRARY EDITIONS:
THE HISTORY OF
ECONOMIC THOUGHT

Volume 10

# PROPERTY MARKETS AND THE STATE IN ADAM SMITH'S SYSTEM

# PROPERTY MARKETS AND THE STATE IN ADAM SMITH'S SYSTEM

ROBERT BOYDEN LAMB

Routledge
Taylor & Francis Group
LONDON AND NEW YORK

First published in 1987 by Garland Publishing, Inc.

This edition first published in 2017
by Routledge
2 Park Square, Milton Park, Abingdon, Oxon OX14 4RN

and by Routledge
711 Third Avenue, New York, NY 10017

*Routledge is an imprint of the Taylor & Francis Group, an informa business*



*British Library Cataloguing in Publication Data*
A catalogue record for this book is available from the British Library

ISBN: 978-1-138-29250-5 (Set)
ISBN: 978-1-315-23288-1 (Set) (ebk)
ISBN: 978-1-138-23059-0 (Volume 10) (hbk)
ISBN: 978-1-315-31798-4 (Volume 10) (ebk)

**Publisher's Note**
The publisher has gone to great lengths to ensure the quality of this reprint but points out that some imperfections in the original copies may be apparent.

**Disclaimer**
The publisher has made every effort to trace copyright holders and would welcome correspondence from those they have been unable to trace.

# PROPERTY MARKETS AND THE STATE IN ADAM SMITH'S SYSTEM

Robert Boyden Lamb

*Garland Publishing, Inc., New York & London*
*1987*

**Library of Congress Cataloging-in-Publication Data**

Lamb, Robert, 1941–
Property markets and the state in Adam Smith's system.

(Political theory and political philosophy)
Originally presented as the author's thesis—London School of Economics, 1970.
Bibliography: p.
1. Smith, Adam, 1723–1790—Contributions in political science. 2. Property. I. Title. II. Series.
JC176.S63L36 1987 320.5′092′4 86-26981
ISBN 0-8240-0823-5

All volumes in this series are printed
on acid-free, 250-year-life paper.

Printed in the United States of America

This book is dedicated to Nancy Lamb.

PROPERTY MARKETS AND THE STATE IN ADAM SMITH'S SYSTEM

## TABLE OF CONTENTS

# NOTE CONCERNING ABBREVIATIONS AND EDITIONS OF WORKS USED

Works of ADAM SMITH

Draft - "An Early Draft of Part of the Wealth of Nations" ed W. R. Scott in W. R. Scott, Adam Smith as Student and Professor (Glasgow, 1937).

Lectures - Jurisprudence or notes from the Lectures on Justice, Police, Revenue and Arms Delivered in the University of Glasgow by Adam Smith in Edwin Cannan ed., Lectures on Justice, Police, Revenue and Arms delivered .. by Adam Smith ... reported by a student in 1763 (Oxford, 1896).

- Lectures on Rhetoric and Belles Lettres Delivered in the University of Glasgow by Adam Smith reported by a student in 1762-3 ed. John M. Lothian (London, 1963).

EPS - Essays on Philosophical Subjects, 1795 (Basil, 1799).

TMS - The Theory of Moral Sentiments: or An Essay Towards an Analysis of the Principles by which Men Naturally Judge Concerning the Conduct and Character, First of Their Neighbours, and Afterwards of Themselves. Twelfth ed. in one volume (London, 1907). To which is added, "A Dissertation On The Origin Of Languages."

WN - An Inquiry into the Nature and Causes of the Wealth of Nations, ed. Edwin Cannon fifth ed. (in two volumes) (London, 1950) (reprinted in the University Paperback series London, 1961).

AR - "Adam Smith on the American Revolution: An Unpublished Memorial," ed. G. H. Guttridge, American Historical Review XXXVIII (1932-3) p. 714-20.

- "A Letter to William Stratham concerning the Death of David Hume, Nov. 9. 1776, "Scots Magazine, January 1777 (edition cited: in David Hume, Essays Moral, Political and Literary ed. T.H. Green and T. H. Grose Vol. I. London 1912).

- A Dictionary of the English Language, by Samuel Johnson Edinburgh Review January 1755 Appendix (anonymous).

- "A Letter to the Authors of the Edinburgh Review," Edinburgh Review July 1755 (anonymous).

Works - The Works of Adam Smith, ed. Dugald Stewart, 5 vols. (London, 1811-12).

# CHAPTER I

## INTRODUCTION

The extraordinary influence of the Wealth of Nations[1] was largely due to the rich complexity of the work. It provided readers of different and even contradictory views with the certainty that in Smith they had found a kindred spirit. Members of Parliament whose corruption and policies Smith had attacked in the book were among those who most fully endorsed it for many of its policies and statements on property rights.

The complexity of the Wealth of Nations reflected the very wide range of Smith's thought, and the absence of any guide in his work as to which theories (out of the many he presented) were the most important.

This book is an attempt to explain one theory - the strange, ambiguous misture of ideas that make up Smith's theory of property. I shall examine it fully to see what Smith said, what

---

1 WN op.cit. in note on abbreviations. Adam Smith's Wealth of Nations although it was first published in 1776 was promised to the public seventeen years previously in 1759, (in the last sentence of the Theory of Moral Sentiments). See John Rae, Life of Adam Smith, ed Jacob Viner (New York, 1965). p. 284. Since 1895 Rae's book has remained the standard biography. Hereafter it will be cited as Life. Jacob Viner has a "Guide to John Rae's Life of Adam Smith" in the 1965 edition cited hereafter as "Guide". See also Dugald Stewart "Account of the Life and Writings of Adam Smith" Extracts from the Transactions of the Royal Society of Edinburgh, Vol. 3, read by Mr. Stewart January 21 and March 18, 1793. (Edinburgh 1793). Stewart's "Account" was appended to Adam Smith's Essays on Philosophical Subjects (Basl 1799) and has since been included in many works of Smith as a biographical introduction.

he really meant, and what can be logically deduced from it.

Since Smith's theory of property was central to his social, economic and political thought it provides a key to understanding the ambuguities and unresolved conflicts in the rest of his social analysis. This book will therefore also attempt to relate some of the ramifications of the theory of property to Smith's general theory of society.

In the Wealth of Nations Smith grappled with most of the fundamental property issues of his age. These were extremely complex. They were complex because of the actual physical changes taking place in the production of property with the industrial revolution, because of the consequent changes in property law, and above all, because the philosophical basis of the theory of property was changing radically.

Therefore, although Smith adopted ambiguous and sometimes conflicting theories to explain these changes in property he cannot be accused simply of random, unsystematic thinking. The real explanation is that Smith was a great eclectic who combined the different disciplines of his age in a comprehensive study of society. In him we find the multitude of currents from the Enlightenment before him, and the flickerings of the methodology of the social sciences which were to follow him. To be such a transitional figure was no mean achievement. Smith epitomised his time - a transitional period in which men were breaking with a way of thinking concerned primarily with moral considerations into a period of empirical enquiry.

Yet., although Smith was wrenching social thought from a metaphysical heritage and attempting to found a new age of positive analysis, his thought was caught up in the midst of this process. Passages of his pure positive analysis seem strangely embedded within a normative argument concerning the improvement of individuals and the state. He was not wholly, or even primarily a positive analyst. Although the framework in which he conceived political economy was that of traditional "moral philosophy",[1] and particularly within that branch known as "jurisprudence," he was not chained by this framework of philosophic thought. The formal traditional structure of his thought was there, but it was not rigidly adhered to, and sometimes it was completely dispensed with. Smith demonstrated that in many ways property theory was becoming too important in modern commerical society, to be dealt with only as a minor sub-section of the formal traditional system of philosophical thought. The actual development of production and transformation of the physical landscape of Britain was imposing itself on Smith and other thinkers who attempted to

---

1 TMS. op. cit. The Publication of Adam Smith's Theory of Moral Sentiments in 1759 was the distillation of many years university lectures. It brought Smith almost immediately a considerable acclaim as one of the foremost moral philosophers of his time. See Life p. 141-150 for current opinions of the work during Smith's life. See A. L. Macfie, "Adam Smith's Theory of Moral Sentiments" in Scottish Journal of Political Economy VIII (1961) p. 12-27, for a description of how seriously Smith's moral theory is still taken.

theorize about property in the traditional manner. This property development and change were not explained by, nor fully included within, previous scholastic thought.

II

Adam Smith belonged to a group of Scottish authors in the 18th century which is now known as "The Scottish Historical School".1 This group, of which Smith was a key member, consisted of social theorists who believed that historical progress was founded upon "the change in the nature of property". Because property ws constantly changing, Smith offers only one static or semi-legal definition of property for his students in his lectures at Glasgow University.

> Property is our posessions of every kind, which if any way lost, or taken from us by stealth or violence, may be redemanded a quocemque possessore.2

However, a legal definition of property such as we find in 18th Century Scottish legal texts, dealing with "personality and

---

1 To be discussed in the following chapter.

2 Lectures, p. 4. For a history of Smith's Lectures see Edwin Cannan's Introduction. These Lectures were first published in London in 1896. They were neither written nor approved by Smith and were unknown until discovered by Cannan. They had been recorded and compiled by a student from Adam Smith's spoken lectures delivered at the University of Glasgow about 1763, the final year of Smith's professorship. For additional information about Smith's Lectures and for a comparison of this version of them with those recollections of other students see "Account" xvi-xix and "Guide" pp. 10-12.

reality",[1] "movables and immovables" is not what Smith was investigating. Nor was this the way he used the term property after the introductory remarks in his lectures.

Smith and the Scottish Historical School as moral philosophers and historians were concerned with "the change in the nature of property". They began with the assumption that a general definition of property or property rights in thirteenth century feudal Britain would not be identical with the definition in the commercial age of Britain in 1776. For this thesis, however, some preliminary definition of property may be useful to orient our subject.

A dictionary definition of property as "thing owned, possession(s)"[2] is too brief. Likewise, the general definition in The International Encyclopedia of the Social Sciences: "What is owned is property"[3] takes too much for granted. They both require the reader to investigate "ownership".

---

1 Peter Stein "The General Notions of Contract and Property in 18th Century Scottish thought." Judicial Review (1963) pp. 1-13 "Legal Thought in Eighteenth Century Scotland", Juridical Review, (no Vol.) (1957) pp. 1-20. And see K. E. Digby, An Introduction to the Law of Real Property (Oxford, 1892) pp. 176, 301. And see John C. Grey, Restraints Upon the Alienation of Property (Boston, 1895) Introduction.

2 The Concise Oxford Dictionary, fifth ed. (Oxford, 1964), p. 981.

3 International Encyclopedia of the Social Sciences. (Urbanna. Ill. 1968) Vol. 12, p. 590.

No definition beyond "ownership" or "thing(s) owned" is stated by Richard Schlatter in his Private Property: The History of an Idea.[1] Ernest Beaglehole, in his book Property restricts property to "appropriation" by persons "capable of enjoying it".[2] Adam Smith considered labour to be man's fundamental property, but he argued that it was certainly not necessarily enjoyed, nor was it appropriated, but was naturally part of each man.

Finally, L. T. Hobhouse's definition in Property, Its Duties and Its Rights, is perhaps the best we can hope for to make clear that property is a fundamental relationship between man, yet capable of constant change and development. Hobhouse says:

> Property is from the first ... a right recognized [by others determining] what sort of exclusive control is exerted over things and by whom.[3]

Having settled on a general definition of property we come then to what is a theory of property and what must it answer? Schlatter insists that the general questions it must answer are:

> What reasons can a man give for calling a thing his own? How are we to distinguish valid claims of ownership from those which

---

1 Richard Schlatter, Private Property: The History of An Idea (London, 1951).

2 Ernest Beaglehole, Property (London, 1931) p. 132.

3 Property, Its Duties and Rights: Historically, Philosophically, and Religiously Regarded. Essays by Various Writers ed. Charles Gore (London, 1922) p. 12. L. T. Hobhouse's chapter entitled "The Historical Evolution of Property in Fact and Idea."

> are unjust? A history of the answers to these questions is a history of the theory of property.[1]

Another simpler definition has been suggested by Mark Blaug: "A property theory must explain who owns what and why and how ownership can be transferred?" This definition appears useful for our investigation if we recognize that it leaves open the question of "what" is or can be owned. That is, the exact form of property is left free to change. And second, this definition leaves open what is meant by "to own" or "ownership".

III

This book will analyze the property theory of Adam Smith from the standpoint of political philosophy and economic theory. I will be especially concerned with Smith's theoretical formulation of the relations between the possession of property and the creation, the control, and the improvement of the state.

From the time of Plato and Aristotle the relation between property and government has been one of the vital mainsprings of Western political thought. Plato's famous search for justice in his Republic led him to stipulate that the "guardians" with no private property must govern the lower orders and artizans who had small amounts of property. Plato thus set many of the terms of the arguments of political theory which have raged ever since

---

1 Schlatter, op. cit., p. 9.

concerning property owners and control of government; political rights and possession of wealth; property as a natural or a state creation; and the form of property and mode of its exchange or distribution in the ideal state.

What were the questions about the state's relations to property which were current in Smith's time? Except for discussions of mercantile state policy and some theoretical discussions of currency and legal property questions, property theory had for centuries been part of scholastic Moral Philosophy; an abstract subject conversed upon in the universities and the church, and to some extent in clubs and social gatherings. These discussions in the universities1 centred upon theories of greater or lesser antiquity: notably of Aristotle, St. Augustine, Puffendorf, Grotius, and the more modern theories of Locke, Harrington and Montesquieu. The works of both Mandeville and Hobbes were usually omitted from university curricula because of their religious and moral views.2

In 1700 the theoretical discussion of "Property" in English universities was not generally concerned with facts or with an

---

1 Life, pp. 9, 15, 54-56.

2 The narrowness and decadence of the English universities in an age of vigorous intellectual writings is accounted for by George Macaulay Trevelian, History of England (London, 1937) p. 322. "It is to be explained in part by the exclusion of Dissenters; in a few exceptions, to the clergy, in a time of great scholarly enthusiasm among laymen." Also see Life pp. 18-28 "At Oxford" esp. p. 24.

analysis of actual production, distribution or markets. It was still largely a discussion of doctrine. These discussions of "property" doctrines were but a small department of formal political enquiries. Locke's theory of the origin of property in men's labour had taken precedence over the theological, or feudal doctrines of property. But the labour theory was contested by adherents of Grotius' and Puffendorf's traditional belief in property's origin from social conventions and civil laws. The prevailing mercantile policy of Britain served to reiforce those property theories which argued for rigid state control over all legal property arrangements, and over foreign and domestic trade.

IV

It is with this as the scholastic background that we must view the significant advance that was made by Francis Hutcheson[1] not only in teaching about and polemically advocating the free

---

1 Francis Hutcheson was Smith's professor of moral philosophy at Glasgow University. See Life pp. 11-15. On Hutcheson's life see the biography in William Leechman's Introduction to Francis Hutcheson, A System of Moral Philosophy. 2 vols. (Glasgow, 1755). Hereafter this work will be cited as System. It is based upon his university lectures and includes the most relevant material for a study of his influence on Smith. Its three parts consist of a discourse on Human Nature, The State of Nature, and third, mainly on Government (with some economy). Hutcheson's philosophy was very much an extension of, and depended far more than Smith's or Hume's, on 17th and 18th century philosophy, economy, and jurisprudence. The great influence of Locke upon him will be examined in detail in a later chapter. Hobbes and Mandeville also exercised an important influence on him as shown by his extensive criticism of them, on their own terms. Shaftesbury is another obvious influence. Hutcheson's works and commentaries upon him are included separately in the bibliography of this thesis.

market, but in partially attempting an empirical method. Hutcheson accepted both the Lockean arguments; concerning the origin of property in each individual's labour,[1] and the original contract of government[2] (though sometimes he believed it to be a useful fiction).[3] And he also accepted the Lockean "Empiricism" whereby man's mind at birth was by natural endowment but a tabula rasa upon which wisdom was written only by gradual learned sensory experience.[4] Property in this theoretical framework was observed not only from the conjectural viewpoint of original labourers but studied empirically in terms of the factual observations and the obvious 'truths' of human psychology.

Property, though still a subsidiary subject in Hutcheson's study of Moral Philosophy was of greater importance than it had been to his scholastic predecessors in the university. Gradually property theory was moving closer to the centre of attention. Conjectural and moral discussions of property began to blend with empirical discussions of the market.

Hutcheson was primarily a moral theorist and it was only a portion of his lectures or writings which was devoted to property

---

1 System, Bk. II, ch. V, p. 294.

2 Francis Hutcheson, Introduction to Moral Philosophy (Glasgow, 1747) p. 285. And see System Bk. II, p. 225 Sequence.

3 Gladys Bryson, Man and Society. The Scottish Inquiry of the 18th Century (Princeton, 1945) p. 161.

4 Ibid. Exp. p.189, 115. And W. R. Scott Francis Hutcheson (Oxford, 1900). Esp. Introduction.

or questions of political economy. However, his influence was extraordinary and, as we shall see, Smith drew considerably upon the broad outlines of Hutcheson's courses and his System of Moral Philosophy to orient his own thought. Smith kept much of the schematic divisions and some of Hutcheson's moral concepts in his own later writings.1

V

Property theory again took a step forward with the Treatises, Enquiry and Essays of David Hume2 which had a significant influence upon Smith and other members of the Scottish School. Hume, like Hutcheson, was not primarily an econmist but the few sections of his works, especially of his Essays, devoted to economic questions were to lay down many of the fundamental

---

1 See especially Life p. 11 where Rae quotes Dugald Stewart. "The lectures of the profound and eloquent Dr. Hutcheson, which he (Smith) had attended previous to his departure from Glasgow, and of which he always spoke in terms of the warmest admiration, had, it may reasonably be presumed, a considerable effect in directing his talents to their proper objects." We are told by Stewart (and more biographical and bibliographical proof is offered by Rae, Scott, and others) that when Smith first came to give his lectures at Glasgow he formed his courses by means of notes and recollection of these of Hutcheson.

2 David Hume, Treatise of Human Nature, 1793 ed. L. A. Selby-Biggs (Oxford, 1960). David Hume, Enquiry Concerning Human Understanding and Concerning the Principles of Morals, ed. L. A. Selby-Biggs, second ed. (Oxford, 1927). (First part originally published 1748; second part 1751). David Hume Essays Moral, Political and Literary, ed. T. G. Green and T. H. Gross (London, 1912). (First part originally published 1741-2, second part 1752) Hume's economics and especially Hume's relation to Adam Smith are dealt with peripherally in the many works on Hume's total philosophy. But this relation of Hume to Smith is dealt with

presuppositions of these later thinkers. Harold J. Laski in his Political Thought in England from Locke to Bentham has argued that Hume's discourses were: "the most powerful dissolvent the century was to see."[1] In fact, says Laski, "The Wealth of Nations would less easily have made its way had not the insight of Hume prepared the road for its reception."[2] Smith and his circle of Glasgow and Edinburgh friends adopted much of his utilitarian approach to state policy (though each with numerous individual qualifications.)

Hume, like Hutcheson, was a firm believer in free trade and the abolition of much of the mercantile policy of restriction, yet he was an advocate of far stronger government and of the subor-

---

especially by Eugene Rotwein in his introduction to Hume's Writings on Economics (Madison, Wisconsin, 1955) esp. Introduction. And Glenn R. Morrow, "The Significance of the Doctrine of Sympathy in David Hume and Adam Smith." Philosophical Review XXXIII (1923).

For discussions of Hume's and Hutcheson's relationship to Adam Smith see especially W. L. Taylor, Francis Hutcheson and David Hume as Predecessors of Adam Smith (Durham, N. Carolina, 1965). See also W. L. Taylor "Eighteenth Century Scottish Political Economy. The Impact on Adam Smith and his Work, of his association with Francis Hutcheson and David Hume "South African Journal of Economics XXIV (1956) pp. 261-276. See also O. H. Taylor: A History of Economic Thought. New York, 1960. pp. 39-48 and Glenn R. Morrow, The Ethical and Economic Theories of Adam Smith, pp. 12-27. (Cornell University Studies in Philosophy, No. 13) (New York, 1923) pp. 12-27. Hereafter cited as Theories. A. L. Macfie, "The Scottish Tradition in Economic Thought", Scottish Journal of Political Economy II (1955) pp. 81-103.

1 Harold J. Laski Political Thought in England from Locke to Bentham (London, 1937) p. 143.

2 Ibid. p. 155.

dination of all questions of property to the civil laws. The extent to which Smith followed his great friend in this advocacy provides one of the key questions of this book.

Throughout Hume's Essays we find the elucidation of a theory of property that rested firmly on empirical and factual evidence. In contrast, we find the property theories of Smith and the Scottish Historical School were far more a blend of moral and empirical thought than was Hume's. Hume was far more detailed than even Smith in the examination of money, interest, credit and even in certain respects in his consideration of the balance of trade. Why Smith did not in his Wealth of Nations go into such great detail on these most important forms of property relations, remains puzzling, especially to those who view Smith as a modern analytical economist. Nor is the explanation for Smith's reticence on interest and money simply that he and Hume were in total agreement and no clarification by Smith was necessary. They disagreed on several currency matters, as is shown by their correspondence. Even in Hume's final letter to Smith just after the publication of the Wealth of Nations in 1776 and soon before Hume's death, he says, "if you were here at my fireside, I should dispute some of your principles."[1]

---

1 David Hume, The Letters of David Hume, ed. J. Y. T. Greig, 2 vols. (Oxford, 1932) Vol. II, pp. 311-12. For an appraisal of this slight disagreement between Smith and Hume see Dugald Stewart "Account" p. xlviii. This passage above is not meant to deny Smith's overall agreement with, and debt to, Hume. As Stewart says: "The political discourses of Mr. Hume were evidently of

The contrast between Hume's incisive discussion of the currency question and Smith's more diffuse treatment of this topic suggests a broader difference in their methods. In theorizing about property Hume used the analytical method almost exclusively, whereas Smith's main emphasis is historical. Of course, Smith used the analytical method also, as in the first two books of the Wealth of Nations which are the basis of classical political economic analysis. But when discussing questions of property, Smith's usual approach was to describe the history of this or that form of property from its origins to the present, not simply to analyze its function abstractly in the present market as Hume was more wont to do.

In discussions of property which Smith engaged in, Hume's analytical view of property probably vied with Hutcheson's moral view. And both of their free market views would naturally have conflicted with the Mercantilist and traditional scholastic views of property and sovereignty. These form the background for Smith's discussions of property theory.[1]

---

greater use to Mr. Smith than any other book that had appeared prior to his lectures." Dugald Stewart, Collected Works, ed. Sir William Hamilton, 11 vols. (Edinburgh, 1854-60) x p. 67.

1 For the broad intellectual background of the 18th century from which these discussions were drawn see Leslie Stephon, op. cit. Vol. II, pp. 47-52, and also see Basil Willey, The Eighteenth Century Background (Harmondsworth, 1962) pp. 117-18, 186-9, 193-8.

## VI

The sorts of questions asked about property in Smith's time thus fell into three distinct categories by modern logical standards. The first set of questions originating in traditional philosophical enquiry were concerned with the "essential" qualities of property and asked: "For what ultimate end was it created?" These "essential" questions about property today might belong strictly to the realm of metaphysical philosophy, if they are still asked at all.

The second kind of questions asked about property in Smith's time were "factual" questions about property ownership: how it was obtained and made legitimate, and how alienated or transferred. Such factual questions of ownership and property control might today be called legal or included under Harold Laswell's definition of the concerns of "Politics" - the study of "who gets what, how, when, and where."

The third type of questions asked about property in Smith's time might today be considered "functional" questions - the province of the economist, who is not primarily interested in who gets what or who owns what, but with whether this or that form of property is more productive, or has an economic function to perform.

The first set of questions concerning the "essential" character of property were typical questions of the seventeenth and eighteenth centuries, although they may seem quite remote from our present interests. Today we are almost totally concerned with the functional and factual aspects of property. In this thesis on Smith's theory of property it is important that functional, factual <u>and</u> essential questions be asked about property because Smith and the other members of the Scottish Historical School were at that juncture of social thought where all three sorts of questions were considered of equal pertinence. Only by considering all three kinds of questions can we hope to understand Smith's entire theory of property or be able to explain its ambiguities. For Smith combined these three studies - philosophy, politics and economics in his "political economy."

## VII

Studies of Smith are plentiful,[1] yet, omitting a handful of exceptions these many works devote only passing reference to Smith's property theory. In the few major works on Smith's thought there is little attention focussed on his property theory specifically. In them, however, certain aspects of Smith's philosophical views of the economy, government and society are explored in detail, and repeatedly touch on his property theory. Therefore, it is these following works which have been most helpful for the preparation of this thesis. Edwin Cannan's two

---

1 Burt Franklin and Francesco Cordasco, <u>Adam Smith A Bibliographical Checklist: An International Record of Critical Writings and Schollarship Relating to Smith and Smithian Theory 1876-1950</u>. Burt Franklin Bibliographical Series III (New York, 1950).

introductions, one to his edition of Smith's Wealth of Nations,[1] and the second to his edition of Smith's Glasgow Lectures on Justice, Police, Revenue and Arms,[2] are of the utmost importance. W. R. Scott's Adam Smith as Student and Professor[3] provides not only important biographical information, and Smith's "Draft of the Wealth of Nations", but also a commentary on Smith's entire social thought.

Four other modern works investigate the interrelations of Smith's economic and philosophic ideas, and have raised some of the questions which this thesis has attempted to answer. These writings include: Jacob Viner's "Adam Smith and Laissez Faire,"[4] Glenn R. Morrow's The Ethical and Economic Theories of Adam Smith,[5] Joseph Cropsey's Polity and Economy,[6] and A. L.

---

1 WN edition already cited.

2 Adam Smith, Lectures op. cit. Introduction.

3 W. R. Scott, Adam Smith as Student and Professor (Glasgow, 1937).

4 Jacob Viner, "Adam Smith and Laissez Faire" first published in Journal of Political Economy, XXXV (1927) pp. 198-232. Though it was reprinted in Adam Smith 1776-1926. ed. John M. Clark, (Chicago, 1928) and in Jacob Viner, The Long View and the Short (Glencoe, Ill, 1958). I will hereafter cite it as "ASLF" and its original page references in JPE to distinguish this article from others in these two later works.

5 Morrow, Theories, op. cit.

6 Joseph Cropsey, Polity and Economy: An Interpretation of the Principles of Adam Smith. (The Hague, 1956).

Macfie's Individual in Society, Papers on Adam Smith.[1] However although these writings have touched on various aspects of theory and policy, the need for a work dealing with Smith's comprehensive theory of property and its relation to the state has not been filled by them.

## VIII

The argument of this book is that Adam Smith's theory of property is the core of his thought. From its ambiguities stem many of the tensions in the rest of his theories. This study examines the ambiguities of his property theory from the standpoint of Smith's background and his objectives.

The Scottish School to which he belonged is considered in order to assess the importance and meaning its members attached to "the history of property and manners." The current developments in agriculture and industry in his time are looked at to see the extent to which these affected his theory of property.

Smith, like John Locke, proclaimed the doctrine of the origin of property in men's labour, and yet justified the inequality of civil property because he accepted the theory that social conventions and the tradition of civil laws were also a proper foundation of property rights. Smith never completely adhered to one of these doctrines exclusively, and at times they tended to conflict.

---

1 A. L. Macfie, Individual in Society, Papers on Adam Smith (London, 1967).

Smith believed that the public "sympathized"[1] with a man's reasonable expectation of reward. Public "sympathy" was therefore the measure by which various claims to property ownership could be judged; whether such claims were based on laws, customs, or the "natural rights" of the labourer. Although Smith said self-interest was the rational motive for acquisitiveness, each man's fundamental desire was to receive the positive "sympathy" of others for his economic situation and eventually to acquire dignity in their eyes. Public "sympathy" was a necessary condition for the persistence of private property and for claims to its rightful ownership.

Smith's property theory was part of his entire system of moral philosophy, and property's self contradictions often stemmed from his conflicting moral, and empirical first principles. How this ambiguity manifested itself is shown by the consideration of his description of property's origin, its existing condition, and its future. These are then related to the original, present and future government which he describes.

This study attempts to show: first, that Smith's primary quest in his property theory was to discover which changes in property were beneficial to men and government and which changes in property were harmful. Secondly, attention is given to the

---

1 Smith's particular use of the term "sympathy" will be discussed in Ch. IV.

kinds of alienation experienced by labourers in tasks with extensive division of labour. Thirdly, this book argues, that according to his various economic theories and political theories, Smith expected that at times strong interventionist government would always be required.

# CHAPTER II

## PROPERTY DURING ADAM SMITH'S LIFETIME: A BRIEF SURVEY.

In the Scottish Universities of Glasgow and Edinburgh of the second half of the eighteenth century there developed a mode of social inquiry based upon the historical, empirical, and conjectural study of property relations. Opinions vary as to how wide was the circle of men meaningfully designated by what Roy Pascal referred to as "The Scottish Historical School."[1]

---

1 Roy Pascal, "Property and Society - The Scottish Historical School of the 18th Century", Modern Quarterly (London) Vol. 1 (1938) pp. 167-178. I use the term "school" for the sake of convenience. Whether there were a sufficient number of shared doctrines, views, methods of analysis or types of similar writings among these Scottish authors to constitute a school is not within the scope of this thesis to analyze. The school is sometimes referred to as "The Common Sense School of Moral Philosophers" and at other times referred to simply as "The Scottish School." I have chosen Pascal's designation of The Scottish Historical School because he uses it to refer to primarily the four authors I will discuss. Pascal considered the characteristic view of property which Adam Smith, Adam Ferguson, John Millar and William Robertson shared to a considerable extent and this is what I will also be concerned with throughout this study. In addition to these authors who will be discussed in this work there were others in the school who wrote on social subjects primarily. These included Lord Kames, Lord Monbodo, James Dunbar, and Gilbert Stuart who also studied various aspects of "Conjectural History". In addition there were other members of the broadly defined Scottish School whose writings were primarily literary criticism or poetry. These included Hugh Blair, Alam Ramsay, William Hamilton and John Home.

By far the most detailed and comprehensive of the studies of the school is Gladys Bryson, Man and Society: The Scottish Inquiry of the Eighteenth Century, op. cit. Three other books in general touch on the School as part of the "Scottish Enlightenment." These are, Charles Ryle Fay, Adam Smith and the Scotland of his Day (Cambridge, 1956) Douglas Young and others, Edinburgh in the Age of Reason (Edinburgh, 1967) David Daiches, The Paradox of Scottish Culture: The Eighteenth Century Experience (Oxford,

Nevertheless the principle members of it are usually said to be Adam Smith, Professor of Moral Philosophy at Glasgow, Adam Ferguson, Professor of Moral Philosophy at Edinburgh, John Millar, Professor of Law at Glasgow, and William Robertson, Professor of History and Principal of Edinburgh University. Since the moral premises and psychology of this "School" were taken largely from their immediate predecessor Francis Hutcheson and their close colleague David Hume I do not think that they should be exluded from "The School". There are certain grounds, but I would argue insufficient ones, for distinguishing Hutcheson and Hume from the Scottish School since far less of their work is concerned with the history of property. But to fail to recognize fully Hutcheson's and Hume's vital significance to the School's, especially to Smith's general System of Moral Philosophy in which property

---

1964). The other literature on the school is contained in articles. The major ones are Ronald L. Meek, "The Scottish Contribution to Marxist Sociology" in John Saville ed. Democracy and the Labour Movement (London, 1954) reprinted in Ronald L. Meek, Economics and Ideology and Other Essays: Studies in the Development of Economic Thought (London, 1967). References will be to the Saville ed. ch. 3 pp. 84-103. A. L. Macfie, "The Scottish Tradition in Economic Thought", op. cit. pp. 81-103. Duncan Forbes, "Scientific Whigism: Adam Smith and John Millar", Cambridge Journal VII (1954) pp. 643-670. Andrew Skinner, "Economics and History - The Scottish Enlightenment," Scottish Journal of Political Economy, 12 (1965) pp. 1-22. William C. Lehmann in his book Adam Ferguson and the Beginnings of Modern Sociology (New York, 1930) considers some aspects of the school. Also Chapter 10 "Eighteenth Century Scottish Thought" in William C. Lehmann, John Millar of Glasgow 1735-1801 (Cambridge, 1960). James Lorimer, "The Economic and Social Philosophy of Adam Smith" submitted for the degree of Ph.D. in the University of London, 1966. He lists the views of several members of the school.

theory was but an integral part, would be to continue the trend of viewing the Scottish School as a somewhat rootless and branchless phenomenon occurring in mid-18th century Scotland. For this study of Adam Smith's theory of property, the relevance of Hume and Hutcheson will be important as sources of influence on Smith; whereas the work of Ferguson, Millar, Robertson, are relevant primarily as colleagues and students who pursued similar modes of thought to Smith.[1] Both groups, to varying extents, shared his method and presumptions. But only the latter developed an historical view that attempted to understand fully society and its change by means of studying empirical and conjectural property development.

A few 18th and 19th century observers as well as several recent ones have noted that the enquiries of these Scottish authors were based on one or two common themes. Dugald Stewart in his original commentaries[1] stated that they shared a certain approach to history, and suggested that property played a significant part in their studies. One recent analyst, Roy Pascal, in his article "Property and Society,"[2] has said that "property" was <u>the key</u> concern of their approach to history. And others, such as Ronald Meek in his article "The Scottish Contribution to

---

1 Dugald Stewart. <u>Works</u> op. cit. X, pp. 67-8.

2 Pascal, op. cit. p. 167.

Marxist Sociology",[1] have included "property" among the central focal points of their work.

Meek and Pascal have stressed that the Scottish School's treatment of property and society was primarily "empirical" and "scientific" and "established the study of modern sociology". On the other hand, the language and the particular moral philosophic context of the Scottish School make it clear that they viewed property theory not simply in scientific or empirical terms but in moral and conjectural terms as well. In fact, Dugald Stewart, their first chronicler, described their method specifically as "Conjectural History". The explanation for this direct clash of traditional vs. modern appraisals is quite understandable. The Scottish School (and Dugald Stewart himself) was largely anchored in the conjectural method and the all encompassing moral philosophic systems of the 18th century. Yet as Meek and Pascal have suggested they also sought and found empirical evidence of men's actual historic property relations and did consciously attempt to establish a new scientific method of social and historical enquiry.[2]

If, as we have suggested, property theories are concerned with who owns what and why, and how ownership is transferred, it

---

1 Meek, "The Scottish Contribution". op. cit. p. 84.

2 It will be shown later that the tendency to blend conjectural and factual methods of enquiry troubled Ferguson, but it appears not to have been recognized completely by others.

may be important to enquire into why they considered property theory so particularly relevant in their time, and so vital to every area of social investigation from Millar's study of feudal chastity laws to Smith's discussion of the Scottish parish schools. What were the questions they asked about property and the disputes they engaged in among themselves regarding the meaning or application of particular property theories? What did they mean by the term property, and what were the actual conditions of property relations they witnessed and were part of during their own times?

We will begin by showing the ways they actually spoke of "property"; and then by describing the actual property conditions they experienced. Smith asserted at the beginning of his Lectures,

> Property and government very much depend on one another ... and the state of property must always vary with the form of government.[1]

The central point of Adam Ferguson's system is that, with the existence of private property, a principle of political development is given; the simultaneous transformations in property and states is thus the focus of his moral and historical enquiries. As he says in The History of Civil Society[2] "property is a

---

1 Lectures, p. 8.

2 Adam Ferguson, An Essay on the History of Civil Society, ed. Duncan Forbes (Edinburgh, 1966) (originally published Edinburgh 1766) p. 82. Hereafter this work will be cited as History.

matter of progress". Property is nowhere static. Property is evolving and with its development it produces "civil antagonisms" between classes which in turn direct social growth and in turn initially cause and then influence Government. "Forms of government make their rise chiefly from the manner in which the members of a state have been originally classed."[1] And men are originally classed primarily by their posession of property. His conception of property theory thus deals not with static but with evolving property, not with static human needs or conditions but with "the progress of property and manners", which dictate the mode of political development.

John Millar in his Origin of the Distinction of Ranks, and Historical View of the English Government[2] founds his system on almost exactly the same understanding of evolving property and its control of the forms of government. Millar says that in order to know what is the best form of government we have to study the past. But really to understand the past we must know the circumstances which produce certain social forms. Such circumstances are the fertility or barrenness of the soil; the nature of the

---

1 History p. 206. And see Pascal, op. cit. p. 174, who notes that "These [class property relations] are the mainspring of social movement," for the entire Scottish School.

2 John Millar, Origin of the Distinction of Ranks, in John Millar of Glasgow op. cit. also in this book is John Millar, Historical View of the English Government. Both these writings by Millar in this book will hereafter be cited as Millar. The chapters by W. C. Lehmann in this work will be cited by the full title John Millar of Glasgow.

labourer required; the size of the population; the proficiency in the arts; the advantages accruing from mutual transactions.1

Millar believed that property was "the foundation of all hereditary influence", the chief basis of "the distinction of permanent ranks in society" and was "the principal circumstance that contributes to reduce [men] under civil government."2 Once again, changes in property relations for Millar, as for Smith and Ferguson, are the motive forces behind social and political change or "progress".3

In general William Robertson's work followed the traditional pattern of historical narrative. However, in several of his works - his History of America,4 History of the Reign of Charles V,5 and even in his general conception of his History of Scotland6 -

---

1 Millar p. 175. In Historical View Millar examines three "natural periods" each from the economic viewpoint. The Anglo-Saxon period for example shows "the effects produced by the gradual acquisition of property" the accumulation of political power, "the usual attendent of property."

2 Millar, p. 122.

3 Millar, p. 175.

4 William Robertson, The History of America in Works, 12 vols, (London, 1812) Vol. VII.

5 William Robertson, The History of the Reign of Charles the Fifth With A View of the Progress of Society in Europe from the Suppression of the Roman Empire, to the Beginning of the Sixteenth Century. 2 Vols. (London, 1857).

6 William Robertson, History of Scotland During the Reigns of Queen Mary and of King James VI till his accession to the Crown of England With a Review of the Scottish HIstory Previous to that Period (Edinburgh, 1840).

we find this same presupposition that change in property relations is the motor of historical development and the cause of political transformation. In _Charles V_ Robertson speaks frequently of "revolution in property"[1] and at one point states the key reason for his interest in such changes in property:

> Upon discovering in what state property was at any particular period, we may determine with precision what was the degree of power possessed by the king of by the nobility at that juncture.[2]

Therefore we may conclude that tracing the effects of changes in property relations on politics and society was a central theme of these four principal members of the Scottish Historical School. It was Smith's particular elaboration of this theme by which The Scottish School was to become known. That is, Smith distingushed four stages[3] in the "History of Civil Society," each distinguished primarily by its mode of property relations. These historic ages of hunting, herding, farming and commerce, will be analyzed at length in later chapters. Suffice it for the present to say that these four historic ages were described by the various members of the school. The principle for distinguishing one age from another in each of their works was "the mode of property relations." The traditional historical periodization into

---

1 Robertson, _Charles V_, op. cit. Vol. 1, p. 355.

2 Cited by Pascal, op. cit., p. 170.

3 WN II, pp. 313-322.

"Barbarian, Greek, Roman and Feudal" ages etc. was not done away with but incorporated into the new "progress of property" scheme which led to comparisons between different kinds of agricultural societies, and different kinds of herding tribes. Into the hunting stage might fit certain ancient societies or certain contemporary Tribes of American Indians. Property history thus cut across the traditional divisions of "ancient" and "modern."1 According to the Scottish School "rude" or "primitive" societies developed into "advanced" or "polished" societies signifying a single line of progress which they called "the natural progress of opulence." Societies, whether supported by hunting since the beginning of human history or currently based upon an advanced form of machine industry, could not only exist at the same time, they could be compared and directly contrasted according to a rough yardstick of co-equal social endeavours know as "the mode of subsistence", or "the state of property and manners".

In their brief speculative efforts to discover the reason for the sudden blossoming of the Scottish School, Skinner, Daiches, Bryson, Meek, Pascal and Lehmann all in passing indicate that the

---

1 Robertson suggests this when he says, Charles V, op. cit., p. 7. "It is not my province to give a minute detail of the progress of government and manners in each particular nation, whose transactions are the object of the following history ... It is necessary to mark the great steps by which they advanced from barbarism to refinement, and to point out those general principles ... [which caused that improvement]. I contend that each of these principle members of the Scottish School sought in history for "principles" of development, more than for a definitive understanding of "singular events."

rapidity of economic advance in Glasgow and Edinburgh must have been a key factor. From the Firth of Forth to the Firth of Clyde commercial and agricultural development was so dramatic, in contrast with the totally isolated areas of the Highlands, that changes in property were bound to fascinate 18th Century Scottish authors. In addition, the growing knowledge of the Indians of North America and of feudal practices still current on the Continent of Europe gave these authors an immediately visible contrast of different forms of social organization with which to compare their own radically changing society. Pascal makes an observation which is characteristic of these recent commentators on the Scottish School when he says:

> Smith and Millar had before their eyes the effects of rapid commercial development; and, as we shall see, the increased interest in and knowledge of the North American Indians gave a real basis to speculations deriving from the contrast between primitive and advance civilization. The close association of the commercial world and the university is illustrated by the number of clubs which sprang into being from the middle of the century, where merchants and professors met. The spirit of enterprise infected the university, and at the time when Smith was giving his famous lectures, Joseph Black discovered the existence of latent heat, and James Watt was working under the protection of the university and was on the eve of perfecting the steam engine.[1]

One cause why property theory was considered so vitally important in the social theories of the Scottish School could certainly

1 Pascal, op. cit., p. 169.

be that the change of property relations they witnessed[1] were a constant subject of dispute and unrest among all groups of the population. The greatest change in property relations affecting the great mass of the people agriculturally, commercially, industrially and legally was the enclosure of the commonlands.

Though the enclosure movement had been long in progress and many of the first English Parliamentary Acts of Enclosure were well over a hundred years old, it was only after 1750 that the vast majority of the individual enclosure acts in England were

---

1 The historical and economic historical material used for this Chapter is drawn primarily from Henry Hamilton The Industrial Revolution in Scotland (Oxford, 1936) and his An Economic History of Scotland in the 18th Century (Oxford, 1963) John Rae: Life of Adam Smith, Viner Guide to the Life of Adam Smith, op. cit., R. H. Campbell, Scotland Since 1707 "The Rise of an Economy 1750 - 1850 (Edinburgh, 1957). An excellent summary of most of the recent conclusions reached in current histories of 18th century Scotland is provided by S. G Checkland, "Scottish Economic History: Recent Work", Economica 31 (1964) pp. 296-313. Alexander Campbell, Journey From Edinburgh Through North Britain 2 Vols. (London, 1801) James Mackinnon, The Social and Industrial History of Scotland From The Union to the Present Time (London, 1921).

Concerning the Economic History of Great Britain in General I have found most helpful: T. S. Ashton The Industrial Revolution 1760-1830 (London, 1962) T. S. Ashton An Economic History of England in the 18th Century (London, 1966) Phyllis Deane, The First Industrial Revolution (London, 1967) Charles Wilson, England's Apprenticeship 1603-1763 (London, 1966) Arhtur Bedford, The Economic History of England 1760-1860 (London, 1965) C. P. Hill, British Economic and Social History 1700-1939 (London, 1966) Arthur Birnie An Economic History of Europe 1760-1939 (London, 1964) Eric Hobsbawm, Industry and Empire (London, 1968) H. A. L. Fisher, A History of Europe Vol. II From the Beginning of the Eighteenth Century to 1935 (London, 1962) Brian Redman Mitchell and Phyllis Deane, Abstract of British Historical Statistics (Cambridge, 1962) Karl Polanyi, The Great Transformation (Boston, Mass., 1957).

pressed through Parliament and brought into force in the mass of individual villages. In Scotland, where there was no necessity for individual Acts of Parliament for enclosure,[1] we find the concentrated effect of common land or "real property" enclosure took place primarily in the second half of the 18th century and forms the background to Smith's and the Scottish School's discussions and theories.

Asthon and others have pointed out the beneficial effects of "enclosure" which brought enormous tracts of land under cultivation for the first time, and which always before had been under common ownership referred to as "The Waste". The enclosures nevertheless did result in the massive shift of population from the South and East to the North and West of Britain, and from the backward rural districts to the new commerical and industrial centres. This progression was not usually over great distances nor in a short space of time but took place in localized waves from the immediate countryside to the nearest town. This was exactly the pattern in Lowland Scotland which had already begun in England. And though the amount of enclosure and the stage of industrial and commercial development was both more primitive and slower to progress in Scotland, the gradual effect on men's

---

1 Two general Acts urging Enclosure but not requiring it, were passed by the Scottish Parliament between 1690-1700 before the Union with England. The division of the land was carried out by the Local Justice of the Peace and the Sherriff. Scottish property law did not allow as many of the broad common rights of the peasants as English Law did.

conception of property was as drastically altered in Ayr and the Lothians as it had been in Suffolk.

The enclosure movement altered the conception of property and property markets as viewed by ordinary people as well as by lawyers, judges, landowners, tennants and legislators. Different forms of enclosure throughout this period became the focal point for new property disputes.[1] The first was of course the division of the "Committee" of "Waste" into separately owned pasture land, then the "common fields" or cultivated scattered strips of arable land which commoners had farmed for centuries in exactly the strip manner and rotation which private farmers and tenants had farmed theirs.[2] Third, there was the effective enclosure of the common roads by townships, companies and even in some cases individuals to make toll roads; then the effective enclosure of the shallower of the most used waterways which could be improved by deepening; and finally, especially in Scotland, the effective enclosure by landowners of the sea shallows off their coastline lands in which grew seaweed (important in the kelp or soda ash extraction industry) or more than normal amounts of fish. Tolls and rents were extracted from the public who had always in the past farmed, fished or gathered freely on the

---

1 John Ramsay of Ochtertyre, Scotland and Scotsmen in the 18th Century 2 Vols (Edinburgh, 1888) (ed. Alexander Alardyce) Vol. II, exp. p. 201. Also see History of Scotland op. cit., pp. 81-85. See also Malcolm Gray, The Highland Economy 1750-1850 (London, 1957) pp. 95-7, 69-70, 79, 81.

2 Hamilton, ibid., pp. 37-45. And see pp. 42, 43, 50, 58, on the "Commities".

common, or had free right of pasage on the roads and waterways.

These countless other lesser forms of private property enclosure from the "Common property" affected the vast majority of the population.1 And the rapidity and concentration of both the enclosures and the successive emigrations to the commercial centres made the change or the "progress of property" relations of central importance to any semi-empirical of scientific study of social development.

In addition to land enclosures which caused emigration to the emerging commercial centres there were also the gradual breakdowns of varying forms of indentured service. Some of these forms of service known as "Statute Labour"2 were light, involving six days a year work on the town roads, but others were more onerous such as the "voluntary slavery" of Scottish miners who were bought and sold with the mines themselves and were unable legally to become free once a boy had first set foot in the pits.3 During the entire last half of the 18th century the lesser forms of indenture were either breaking down, or, where they remained rigid, causing the workmen and tenant farmers to break their

---

1 For the general state of the agricultural populaton and the histroic development of agriculture in the 18th century see James F. Handley, The Agricultural Revolution in Scotland (Glasgow, 1963) and John Prebble, The Highland Clearances (London, 1963.

2 WN II, p. 253 on "Statute Labour".

3 WN I, pp. 116-117, Lectures, pp. 92, 99.

agreements and flee to the towns where they could at last work "as freemen" "for themselves" in the new factories or in trades.[1] These various forms of "service" in Scotland had meant that a workman or a tenant could be called upon almost at will by his landlord,[2] the local laird, the parish kirk, the town council or the millwright. In trades, the rigidly strict statute of apprenticeship which Smith and other members of the Scottish School condemned, caused many to break their agreements of apprenticeship and flee to the new centres where there was a gradual trend towards the breakdown of restrictions and a definite shortening of the number of years "learning" of any particular trade.

Of course these changes in property markets for enclosed land and apprenticeship labor, and the emigration to the towns they both caused were intimately related to the dramatic change in industry which occurred during the 18th century. The "Industrial Revolution" in its emergence in Scotland was far later and far slower to develop than in England but the drastic change it caused in men's conception of property producton was quite similar.[3]

The physical change in the actual landscape of villages and towns from Kirkcaldy to the Clyde valley with the erection of

---

1 And in 1775 the miners "voluntary slavery" was abolished by Parliament.

2 WN II, p. 253, Lectures, p. 116.

3 This raises the interesting question of why these effects on men and government from commercial industrial society were first analyzed in Scotland and not in the more industrialized England.

"works", the expansion of buildings, the construction of roads, canals, and docks led to a great change in the public's conception of progress. Each single "works" erected in a village was watched daily with the keenest interest and its immediate effects on the locality were widely discussed. These were not merely new forms of physical property plant and eqipment but new property relations of workers and a new understanding of "exchange". Though the physical development of industrial and commercial concerns in the cities was enormous it was in the rural districts that the first and most important industrial plants were erected. The "works" sprang up where trees, coal or other fuel or water power were present in abundance. Thus, the centres of the textile, the coal, the iron, pottery, distilling and other industries in Scotland as in England were to develop in rural hamlets which they would utterly transform. This industrialization of rural hamlets provided immediate examples of "the progress of opulence". Moreover, the new markets and labour force and uses of land were shifting the basis of property from service relations to cash relations between individuals and so altering their view of money, and of their work, and of their futures.1

The new importance of cash money was partly camouflaged by the lack of coins and the widespread practice of "notes of

---

1 See Gray, op. cit., Ch. I, Sec. 4, "Money in the Subsistence Economy" pp. 41-56 and Ch. III, Sec. 3, "Money Income: Growth and Redistribution" pp. 141-154.

currency" and "papers of exchange" which men gave each other and traded for their needs and a form of barter occurred in many rural districts. But the new form of property capital and the great new form of capital credit which accompanied the new commerce and new industry was not beyond the Scots awareness. As Ashton makes clear:

> The deep mines, solidly built factories, well constructed canals, and substantial houses of the industrial revolution were the products of relatively cheap capital.[1]

In conclusion, it was the enclosure movement which first led to the general change of property relations during Smith's time. The transformation to the Market economy was fostered by the enclosure, sale, and exchange of the common land and the displacement of rural agricultural workers to the new industrial areas. The division of labour brought about increased productivity in industry and led to the increasing use of machines and the development of factories. Finally, the tremendous increase in cash exchanges, and the increased foreign and domestic trade; along with the growth of cheap capital for investment encouraged the general expansion of the entire economy and hence an expansion of total property markets in all their forms.

Though most of the members of the Scottish Historical School were professors at Glasgow and Edinburgh (of moral philosophy, history and law), they were not parochially Scottish in their concerns, nor merely theoretical in their interests. They each

---

1 Ashton, Industrial Revolution, op. cit., p. 11.

viewed the rapid economic development of industrial Britain and her relations with Europe and colonies with unusual breadth of interest, and depth of general knowledge. But for a study of their views of property it is perhaps best to describe the property relations of eighteenth century Scotland or more particularly the Lowland area from the Firth of Forth to the Firth of Clyde that formed the setting for their lives.

In Scotland from 1723 till 1790 (the span of Smith's life) the gradual shift of property relations from traditional rural agriculture towards urban commerce and industry never involved the total population of Scotland and it is wise in the following descriptions of the dramatic changes of property forms and relations to keep in mind that Scotland remained predominantly agricultural and dependent on the raising of cattle throughout Smith's life. The change in property relations which Smith witnessed and extensively described in his Wealth of Nations and other works was at all times concentrated in the area between the Clyde and the Forth where the experience of the industrial revolution and commercial and agricultural improvements were telescoped into a short period.

The facts of Smith's life are in broad outline well known.[1] Born at the small Scottish port of Kirkcaldy in 1723, the only son

---

1 Those who have written extensively on Smith's life include: Dugald Stewart in Account of the Life and Writings of Adam Smith" op. cit. John Rae, Life of Adam Smith, op. cit. Jacob Viner "Guide" to John Rae Life of Adam Smith op. cit. W. R. Scott, Adam Smith as Student and Professor, op. cit. Edward Cannan in his introduction to Smith Lectures on Justice Police Revenue and Arms op. cit.

of a widowed mother and the former controller of customs, he was well educated in classics and mathematics at the local parish school till at 14 he travelled to Glasgow to study at the University. He stayed for three sessions studying mathematics, Greek, Latin and natural and moral philosophy. It was in moral philosophy as taught by Francis Hutcheson that Smith was to take the keenest interest,[1] and thus in 1740 he won a Snell Exhibition to Balliol College, Oxford, reading supposedly in preparation for the ministry. After six dull and sometimes unpleasant years,[2] he left without taking up the ministry and returned to Scotland. A series of lectures on Belles Lettres,[3] arranged by Lord Kames in Edinburgh, led to his appointment to the chair of Logic at the University of Glasgow in 1751, moving to the chair of Moral Philosophy in 1752, when it became vacant, as this was closer to his real interests. For these "happiest years" of his life he taught, wrote and met with friends in this thriving commercial centre.[4] In 1757 the publication of part of his Lectures entitled _The Theory of Moral Sentiments_ immediately established

---

1 _Life_, p. 11.

2 _Life_, "At Oxford" pp. 18-28, esp. 24-28.

3 _Life_, Ch. IV, "Lectures in Edinburgh" pp. 31-40. See also W. R. Scott, _Adam Smith as Student and Professor_ op. cit., for fragments of Smith's Edinburgh Lectures

4 W. R. Scott, "Adam Smith and the City of Glasgow," _Proceedings of the Royal Philosophical Society of Edinburgh_, LII (1923) pp. 138-148.

him as one of the foremost philosophers of his time.[1] In 1763 at the end of years of teaching at Glasgow, Smith wrote a first draft of the Wealth of Nations[2] to secure the post of tutor to Lord Townsend's nephew, the Duke of Buccleuch.[3] Smith travelled with the Duke in France from 1774-1776. Although most of their time was spent in Toulouse, in Paris Smith became acquainted with Turgot, the Physiocrats and Voltaire.[4] Returning to London in 1776 Smith became assistant to Lord Townsend, the Secretary of the Treasury, specifically engaged in Colonial policy.[5] In 1767 Smith left, perhaps in dissent with Townsend's policies. Because there are scarcely any records this explanation is but a deduction

---

1 A. L. Macfie, "Adam Smith's Moral Sentiments as foundation for his Wealth of Nations," Oxford Economic Papers 11 (1959) pp. 12-26. James Bonar, Moral Sense (London and New York, 1930) Chapters on Smith. James Bonar "The Theory of Moral Sentiments by Adam Smith, 1757, Journal of Philosophical Studies. I. (1926) pp. 333-53.

2 W. R. Scott, Adam Smith as Student and Professor (Glasgow, 1937). See pp. 317-20 especially where Scott sets forth his justification for 1763 date of the Draft, and the proof that it was written for securing the position Lord Townsend had suggested.

3 Scott, ibid,. pp. 317-30. Smith's close friendship with the Duke of Buccleuch was to last till his death and was to provide Smith with 500 pounds a year till that time. The Duke was important in Scottish Banking, Land, and Politics.

4 Smith's relationship to the Physiocrats has been a subject much debated. For the most recent state of this controversy see Viner's Guide to the Life of Adam Smith, and W. R. Scott, ibid., pp. 105-11.

5 W. R. Scott, "Adam Smith at Downing Street, 1766-1767" Economic History Review, VI (1936) pp. 79-89.

from Smith's stand on colonial policy in the Wealth of Nations ten years later where Smith differed from Townsend's views so markedly. For the next nine years Smith worked solidly and in partial seclusion upon the manuscript of the Wealth of Nations which finally appeared in 1776 and won him almost immediate fame. He spent another year in London society before returning to take up his appointment as Controller of Customs and Collector of the Salt Tax for Scotland. These were difficult jobs, if not very rewarding intellectually and many have lamented his taking them up instead of continuing his writing. He died in 1790.

Because of the rapid expansion of property from and market relations in the three places where Smith spent the most of his life (Kirkcaldy, Glasgow, and Edinburgh), these changes can be reasonably argued to have influenced the development of his theory of property.

Kircaldy, the seaport town where Smith lived his formative years was a small but historic settlement of 1500 people, whose population, industry, and trade steadily expanded during Smith's life. It is situated on the eastern coast of Scotland in the Firth of Forth which "for many centuries" was the "Cradle of Scottish economic life." Its historic significance as one of the "important ports" for the North Sea commerce with Holland, Germany, and the Baltic countries was responsible for its being among the first areas in Scotland to feel the effects of the industrial revolution. Scotland's sea transport was the principal form of communication and hence the seaports were the main centres of commerce. It was natural that in these port towns the new industrial methods from England and the Continent would first be learnt and put into practice. They were often the first towns to receive the capital investment and labour force which these new methods were to inspire and organize into commercial enterprise. According to the various histories of Scotland and Rae's biography of Smith, the period from 1723 to 1737 witnessed a growth of Kirkcaldy's population, trade and industry far greater than most comparable towns not on the coast or near the Firth of Forth. Kirkcaldy's name is repeatedly listed in histories of the Scottish coal, linen, woolen, or distilling industries. Kirkcaldy's inhabitants were ideally suited for the coal and iron industry being "supplied from pits within a mile or so" of their dwelling houses and industrial workshops. This should serve to place in historical perspective Smith's various reflections on cheap and accessible coal. Yet Smith's Kirkcaldy was also important in the employment of the newest hand looms and spinning devices before factory production was instituted. It was reckoned outside of Glasgow and Edinburgh throughout the century to be among the leading textile centres possessing far more domestic looms and heavy equipment than any but a handful of comparably sized towns. And unlike other towns this equipment was locally owned and managed and not under the control of Glasgow or Edinburgh. The development of industry in Kirkcaldy led steadily to an increase in population from 1500 to 1723 at Smith's birth to 2296 in 1755 to 3248 in 1801. The types of industry which expanded included the few large licensed distilleries which stood out since most distilleries in Scotland were small and illegal. The fishing industry also developed in Kirkcaldy. Foreign trade continued to expand there even though many other port towns on the East coast of Scotland were shrinking in size and foreign tonnage as the ports along the Firth of Clyde on the West of Scotland expanded. Kirkcaldy increased her trade steadily throughout the American War of Independence. It is interesting to note that when the Chamber of Manufacturers was established in 1785, Kirkcaldy provided some of the few members to come from outside the great cities of Edinburgh and Glasgow. Campbell's and Rae's statements that Smith "was fond of visiting" or probably followed the custom of stopping in at the "Nailery" or some small industrial works to see work going on is thus by no means far-fetched.[1] Before he travelled to Glasgow to college and saw a really thriving city, Smith could have had a clear idea of the remarkable effects of machinery and commerce.

However, Rae aserts that it was Smith's experience in Glasgow during its great expansion that made Smith the eminent economist and perhaps decided him to become a political economist at all.[2] Between 1736, the time that Smith at 14 travelled to Glasgow as a

---

1 Rae, Life, p. 8. Campbell, Journey from Edinburgh through North Britain, op. cit., II, p. 49. See also W. R. Scott, Adam Smith as Student and Professor, op. cit., esp. p. 333.

2 Life, p. 87.

student, and 1751 when he returned there to take up the professorship of Logic, the population had risen from near 15 thousand to near 23 thousand "and thereafter the rate of increase quickened;" in 1780 it was 42 thousand and by Smith's death it had nearly doubled again. As Hamilton says "the growth of population took place in response to the needs of a rapidly expanding economy." This progression of population which Smith witnessed in both Kirkcaldy and Glasgow thus seemed directly caused by the demand for labourers as his subsequent theory of population asserted.[1]

Smith in both his Lectures and in the Wealth of Nations took note of the rapid and extraordinary development of Glasgow,[2] but he was always careful to keep these discussions firmly within the larger setting and discussion of British industry and trade and never treated Glasgow or Edinburgh or Scotland in an isolated and parochial way. For example, he discusses the rise of wages of Scottish labourers but stresses that this increase in wages occurred:

> ... in the counties which border upon England, probably on account of that neighborhood and in a few other places where there has lately been a considerable

---

1 WN, I, p. 89.

2 Smith's Lectures because they were delivered at Glasgow could be expected to devote excessive space to examples from the city which would be readily apprectiated by his 14-18 year old students. But his Wealth of Nations published for a far larger audience still devotes a number of passages to this city's progress to illustrate several different facets of commercial and industrial development.

> rise in the demand for labour, about Glasgow, Carron, Ayrshire & co. In England the improvements of agriculture, manufacturers and commerce began much earlier than in Scotland. The demand for labour and consequently its price, must necessarily have increased with those improvements.[1]

Nevertheless, Smith was made aware of the particularly extraordinary development of Glasgow not only by his own observations of industry, foreign trade and agriculture which are numerously documented in his own works,[2] and by others,[3] but also by the continual enlightenment of close friends such as Lord Kames, and James Watt,[4] and in general by the numerous and well attended clubs[5] to which he belonged. Smith was among the organizers and most active members of these Glasgow and Edinburgh clubs where merchants and academics met together to discuss and encourage the development of Scottish industry and a variety of other interests.

The tobacco trade with the Plantations in America was bringing great wealth to Glasgow, while the development of first

---

1 WN, I, p. 86.

2 See WN, I, p. 86, 315 doubling of trade in 15 years and 358 why Glasgow's trade had increased so rapidly.

3 W. R. Scott, "Adam Smith and the City of Glasgow", op. cit., pp. 138-48. Rae, Life, pp. 87-99. "Among Glasgow Folk." Ch. VII W. R. Scott, "Adam Smith and the Glasgow Merchants," Economic Journal XLIV (1934) pp. 506-8.

4 W. R. Scott, Adam Smith as Student and Professor, op. cit., esp. pp. 333-9.

5 J. P. Bell, "Adam Smith, Clubman" Scottish Journal of Political Economy VII (1960) pp. 103-116. esp. pp. 113-115. The two most important of the many clubs Smith belonged to were the "Political Economy Club" of Glasgow and the "Select Society" of Edinburgh.

the linen and later the cotton industry also served to increase income and create an expanding market for labour.[1]

> Under such highly favourable economic circumstances, it is not surprising that there was great building activity throughout most of the century. From its ancient centre in the Trongate and High Street, the city expanded in all directions as new streets were constructed, while what had hitherto been small rural villages of the perimeter were absorbed into the urban area. In this period of expansion, enterprise and capital were not lacking.[2]

Glasgow trade had for centuries been small compared to the towns surrounding the coastline of the Firth of Forth which traded constantly with Holland and the Continent. Glasgow was badly situated for any but Irish and French trade, but even this remained small, and it was not until the development of the tobacco trade with the American colonial plantations that Glasgow became truly prosperous. Before the Union of Scotland and England in 1707 the Scots were prohibited by the Navigation Acts from trading with the English colonies in North America and so only a small and illegal trade was carried on.[3] But after the Union, Glasgow's Tobacco trade multiplied itself many times over till it imported more than London. Between 1771 and 1775 imports of tobacco more than trebled in the City of Glasgow. Her success was

---

1 Life, pp. 87-99, Ch. VII "Among Glasgow Folk."

2 Hamilton, Economic History of Scotland, pp. 18-19.

3 Except for the settlement at Darwin, Connecticut.

due to several factors. She had a four to six weeks shorter round trip sea voyage to the colonies than London. And Scotland's boats had immunity from attack during war, and this reduced their insurance until the "Seven Years War." But Glasgow's chief advantages were less rigid customs duties, cheaper manufacturers to trade with the colonists, and the establishment of Scottish agents in the Plantation towns to buy tobacco before the ships arrived.

The tobacco industry represented more than 85 per cent of Glasgow's imports and was by far the largest industry of the city. Its prosperity was supported by commercial and banking facilities in Glasgow which were intimately bound up with the success of the tobacco importation. Since large capital sums were invested over long periods of time, the result was a steady accumulation of capital. This supported the growth of subsidiary industries.

> Both coal-mining and the extension of the iron industry involved heavy capital outlay, and in addition there was considerable investment of capital in harbour works, in deepending the Clyde, and in house-building in Edinburgh, Glasgow and elsewhere.[1]

Gradually sugar, rum and cotton were to add to the more general growth of imports which further spurred on the development of Glasgow industry and commerce. But during Smith's life it was the tobacco import business which was without rival in its effect on trade and the general influx of capital into Glasgow.

---

1 Hamilton, Economic History of Scotland, p. 330.

Smith was well aware of these developments in Glasgow and in both his Lectures and in the Wealth of Nations he considered the facts of and reasons for this extraordinary development.

> I have heard it asserted, that the trade of the City of Glasgow, doubled in about fifteen years after the first erection of the banks there; and that the trade of Scotland has more than quadroupled since the first erecting of the two public banks at Edinburgh, of which one, called the Bank of Scotland, was established by Act of Parliament in 1695; the other called The Royal Bank, by royal charter in 1727. Whether the trade, either of Scotland in general, or of the city of Glasgow in particular, has really increased in so great a proportion, during so short a period, I do not pretend to know. If either of them has increased in this proportion, it seems to be an effect too great to be accounted for by the sole operation of this cause. That the trade and industry of Scotland, however, have increased very considerably during this period, and that the banks have contributed a good deal to this increase cannot be doubted.[1]

Smith in this paragraph may not have included the extraordinary impetus accorded to the tobacco industry which was caused by the creation of the Ship Bank and the Arms Bank in Glasgow itself in 1750 and of the Thistle Bank some years later, all intimately related to the tobacco importation. Yet since Smith lived in Glasgow from 1751-1763 he was well aware of the continued progress of banks, industry and trade. He takes note of these developments in many places and at one point contrasts the development of Edinburgh, long the seat of the Scottish Parliament until its

---

1 WN, I, p. 315.

abolition by the "Union" with England, was the residence of the nobility. It was still the residence of the law courts and of the excise administration - and hence the recipient of large amounts of revenue. But it was not an equal commercial and industrial centre to Glasgow where the population "are chiefly maintained by the employment of capital."[1]

Smith spent a good deal of the last part of his life in Edinburgh as the Controller or Commissioner of Customs and Collector of the Salt Tax,[2] and in these capacities Smith was more than ever in touch with the empirical evidence of changing property relations as he revised his writings. In Edinburgh itself the transformation was among the most remarkable for it involved the creation of an entire new section of the city which for hundreds of years had been confined within the narrow space of the ancient walls. Buildings crammed into this steep and ancient hillside fortress had built up ten and twelve storey tenements, so overpopulated by rich and poor alike that the city was known as the dirtiest and most unlivable in Europe. Though the poor lived in cellars and attics and the rich on the middle floors of the same building the life of all Edinburgh's inhabitants appears to have been thoroughly squalid. It was therefore an incredible

---

1 WN, I, p. 358.

2 These two important political posts yielded respectively f500 and f100. In addition Smith received f500 a year from the Duke of Buccleuch.

transformation when in 1766 the plans for the new town submitted by James Craig were embarked upon, with building construction continuing for the last forty years of the century. Spacious new squares, public buildings, and private houses were constructed and roadways (specially to Leigh, the coastal harbour for the city) were extensively improved.[1] The resulting effect on general property relations between employers and employed of this new town was even more relevant to Smith's theory of class relations, for:

> The character of the Old town was rapidly changed as the well-to-do left their old quarters in the High Street and Cannongate for the more elegant houses in the New Town. Their old residences were sub-divided and their gardens built over to be occupied by the humbler members of the trading classes. Thus the Old Town, which had housed so many distinguished people, came to be occupied almost exclusively by ordinary people, and the New Town was possessed almost exclusively by middle and upper-class people.[2]

Smith was well aware long before he became Comptroller of Customs in 1780 of the development of property relations in Edinburgh. Through his own visits, and frequently attended clubs such as the famous "Select Society", and the trips to his friends Hume and Ferguson, he had a long familiarity with the city. There are many indications of his comparative inquiries into existing property relations, in his localities - Edinburgh, Glasgow, Kirkcaldy and London. For instance he relates the low wages in Edinburgh (only

---

1 For example Hamilton, Economic History of Scotland, p. 25.

2 Hamilton, Economic History of Scotland, p. 25.

half of what they were in London) to the price of lodging which was much dearer than in London. He reflects on the reasons merchants of Edinburgh have an advantage over London and he attributes the improvement of trade to the removal of the Scottish Court and Scottish Parliament from the city.

Everywhere he emphasizes the comparative poverty and backwardness of Scotland in comparison with England.

> England is a much richer country than Scotland... The money price of labour is lower in Scotland than in England, because the real recompense of labour is much lower; Scotland, though advancing to greater wealth, advancing much more slowly than England. The frequency of emigration from Scotland, and the rarity of it from England, sufficiently prove that the demand for labour is very different in the two countries.[1]

At other points Smith goes into detail on many aspects of English - Scottish comparisons: of the price of corn; of cattle, of apprenticeships and corporations, of linen and wool manufacturers, of rent, luxuries, improvements and backwardness. These serve to indicate Smith's detailed historical and factual knowledge of Scottish and British property relations and to emphasize the enormous importance his thought attributed to factual evidence of historical property development. The factual discussion of economic history in the Wealth of Nations is far greater than the portions devoted to pure economic theory, (notably the first two books). The relations between his theories and his economic

---

1 WN, I, pp. 210-11. See also esp. p. 101.

historical data is usually, but not always, clear. His argument in theory is often built upon and buttressed with his factual data of historic property relations. The work is so overflowing with material that frequently Smith engages in "Digressions" on various histories of specific property practices which he does not attempt to integrate with, nor use to support his more purely theoretical argument. Smith uses Scottish economic history sometimes to indicate his theoretical propositions (on profit and wages and advancing and declining societies) and at other times simply as examples of interesting historical information.

In conclusion, the theories of the Scottish School centred upon the dynamic evolution in property relations throughout history. These authors who witnessed the division and enclosure of the common lands, waterways, roads and shallows of the sea were well placed to differentiate between societies before and after the appropriation of private property. Similarly their theories of the shift from the agricultural to commercial society had a direct relevance to the experience of the Scotland of their times where this was happening. Their historic writings and examples bear out this influence of contemporary property transformation.

This chapter has attempted a general historical introduction. It has also provided a summary of several themes of the Scottish Historical School which will be discussed in detail in the following chapters. These themes were: stages of property development - empirical and conjectural views of property -

changes in the nature of property which cause and direct changes in social relations and in the form and activities of the state. These will be the central focus in this study of Adam Smith's theory of property and the state.

# CHAPTER III

## THE INFLUENCE OF JOHN LOCKE ON ADAM SMITH'S THEORY OF PROPERTY

This chapter will attempt to show that Smith accepted both Locke's doctrine that property rights originated in men's labour, and he also accepted Locke's other theory that custom and state laws were the proper determinant of property rights.[1] I hope to show that Smith never conclusively decided which of these two theories should be adhered to.

### I

The search for "influence" on Smith's property theory would encompass countless predecessors whose writings and ideas he knew quite thoroughly and in many cases taught in his courses.[2] He was also influenced by contemporary theories of Scottish, English, French, and American authors he knew and upon which his circle of friends would discourse. Because his property theory was an intimate part of his integrated system of economics, as well as his political theory and was crucial to his entire system of moral

---

1 John Locke, Two Treatises of Government, ed. Peter Laslet (Cambridge, 1963). (Hereafter cited as Two Treatises).

2 Both in Smith's Lectures and in his other works drawn from his Glasgow lectures (1751-63) we find the description of and commentary upon the theories of political and moral philosophers of all ages. At times as in his Lectures, Moral Sentiments, and his Essays on Philosophical Subjects Smith describes these other thinkers' theories in detail contrasting them not only to his own but to one another. At other times as in the Wealth of Nations Smith mentions and makes passing allusion to the theories of others which may have affected his own.

philosophy, a comprehensive search for predecessors would be nearly endless even if we were to limit our discussion strictly to property theory alone. Although the study of influences on his property conceptions has not been the subject of thorough investigation, a few aspects of such a study have been touched on in works which deal with forerunners of Smith's total system. Predecessors and contemporaries who are known to have shaped Smith's thought usually include Hutcheson, Montesquieu, Mandeville, Hume, Lord Kames and the Physiocrats, and are the subjects of numerous studies.2

These authors to varying degrees, and each in different ways, affected Smith's method and total philosophy, as well as providing him with principles and presuppositions of human psychology, morals, politics and indeed many of the terms of economics. However, these were not the prime influence on his theory of property, which was drawn from a relatively distinct source: the property theory of John Locke. Locke's theory, in fact pervades the thinking of Smith's immediate predecessors, Hutcheson, Montesquieu, and Lord Kames, and in a more oblique way even the works of Mandeville, the Physiocrats, and Hume.

---

1 As mentioned in the two foregoing chapters Dugald Stewart, Rae, Viner, Bell, Bonar, Cannan, Scott and Robbins have all dealt with this vast subject of contemporary and literary influences upon Smith's thought in their extensive writings. Current opinion on the exact amount of influence of each of these men upon Smith remains in dispute, but nevertheless each of the various influences is evaluated in depth in Viner's "Guide", passim.

2 The Appendix considers in general these numerous studies of the many authors who have influenced Smith's theories.

There is general unanimity among the secondary sources regarding Locke's persistent influence on both popular and academic discussions of property theory during Smith's life. As R. L. Meek states:

> No one would wish to deny, either, that the Lockean theory of property rights contributed largely to the building up of the political atmosphere in which the classical labour theory of value was eventually able to flourish ... 1

As Schlatter says:

> John Locke's theory of property became the standard bourgeois theory, the classical liberal theory.2

Schumpeter insists:

> This doctrine, restated in its boldest as well as most influential form by Locke, did command almost general assent.3

This "general assent," to the Lockean property doctrine is indicated by many legal property treatises,4 Blackstone's

---

1 Ronald L. Meek, Studies in the Labour Theory of Value (London, 1954) p. 125.

2 Schlatter, Private Property, op. cit., p. 151.

3 Schumpeter, History of Economic Analysis, op. cit., p. 119. That the Lockean formulas were woven into the entire assumptions of political economists of the English Classical School was so clear to Marx that in his Theories of Surplus Value (Moscow, London 1956) part I, p. 356, he stated that "His (Locke's) philosophy served as the basis for all the ideas of the whole of subsequent English Political Economy." As Marx says, it was not only Locke's property doctrine but his entire 'philosophy' which served as the basis for "political economy". Locke's property theory was simply the central theme.

4 Grey, Restraints upon the Alienation of Property, op. cit. Introduction.

revised version of Lockean doctrine,[1] academic lectures,[2] and legal trials,[3] of the period. In these, statements of man's right to things with which he had mixed his labour were expressed as self-evident truths. Soon after Smith's Wealth of Nations was published, we find the 1778-1783 edition of the Encyclopedia Britannica stating not only in its article on "property" and on Locke the now familiar "doctrine", but including as a prime article of faith the statement that the British by birth had "three great and primary rights of personal security, personal liberty, and private property." Nor was the Lockean doctrine less well known or less well respected in Scotland during this period. Because of the quality of Scottish general education[4] and a greater spirit of political independence,[5] it was more ardently voiced there than in England. (Simultaneously, though the Scottish scholars, as historians, disputed Locke's original contract of government, they nonetheless, as members of the "Poker Club" dedicated themselves to the Lockean political doctrines of the right to bear arms and the right of Scotland to have a

---

1 Edward P. Thompson, The Making of the English Working Class, (London, 1963) pp. 80-88.

2 Hutcheson, System, sec. 2.

3 Thompson, op. cit., p. 128.

4 WN, II, pp. 306, 335.

5 Bell, "Adam Smith, Clubman" op. cit., pp. 113-115. Bell gives the background of the "Poker Club" which was the clearest expression of this political indepenedence.

standing armed militia. They demanded ultimately the theoretical right to rebellion if England should ever tyrranize Scotland under the Act of Union. That is, they recognized an implicit or effective contract of government.)1

In his Lectures Smith appears to have drawn his property conceptions in the first chapter directly from Hutcheson's System of Moral Philosophy, at times even paraphrasing whole segments of Hutcheson's Book II. Hutcheson's essential points were that: property's origin was in men's labour; labour was the fundamental property; the labourers had a right to the produce of their labour; and labour is the principal source of all wealth.2 Thus, the adherence of Smith to Hutcheson's property theory is largely an agreement with the Lockean principles which lie behind Hutcheson's own views. (Smith's and Hutcheson's treatment of "Acquired rights" and the civil condition of property will be dealt with later in this chapter.)

In the case of Hume, another writer whose thought is intimately associated with that of Smith, we find again that the

---

1 Bell, ibid., pp. 113-115.

2 For example see Hutcheson, System, Bk.II, ch. V. "Of the Private Rights of Men." p. 294. "'Tis plain each one has a natural right to exert his powers, according to his own judgement and inclination, for these purposes, in all such industry labour and amusement." But even more important we find that Hutcheson believed "Each one fitted for the common use of all: (of which hereafter) and has a like right, by any innocent means to acquire property in such goods as are fit for occupation and property and have not been occupied by others." System, p. 298.

Lockean influence is sometimes apparent. This is true, for example, of Hume's "utility theory", that the laws of the state control property for maximum social happiness. In fact this theory, emphasizing the common expectations of men that they will continue in possession of those things which they have long enjoyed, also indicated the common expectation of men to a just portion of that property which they have produced with their own labours.[1] This view was the same as Smith's,[2] who did not accept the utilitarian basis of Hume's thought. Some aspects of Smith's justification of property distribution in line with reasonable expectations are discussed by Millar, Dugald Stewart and James Bonnar.[3]

It would be fair to say that Locke's conventional property theory had given a foretaste of Smith's and Hume's idea that property laws must fulfill general expectations. Yet, in terms of his total property theory, Smith was closer to Locke than was Hume, since Hume did not base his theory on the Lockean principle of the existence of original property rights in man's labour. This principle was firmly held by Smith who says, "Labour, as it

---

1 Hume, Essays, op. cit., II, p. 189. "Who sees not that whatever is produced or improved by a man's art or industry ought forever, to be secured to him, in order to give encouragement to such useful habits and accomplishments?"

2 Lectures, p. 108.

3 See James Bonnar, Moral Sense (London, 1930) p. 204, for his discussion of the moral basis of Smith's theory of property.

is the original foundation of all other property ..."[1] Where Hume admits that in general it is best to let men receive the fruits of their labour (that is, tacitly accepting the Lockean theory) he does so on the grounds of utility. Yet the reason Smith disagreed with Hume was that he believed such social utility is not apparent to all individuals. It could thus not serve as a general moral or social guide to action. Utility, for Smith, is thus not a security against invasions of individual's possessions and property. Smith believed that it is only by declaring rewards as rights which are to be socially observed and legally enforced that men will gradually appreciate the social utility of them.

In summary, we find that Smith accepted the Lockean conception of property rights originating in men's labour and accepted it not in terms of social utility but in terms of natural rights and natural expectations of the individual. Nevertheless, Hutcheson, Hume and other authors did help to shape that particular conception of the Lockean view of property Smith was to learn.

---

1 WN, I, p. 136.

II

Locke held two theories of property.[1] The first was based on the individual's labour in an original "state of Nature," the second was based upon civil laws, conventions, or traditions.[2] (According to the definition of property I advanced in the Introduction it is questionable whether tradition or convention can constitute a theory of property at all. However, Richard Schlatter demonstrates that there is a long and respectable heritage behind the theory that conventions were the source of property rights[3] so that it would probably be beside the point to elucidate the illogic of considering convention or tradition as a "theory" of property.) Locke was by no means fully clear or

---

1 Both of Locke's two theories of property are expressed in Ch. V Of Property of the Second Treatise; see Two Treatises, pp. 303-320.

2 Locke's two theories of property stem from his comprehensive political philosophy and it is not entirely fair to take them from that context. Locke's entire political argument was ostensibly an attack on Robert Filmer's Petrarchia and its assertion of the Divine Right of Kings. In Locke's attempt to prove that men had rights before there were kings or government he conjectured an original "State of Nature" before any state had come into being. Foremost among those "natural rights" which Locke asserted to be man's possession in that state of nature, was their right to property. By this Locke meant the right to own or possess themselves and their labour. Locke then postulated that a man also had a natural right to those things which he found in these natural surroundings if he mixed his labour with them and thus made his own. It was because of men's desire to preserve their property that men formed government. Yet, once governments were formed property rights were based on laws not labour.

3 Schlatter, op. cit., pp. 128-131, 145-149.

consistent in his use or delineation of these two theories of the source of property rights. But for this chapter which traces certain influences of these two theories upon Adam Smith's thought it may be useful to define them.

Because Locke believed "Government has no other end but the preservation of Property,"1 his Two Treatises of Civil Government devoted an important section to a justification of private property and an explanation of its origins.2 John Locke did not begin the practice of enquiring into the origins of property for a justification of unequal possession,3 but Locke did originate the labour theory of property which has come to be associated with his name.4

---

1 Two Treatises, II, p. 347. See also p. 368.

2 Ibid,. the famous Chapter V. "Of Property."

3 Many authors employed this practice including most notably: Puffendorf, De Jure Nature et Centium, English trans. by Basil Kennet (London, 1710) IV, iv, 13. William Petty: "An Essay Concerning the Multiplication of Mankind" in his Several Essays in Political Arithmetic (London, 1682) and Thomas Hobbes, Leviathan ed. Michael Oakeshott (Oxford, 1960) Ch. 13 "Of the Natural Condition of Mankind as concerning their Felicity and Misery" p. 80.

4 The originality of Locke's theory of property as a whole is generally accepted, although the originality of specific parts of that theory is a matter of controversy. (See Peter Laslett's footnoes to the Two Treatises in Chapter V of the Second Treatises esp. pp. 304-8.) Peter Laslett, in his Introduction to the Two Treatises concludes: "But it (Locke's theory of original property) remains an original doctrine, particularly important in its bearing on the way men analyzed social and political origins, and his own judgement must stand - no man has ever done quite this before or since." p. 106.

Since Locke's theory of property has been so extensively discussed by many authors[1] (and since our interest in this dissertation is not Locke's property but that of Smith,) I must limit my discussion of Locke's famous doctrine of property to a skeleton outline of its foremost principles. These are as follows:

> Though the Earth, and all the inferior creatures be common to all Man, yet every Man has a Property in his own Person. This no Body has any Right to but himself. The Labour of his Body, and the Work of his Hands, we may say are properly his. Whatsoever then he removes out of the State that Nature hath provided, and left it in,

---

Concerning Locke's theory of property as a whole Richard Schlatter in his Private Property, op. cit., p. 152 states, "The new and original part of his work (Two Treatises) was the theory of property."

1 This "original" property theory of Locke has been extensively discussed by many authors. See for example: Pashell Larkin, Property in the 18th Century, with Special Reference to England and Locke (Cork, 1930), C. J. Czajkowski, The Theory of Private Property in Locke's Political Philosophy (Notre Dame, Ind., U.S.A., 1941), Willmore Kendall, "John Locke and the Doctrine of Majority Rule" Illinois Studies in the Social Sciences, Vol. XXXVI, no. 2 (Urbana, Ill, 1941), J. W. Gough, John Locke's Political Philosophy, Eight Studies (Oxford, 1950), Leo Strauss, Natural Right and History, pp. 202-51 on Locke. (Chicago, 1953), M. Cherno "Locke on Property" Ethics 1959, C. H. Monson, "Locke and his Interpreters" Political Studies VI (1958), Raymond Polin, La Politique Morale de John Locke (Paris, 1960), C. A. Viano, John Locke, dal Razionalismo al Illuminiamo (Turin, 1960) deals with Locke's theory and Lord Shaftesbury's policy on property. C. B. Macpherson, "Locke on Capitalist Appropriation", Western Political Quarterly VII, I (Salt Lake City, Utah, U.S.A.) 1951, and Macpherson's article in the same journal X (1954), entitled "The Social Bearing of Locke's Political Theory," and Macpherson's book The Political Theory of Possessive Individualism (Oxford, 1962). Laslett's Introduction to Two Treatises also considers property.

> he hath mixed his Labour with, and joined to it something that is his own, and thereby makes it his Property.1

This original property of men included:

> Lives, Liberties, and Estates, which I call by the general Name, Property.2

Individual labour gave exclusive title to property rights in all natural substances with which it was "mixed", only so far as:

> ... at least where there is enough, and as good left in common for others.3

Locke approached the subject of property from the standpoint of men in an original "State of Nature", probably because it was the prevailing practice to explain and justify social phenomena in terms of an inquiry into their essential characteristics or historic origin.4 Yet Locke's discussion of the origin of property was to supersede that of his predecessors.

The second theory of property Locke described is hardly mentioned even in works on Locke5 and is virtually unknown in

---

1 Two Treatises, pp. 305-6.

2 Two Treatises, p. 368. At the moral basis of this theory is Locke's conviction that man was God's "Property."

3 Two Treatises, p. 306.

4 See Laslett's Introduction to Two Treatises, Otto Gierke, Natural Law and the Theory of Society, trans. Ernest Barker (Boston, 1957), pp. 101-4, 293-5.

5 Ernest Barker, Social Contract: Locke, Hume, Rousseau (London, 1968) pp. xvi-xxxv.

the popular Histories of Political Thought.[1] This second theory refers to what we will call "civil property". After the state of nature Locke describes two occurrences taking place which appear to be responsible for the establishment of modern civil property relations as we now understand them. The first was the famous convention by which men agreed to the use of money.[2] The second convention was the establishment of civil laws. Men consented to laws after they had agreed to the original contract or compact by which the state or the sovereign was brought into being. As Locke says:

> The several Communities settled the Bounds of their distinct Territories, and, by Laws, within themselves, regulated the Properties of the private Men of their Society, and so by Compact and Agreement settled the Property which Labour and Industry began; ... [3]

Many passages in Two Treatises refer repeatedly to this fact that although property originally could be natural it is now "conventional" and rights once created by men's labour are now valid only because men have agreed by compacts to abide by them. For example see Bk. I, sec. 88-94, compared with Bk. II, secs. 63-73 and especially Bk. II, chapter V, sec. 38.

---

1 e.g. G. H. Sabine History of Political Theory (London, 1963) fails to mention Locke's civil theory of property. See ch. XXVI, pp. 526-8.

2 Two Treatises, Bk. II, Sec. 45-9, pp. 318-9.

3 Ibid., Bk. II, Ch. V., section 45, p. 317.

> [Men] settled themselves together, and built Cities, and then, by consent, they came in time to set out the bounds of their distinct Territories and agree on limits between them and their Neighbours, and by Laws within themselves settled the Properties of those of the same Society.[1]

This conventional theory of property was drawn almost entirely from the traditional theories of property of Puffendorf and Grotius and this is perhaps the reason it has been somewhat unnoticed in the general literature in comparison with Locke's original "doctrine of property."[2] Most writers in Locke's own time[3] and virtually all commentators since have not distinguished between rights of property in natural vs. civil society. And thus now only the doctrine of the origin of property in men's labour is called "Locke's property doctrine". It has come down to the present as albeit ambiguous, yet still probably the foremost philosophical justification for unequal distribution and the complex rights of conflicting individuals in western society.

---

1 Ibid., section 38, p. 313.

2 This conventional theory of civil property is mentioned by a few authors not specifically dealing with Locke's property theory such as David G. Ritchey, Darwin and Hegel, With Other Philosophical Studies (London, 1893) exp. Ch. VI.; Leslie Stephen, English Thought in the Eighteenth Century, op. cit., II, pp. 141-2 and Richard Schlatter, Private Property, op. cit., pp. 157-8.

3 The one interesting exception was Locke's friend James Tyrrell who perhaps because of his friendship adhered strictly to Locke's two theories of property in his Brief Disquisition of the Laws of Nature (London, 1701).

Because Locke was not clear or consistent in his use of these two theories of property,[1] and because Locke's "conventional" theory of property was drawn from the more traditional theories it is difficult to assess whether Hume and others who enunciated theories similar to Locke's conventional theory of property were in fact following him or not. Yet, if we simply separate the natural from the civil theories Locke used it is obvious that these were employed respectively and to varying degrees by different members of the Scottish Historical School. The Civil property theory was most fully adopted by Hume. Following his emphasis on the utilititarian aspects of that theory Bentham and later utilitarians elaborated upon Hume's description of government's responsibility for the determination of social property rights and questions of distributive justice. The influence of the other famous Lockean "doctrine of property" (derived originally from labour) was strongest on Francis Hutcheson and through him on Smith. But in both Smith and Hutcheson we find many statements of the theory of civil control over property, blending with the natural labour theory on such questions as inheritance, taxation, navigation acts, and defence.

---

1 For example Locke contradicted himself on inherited property. Compare Bk. I, sec. 88-94 with Bk. II, sec. 65-73.

III

Locke had not only been a political theorist but a vitally important empirical philosopher, economist, and adviser to Lord Shaftesbury (one of the most important political figures of the time). He considered both the universal and the particular aspects of society; the refutation of the existence of innate ideas in his Essay Concerning Human Understanding and at other times the effects of "clipt currency" in his Considerations and Further Considerations on the Lowering of Interest and Raising the Value of Money. This breadth of perspective was, as we shall see, extremely important as a background for Smith. Especially important was the fact that Locke appeared to have integrated principles from various social disciplines into a larger whole, and set men's rational understanding as the foremost human quality for all social activity. Smith to some extent followed Locke in these steps; both in his adherence to empirical psychology and to an idealistic natural rights political philosophy and in his far more successful attempt[1] to establish a single system to integrate all social activity. It is true that Smith based his system (integrating the different social disciplines) on human

---

1 Locke's total thought is notoriously lacking in system and lacks even a basic consistency. There is a disproof of innate ideas in his epistimology and a dependence on innate ideas and innate rights of men in his political philosophy. See Leo Strauss, Natural Right and History (Chicago, 1969) pp. 202-51. Stoughton Lynd, Philosophical Origins of American Radicalism (New York, 1968) pp. 20-22.

sentiments and human passions rather than reason, and proclaimed that society developed throughout history more by blind social and individual drives than by any process of rational decisions. Yet nevertheless, Smith insisted that reason was the most important human attribute and that it was necessary for the "justice" of civil laws and property relations and ultimately responsible for future social improvement.

Even more important than his principles and total philosophy Locke established a mode of "empirical" enquiry which Smith and the Scottish School greatly respected, and attempted to employ in their own social researches.[1] Locke was credited by members of the Scottish Historical School with the founding of the "empirical" approach in social investigation and philosophic thought.[2] However, Locke had not really used what we now call an "empirical method" and thus we must look more carefully at what the Scottish School meant when they praised Locke's mode of enquiry. His and their theories were not based on a purely factual approach to society and social change. Their "empirical" method combined facts with a consultation of "general opinion" of the educated classes and with a good number of "self evident" truths which each theorist found within himself. Gladys Bryson has explained their understanding of the "empirical" approach as:

---

1 See Bryson Man and Society, op. cit., pp. 18,115,122,144,146.

2 Ibid., pp. 18, 115.

> To them, as to Locke, introspection of their own minds seemed an empirical beginning: what he said of ideas they could say of ideas, and sentiments and passions, "Everyone is conscious of them in himself; and Men's words and actions will satisfy him that they are in others." What more indubitable observation could empiricism demand? Here, it seemed to them, was the rock-bottom start for the study of man.1

There was another aspect of Locke's method which was relevant to the Scottish School. Locke entitles his most famous work: "An Essay concerning the true origin, extent, and end of civil government." According to Locke the origin, extent and end of government was the preservation of private property. Therefore Locke's enquiry into property followed directly from his study of government and its mode of investigation followed the same pattern. His famous chapter V dealt with "the true origin of property" in men themselves and their labour. Next, the extent of private property rights was described as being bounded by the amount a man could use before spoiling (until the introduction of money.)2 And finally, the end of property is described as human improvement.3 Thus Locke used this same form of enquiry (origin, extent, end) for both his study of property and government. In part at least one theme to be investigated is; to what extent did Smith follow Locke in this method and how far he can be

---

1 Ibid., p. 18.

2 Two Treatises, pp. 317-319.

3 Two Treatises, pp. 183-188.

said to have adopted these presumptions about the relations of property to government.

Locke's property doctrines, political principles, integrated system, empirical method (and this three part social inquiry into origin, extent and end of property and government) all had a certain influence upon each of the writers of the Scottish Historical School.

However, their interpretation of Locke's ideas as well as their use of them was somewhat different from anything Locke had formulated. First, the Lockean political or property theories they believed themselves to be concerned with[1] were not exactly the theories or issues Locke had stated or meant in 1689, but related to their own experience of politics and property relations of Scotland and England from 1730-1790. The Lockean theories they used were selectively reinterpreted in terms of their historical sociological method and their moral philosphic theories of sentiments and self-interested behaviour, in contrast with Locke's concern with Natural Law and faith in "Reason" as the arbiter of human conduct. By the time of the Scottish Historical School, pure rationalism, and the central position of "Reason" in theories of human psychology and natural laws, had been to a considerable extent replaced by "feelings", "sentiments", and the more

---

1 Lectures, pp. 1-12, 68-72.

instinctive "passions" of men.[1]

The Scots at this time based their theories on "experience" and claimed Locke as their foremost predecessor,[2] in adopting this first principle. Yet, though Locke had attempted to show that knowledge was largely built up through continual contact with "experience" he had never claimed that "reason" (the interpreter of knowledge), had developed through experience. Reason was the individual's expression of the eternal "Natural Law." For the Scots, "Reason" could not form the basis of their social systems, because it was not based on experience. Thus when Locke was cited by the Scottish Historical School and praised for his founding social science on "experience" they were to some extent reinterpreting Locke. Likewise, though Locke had developed an extremely complicated theory of knowledge in his _Essay Concerning Human Understanding_, by the time of Smith, Locke's theory had been reduced to one or two simple propositons. For example:

> It should be remembered that popular interpretation of Locke's contribution had it that most knowledge comes to us from without, by way of our rather passive senses, and that our minds are little more than _tabula rasa_.[3]

---

1 Bryson, op. cit., p. 27. "We find many men of the later Enlightenment, then, and not only the Scottish group, turning from reason to feelings as being at once simpler to explain, surer as items of experience, and more effective as agents of human activity."

2 Bryson, op. cit., p. 18.

3 Bryson, ibid., p. 122.

Finally Locke's Original Contract of Government was hotly debated in Smith's times in terms of its being an historical fact by which men at a certain discoverable date had actually assembled together either to sign or to witness such an agreement between sovereign and subjects. David Hume's "On the Original Contract"[1] is of course the most famous such historical attack on the Lockean theory but there were many others of varying tones of disbelief. Hutcheson was among those who retained the conception of the original contract while suggesting some ambivalence as to whether it was an historical fact or a worthwhile myth. Adam Smith borrowed both Hume's historical disbelief in the factual existence of any original contract, and from Hutcheson borrowed the idea that a contract of government was a useful fiction describing accurately the actual form of the conditions of allegiance.[2] Bryson is in error when she states "Smith opposes the doctrine of contract as the foundation of allegiance to the civil magistrate. He takes his position bluntly ..."[3] Smith did say that "government takes place where it [the contract] was

---

1 See Ernest Barker Social Contract, op. cit. Hume's "On the Original Contract" in his Introduction pp. liv-lix., where he shows that Hume did agree that the original government "if we trace it to its first origin in the woods and deserts", certainly originated in "consent" (though it has since been based on usurpation or conquest.

2 Hutcheson, System, op. cit., sec.III dealing with Government.

3 Bryson, op. cit., p. 161.

never thought of"[1] but he was most emphatic on those terms of agreement between subjects and sovereign which must not be broken. Smith did not shy away from stating the terms and even the kind of taxation which would justify rebellion or the withdrawal of allegiance from a sovereign.[2] This will be dealt with later in the chapters on Smith's conception of government in the present and in the future. Smith like Hume suggested disbelief in any historic factual original contract and agreed that outside of Great Britain there were few examples of contracts of government, recent or original, yet Smith and Hume concurred with Locke in believing in the "effective" or "implied contract" or government between subjects and sovereign.[3]

Although Locke's doctrine of property is most explicitly stated in his Second Treatise of Civil Government, echoes of this same theory appear in Locke's more specifically economic writings which are the works Smith most frequently cites.[4]

---

1 Lectures, p. 11.

2 Lectures, pp. 66-72. "Of the Rights of Subjects, esp. p. 69.

3 It is curious that Bryson should be one of the few to recognize the ambivalence of Hume in his ultimate view of a contract of government yet fail to recognize Smith's ambivalence. She says Hume "admits in the way of contract .. a voluntary submission" Bryson, op. cit., p. 202. But, "Smith takes his position bluntly," against contracts, Bryson says.

4 John Locke Some Considerations of the Lowering of Interest and Raising the Value of Money. Further Considerations Concerning Raising the Value of Money. Collected Works (London, 1714). Hereafter referred to respectively as Considerations and Further

He describes the origin of property in terms clearly reminiscent of Locke's Second Treatise, "Labour is the original price paid for all things", "The produce of labour constitutes the Natural recompense".1 Smith often does not acknowledge and perhaps does not even recognize his debt. Yet, since Locke's property theory was by 1750 embedded in the general public's conception of the origins of property, he may have simply believed they were accepted principles he was enunciating when he put forth the main tenets of Locke's theory of property. However, the similarity of language would suggest Smith owed far more to Locke's actual works than he acknowledges. For example:

Locke says:

> ... though the things of Nature are given in common, yet Man, (by being Master of himself, and Proprietor of his own Person, and the Actions of Labour of it) had still in himself the great Foundation of Property.2

Adam Smith echoes this statement of Locke's exactly when he says:

> The property which every man has in his own labour, as it is the original foundation of all other property, so it is the most sacred and inviolable.3

---

Considerations. Other papers on money by Locke though bound with these will be cited separately.

1 WN, I, Book I, Chapter 8, first sentence, p. 72.

2 Two Treatises, pp. 316-7.

3 WN, I, p. 136.

Many authors have remarked upon Smith's use of the Lockean property in labour doctrine.[1] Yet at the same time that Smith accepts the Lockean Natural Labour origin of property he at other times denies it and instead adheres to the Lockean Conventional theory of property as an acquired right from custom and laws of society. For example:

> His [a man's] rights to his estate are called acquired or _inura adventilia_, and are of two kinds, real and personal.[2]

Such rights were acquired from customs and civil laws for, "Property and civil government very much depend on one another."[3] Smith appears to have drawn his terminology for this expression of The Conventional Property Doctrine from Hutcheson's _System_ where Bk. II, Chapters 6, 7, 8 deal with "Adventitious Right of property real or personal". As shown earlier in this chapter, Hutcheson also held to the other Lockean Doctrine of Property that man has a natural right to himself, his labour, and to mix his labour with natural substance and thus appropriate it from the "Common".[4] Hutcheson shows that such natural rights to common natural

---

1 Schlatter, op. cit., pp. 160-1. Schumpeter, _History of Economic Analysis_, op. cit., p. 310. 'As has been mentioned already, there is plenty of this in the _Wealth of Nations_, much of it, perhaps, inspired by Locke. "The produce of Labour constitutes the natural recompense of wages of Labour".' _WN_, I, p. 72.

2 _Lectures_, p. 6.

3 _System_, Bk. II, pp. 294, 298.

4 _Lectures_, p. 8.

property can be secured not only by Labour but by occupation, "understood sometimes at first discovering by the eye, sometimes touching with the hand."1

Yet, Hutcheson by accepting the two Lockean theories of Property, Natural, and Conventional or adventitious, merely embellished the Lockean Principles with examples of real and personal holdings. Smith, as we shall see, not only accepted the two Lockean Principles but attempted to build upon them as entire historic and political theory.

But how can we reconcile Smith's adherence to both Lockean theories of property? Because of his more complex view of Historical stages Smith could not simply copy Locke's explanation that the labour theory was for property "in nature" and the conventional theory was for property "in civil society." At times Smith could describe Hunting and Herding societies as distinguished by their different property relations, and at other times could describe them as having little or no property at all, or none that required more than two or three days labour. Men in their first primitive hunting tribes had by necessity essential objects for their life and labour which were their property either communally or individually,2 yet their property wasn't abundant,

---

1 System, p. 315

2 Smith and others of the Scottish Historical School described both the historical evidence for primitive communal societies and also employed the conjectural device of the deer and beaver

or in excess of their physical needs. (Smith also describes these societies as without state governments but at other times suggests the basis upon which they do have leaders implying much the same dualism that he implies in deciding whether they have property or not.) Essential objects, men had a natural right to use, and hence there must be natural property. But only beyond that primitive level of society did Smith describe the development of conventional property in excess of essential human needs which was "acquired" by social custom or civil laws.1 Hence Smith accepted both Locke's natural and Locke's conventional theory of property. And like Locke, Smith was not always consistent in distinguishing these two theories and hence has left contradictory opinions of his views.2

---

exchanges of property between individuals. Locke had suggested both these when he described individuals taking things out of "the common".

1 Smith states in his Lectures, p. 8, "The origin of natural rights is quite evident. That a person has a right to have his body free from injury and his liberty free from infringement unless there be a proper cause, nobody boubts. But acquired rights such as property require more explanation. Property and civil government very much depend on one another."

2 Henry J. Bitterman, "Smith's Empiricism and the Law of Nature", Journal of Political Economy XLVIII (1940) pp. 487-520, 703-34, argues that "Smith's 'natural liberty' and 'Sacred rights of private property' do not indicate an acceptance of Locke's theory." ... "The Lectures in various places speak of natural rights, but the term is used to designate personal, as opposed to property, rights, following the usage of Roman law." p. 707. Schlatter, op. cit., p. 182, expounds the far more commonly held view that Smith and his followers "usually took for granted the natural rights doctrine, that ... each individual was owner of the commodities he created by mixing his labour with them."

Second, we find Locke directly influenced Smith's conception of what wealth or property included. On this point Edwin Cannan notes Smith's indebtedness to Locke in the first sentence of the Wealth of Nations:[1] by footnoting Smith's statement that "The annual Labour of every nation is the fund which originally supplies it with all the necessaries and conveniences of life ..." Cannan says: "with this phrase [compare] Locke, ... "'The intrinsic natural worth of anything consists in its fitness to supply the necessities or serve the conveniences of human life.'[2] Though Smith here is defining wealth and Locke, value, the similarity of their use of this expression occurs frequently. Locke and Smith agreed concerning their definitions of wealth as use values supplying necessities, conveniences and enjoyments of human life. This is significant for an analysis of the theory of property Smith advanced and those of political economists who followed him.[3] It is also relevant that Smith echoed Locke's

---

1 WN, I, p. 1.

2 John Locke, Considerations, 1696 ed., p. 66.

3 In at least three instances Ricardo refers to this expression. See David Ricardo, Principles of Political Economy and Taxation, in Works ed. Piero Sraffa, 10 vols (Cambridge, 1962) I, pp. 100, 276, 429. "Wealth, that is to say, the necessaries, conveniences, and enjoyments of the society." p. 400. Moreover, Ricardo credited Smith with this formulation when he said "he has himself defined riches to consist of the necessaries, conveniences and enjoyments of human life." p. 429. See also Karl Marx, Capital 3 Vols. (Moscow, 1961), Capital I, p. 36. Yet Marx's use of these earlier concepts is not merely historical "Use-values become a reality only by use or consumption: they also constitute the substance of all wealth, whatever may be the social form of that wealth." Capital I, p. 36.

definition of property as "Lives, liberties and property,"[1] and included the right to life, liberty and property in "a man's estate."[2]

The third important area in which Smith followed Locke, was in believing that property not only preceded government, but that private property was the essential cause of the establishment of government. As Locke says:

> Government has no other end but the preservation of property.[3]

Adam Smith in his Lectures makes this even more explicit:

> Till there be property there can be no government, the very end of which is to secure wealth and to defend the rich from the poor.[4]

And finally in his Wealth of Nations Smith repeats this more forcefully. It may be noticed in the following as in the foregoing passage that property, for Smith, not only precedes government but appears to be its cause:

> Civil government, so far as it is instituted for the security of property, is in reality instituted for the defense of the rich against the poor, or of those who have some property against those who have none at all.[5]

---

1 Lectures, p. 67.

2 Lectures, p. 8.

3 Two Treatises, p. 347.

4 Lectures, p. 15.

5 WN, II, p. 326.

From these three basic agreements about property between Locke and Smith we find there develops a network of subsidiary agreements regarding the right to alienate one's property as an intrinsic attribute of property itself; regarding contractual property and contractual government; and the right to revolution to protect one's property.[1]

Locke considered the capacity to alienate or dispose of one's property to be central to the proof or certainty that one possessed property.[2] For example:

> Their persons are free by a Native Right, and their Properties, be they more or less, are their own, and at their own dispose, and not at his [sovereign or conqueror] or else it is no property.[3]

Locke makes this statement several times in each of his political and economic writings insisting that usually something which cannot be alienated, is not property. Smith implies this when he

---

1 Regarding property interests as continually controlling government. Regarding the presence of classes in society, regarding the naturalness and probable continuance of subsistence wages, regarding the alienation of political rights and property rights which should be inalienable by workers who cannot control the contract.

2 See Laslett's Introduction to Two Treatises, Macpherson, Political Theory of Possessive Individualism, op. cit., pp.214-22, esp. pp. 215, 218. Macpherson demonstrates that in Locke's theory the labour was not only rightful by civil property law but by Natural Law and therefore originated in natural society and could not be abolished by civil society.

3 Two Treatises, p. 413.

says "You cannot ask it as your property, for you alienated [it]."[1] Although alienability is usually one of the central attributes of property, this did not prevent Locke (or Smith) from describing some property as "inalienable."

Locke and Smith fully recognize the current existence in their time of the emergence of a "market society" in which most forms of property including labour, land, goods, capital, and human attributes and rights could be capable of becoming "commodities" for sale. Indeed, Smith and Locke not only theorized upon the basis of these commodity exchanges but encouraged the expansion of alienable market property. Also they recognized many similar economic developments: concerning employment markets, real estate markets, currency markets etc.

Notice, that similarly to Smith, Locke states repeatedly that labourers are "the propertyless" and the rich are "the propertied". Locke described the "meagre subsistence" and "poverty" of wage labourers in his Considerations[2] and their dependence upon others for their necessities,[3] and their need to labour for money with which to buy their necessities,[4] all in much the same terms that Smith was to begin from when he constructed the theoretical and historical sections of his Wealth of Nations. Though there are many of these two authors' market

---

1 Lectures, p. 135.

2 Considerations, p. 33.

3 Ibid., p. 36.

4 Ibid., p. 36.

descriptions, we sense an enormous gulf in method of economic analysis, historical perspective and general purpose between Locke's inquiry into commercial relations and Smith's later inquiry. By comparison, Locke's theories seem antiquated and primitive.

For example Locke's general argument in Considerations and in Further Considerations advocated maintaining the interest rate and not devaluing the currency on the grounds of Natural Law.[1] Secondly, Locke put forward three economic laws[2] suggesting a pure "quantity" and "vent" (what today is called a supply and demand) theory of prices, wages, and profits, that appeared to be based on a free market with "self regulation" towards equilibrium. However, in most practical cases such as the issues relating to "the poor" and the question of Irish manufacturers, he advocated government intervention.

Nevertheless, many of the same ideas are emphasized by Smith and Locke such as the workers' necessity to accept truck for work instead of wages, and the labourers' complete dependence on employers in the contracts he agrees to. Yet, in each case they had different historical perspectives in mind as well as different opinions of these practices. Locke was, for example, in favour of workers' meagre subsistence whereas Smith was far more in favour of raising wages. Locke was in favour of earlier child labour,

---

1 Ibid., p. 67.

2 Considerations, passim.
1. Intrinsic value of goods is not reflected in price.
2. Market value of goods depends on supply and demand.
3. Price is determined also by quantity or money.

Smith was in favour of its abolition. Hence, their property theories and commentaries upon the facts and situations of their times even where they use the same terms are somewhat different.

V

Concerning Smith's use of Lockean political philosophic principles I have already indicated his dual view of contracts of government. Smith accepted the Lockean conception only so far as it was an implicit, not an historic, contract between subjects and sovereign. Yet Smith did accept much of Locke's natural rights political philosophy[1] which was implicit in Locke's version of the original contract. For example Smith states:

> Among equals each individual is naturally, and antecedent to the institution of civil government, regarded as having a right both to defend himself from injuries, and to exact a certain degree of punishment from those which have done them to him.[2]

How extraordinary similar to Locke is this conception of the "rights" of men before government as if it were drawn almost word for word from Locke's Second Treatise.[3] More important, Smith

---

1 Smith's belief that in primitive hunting tribes there was no government makes his many comments about this period interesting to compare with Locke's description of the State of Nature. Smith directly echoed Locke on p. 1 of his Lectures that Nations confront each other in a state of nature for there are no laws above each of their rulers. But later Smith says Lectures, p. 2, "It in reality serves no purpose to treat of the laws which would take place in a state of nature, or by what means succession to property was carried on, as there is no such state existing."

2 IMS, p. 115.

3 Two Treatises, II, Ch. II, sec. 7-5, pp. 289-94.

accepts Locke's belief that government's duty to protect property rights is the justification of the right of resistance or revolution if these property rights of individuals are usurped or are not protected. It is Smith's frequent echoing of Locke's description of men's political right in original, present and future society which suggests an unacknowledged debt to Locke's political thought. Smith described in detail political rights which have been denied or usurped,[1] as the conditions for the withdrawal of allegiance,[2] and insists that the aim of government must be to protect and promote the rights of individuals and act in their best interest.[3] All these are typical Lockean discussions.

Smith did not accept Locke's entire justification of Revolution or view politics in the Lockean terms of "sovereignty" and measuring governments against identifiable principles of "Natural Law." However, Smith and most of the writers of his time tended to view questions of - the political rights of men, the justifications for revolution, and adherence of governments to an implicit contract - all in the basic terms which Locke had formulated.

---

1 Lectures, p. 68-72.

2 Ibid., p. 68-72.

3 TMS, p. 269.

Finally, the close relation of alienation of property through contract and alienation of political rights of individuals through a social contract, was among the most important conceptions Locke was to bequeath to Smith, however much the latter denied the historical fact of an actual contract. Furthermore, Locke's contradictory views of alienable and inalienable political rights was taken over by Smith in his ambiguous attitude towards the extent of lawful Government taxation,1 the partial enfranchisement of colonists,2 the sale of provinces, colonies, political posts, and of "pocket" boroughs.3 These will be discussed in detail in a later chapter on Smith's view of existing government.

Smith also recongnized the basic Lockean proposition about government that political rights derive from property or land holding and that the propertyless were without political rights. This property basis of politics Smith suggested was necessary for moral, and political as well as economic stability and served to maintain the useful qualities of the "distinction of Ranks." However, Smith wished that this property requirement for enfranchisement and holding office, would be reduced. He definitely intended the reformed electorate to inclue all "leaseholders" as

---

1 WN, II, "Of Taxes" pp. 349-352. Lectures, pp. 69-72.

2 WN, II, pp. 137-8.

3 Lectures, pp. 69-72.

well as "freeholders" and many of the tradesman without land at all. Smith went beyond Locke in his dedication to real political reform.

Smith accepted both Locke's labour and conventional doctrines of property. He never really decided which of these two theories of property he considered primary. The rest of this thesis will attempt to show that many of Smith's ambiguous principles and theoretical self-contradictions in, for example, wages, profit, rent and class theories stem from his indecision concerning which of these two theories of property he really believed in or considered foremost. His labour theory of property led to his critique of current distributions of wealth and to his suggestions of exploitation. His conventional theory of property became the unstated premise of his abstract theories of supply and demand as the "natural" determinants of productive and distributive shares.

# CHAPTER IV

## PROPERTY IN ADAM SMITH'S SYSTEM OF MORAL PHILOSOPHY

It is the individual's paramount desire for the approval of other men which motivates him to virtuous acts and to property accumulation. And this approval or "approbation" which men desire springs from their ability to sympathize[1] with the situation or acts of one another. Although Smith gave numerous indications that self interest was men's rational motive for their acquisition of wealth, their more fundamental desire was to receive sympathy from other men for their material as well as their moral situation. That is, men sought to acquire approval by the acquisition of wealth. Thus I would assert that sympathy rather than self interest was the basis of property in Smith's system. This chapter will attempt to show this key position which property held in Smith's system of moral philosophy.

---

1 "Sympathy" by Smith's definition (TMS, p. 5) was the ability of the individual to enter into or imagine himself in the situation or someone else. "Sympathy", though its meaning was, perhaps, without much impropriety, be made use of to denote our fellow feeling with any passion whatever." TMS, p. 5. Thus an individual could sympathize either positively or negatively. Sympathy forms the basis of Smith's entire *Theory of Moral Sentiments* and it will be considered in detail in the following pages.

I

Adam Smith is so often spoken of as having established a "system" of moral philosophy, and a "system" of political economy,[1] that some clarification of what is meant by "Smith's system of thought" is necessary. By Smith's own definition:

> Systems in many respects resemble machines. A machine is a little system, created to perform, as well as to connect together, in reality, those different movements and effects which the artist has occasion for. A system is an imaginary machine invented to connect together in the fancy those different movements and effects which are already in reality performed.[2]

Smith was well aware there could be separate systems used to interrelate different social changes. An ethical system thus often had a different subject matter entirely from an economic system, and these separate orientations of his two major works (ethics as opposed to economics), have led Ethel Muir and Joseph Schumpeter to describe his system of thought exclusively in one of these two different ways.[3]

However, Smith was also well aware that there could be alternative systems of thought used to describe the same social subject

---

1 Ethel Muir The Ethical System of Adam Smith (Halifax, 1898). Joseph Schumpeter History of Economic Analysis ed. Elizabeth B. Schumpeter (London, 1963), p. 38. "Smith's Wealth of Nations was, in fact as in intention, a system of political economy."

2 EPS, p. 58, and Smith, Works V, pp. 116-7.

3 Muir, passim. Schumpeter, op. cit., p. 38.

such as ethics, or a particular branch of ethics. And in the last section of his Theory of Moral Sentiments, he contrasts his own system of ethical thought with that of others such as Plato, Aristotle, and Mandeville, which are based upon different principles of organization, such as propriety, prudence and benevolence. And in his Wealth of Nations Smith contrasted his own "system of natural liberty" with the economc systems of the Mercantilitsts, and of the Physiocrats. Therefore, there is ample justification for critical discussion of Smith's particular system of ethical and economic thought.[1]

However, Smith was struck by the "beauty and simplicity" of Bacon's and Newton's system of the natural laws of science which had incorporated many narrower and more disparate systems of thought from preceding ages. And Smith and others of the Scottish School consciously attempted to discover the natural and simple and most broadly comprehensive laws of social behaviour as Newton had discovered the system of natural scientific laws. Smith's total system of thought, therefore, was an attempt to incorporate the separate principles of ethics and economics in one great whole. It is in this sense of a total system of social thought that I will use the term "Smith's system" in the following discussion.

Hobbes, Aristotle and others before Smith, had attempted to outline a contemporary theory of social behaviour and he was well

---

1 Schumpeter, ibid., pp. 38-9, 167-97.

aware that there were a variety of quite different systems dealing with the whole of social development. Once again, Smith in an effort to emulate the Newtonian model, concluded that the best or most advanced system of social development[1] was the one which in the simplest terms could describe the most desparate social phenomenon.[2] Therefore, although Smith speaks of a variety of "systems" and a great number of "principles" in all his various works, it is this "Great system," and the "one great connecting principle" that Smith's thought is founded upon. Not only did Smith set this total system as his goal for his writings but periodically throughout his life and even in the amendments to his final editions of his writings he speaks of the extent to which he has succeeded in developing his entire system. Smith concluded that he had not fully accomplished this elaboration upon all the various parts of his system, but that the principles of it are well laid out in his existing writings.[3] An elucidation of his broad system, and the place of property within it, are the tasks of this chapter.

There has been such a wealth of material on Smith's total social system that a brief resume of the existing critical literature is called for before embarking on my own statement of what

---

1 EPS, p. 58, and Smith Works V, pp. 116-7.

2 EPS, p. 58, and Smith Works V. p. 117.

3 Introduction to the 6th edition of Theory of Moral Sentiments, op. cit.

appears to be property's place within his system. Since the time of Smith himself and the conjectures of his friend John Millar, then of Dugald Stewart,[1] and others,[2] there has been an effort made to enunciate the great connecting principles of Smith's system. That this effort is by no means yet exhausted, has been demonstrated by the controversies sparked off by the publication this century of G. R. Morrow's The Ethical and Economic Theories of Adam Smith,[3] and more recently by Joseph Cropsey's Polity and Economy.[4] Nor has the general area of disagreement narrowed to a few minor points with the passing of time. The controversies are surprisingly similar, in this century, to those of James McCulloch's time sixty years after the Wealth of Nations was published.[5]

These controversies appear to result from there being two primary ways of viewing Smith's descriptions of individuals and his attempts to interpret institutions and social change as the

---

1 John Millar's comments are reported in Dugald Stewart's "Account" op. cit.

2 In the 19th century John Rae (not Smith's biographer but an earlier economist) and Hasback, Onekan and several German theorists debated this.

3 Morrow, Theories, op. cit. See also the review of this book by Herbert J. Davenport in Philosophical Review XXXIV (1923) pp. 599-611.

4 Cropsey, Polity and Economy, op. cit., and A. L. Macfie, Individual in Society, op. cit., Ch. 7.

5 See James McCulloch's Introduction to his edition of Smith's Wealth of Nations (London, 1843).

result of instincts, or characteristics which are found in individual men. The second method is to look at the concrete historical order of society which Smith describes and his attempt to interpret the nature of individuals as affected by changes in that social and political order. The first method assumes society is a product of individuals' natures, the second assumes the individual is a product of society.

Joseph Cropsey's Polity and Economy, Henry J. Bitterman's "Adam Smith's Empiricism and the Law of Nature" and Lionel Robbins, The Theory of Economic Policy in English Classical Political Economy, and other economists have attempted to integrate Smith's Wealth of Nations psychology of individuals' passions and self-interest with the comments Smith makes in the Theory of Moral Sentiments on self interested psychology. Smith's system according to these authors is based on market psychology. The prime motivation of the individual is self preservation, and society is a product of individual drives or "passions." Cropsey describes the combined effect of these drives as a "motions effective" type of human development.

On the other hand, there is a traditional integration of the morals and economics of Smith's system described in detail by G. R. Morrow,[1] Ethel Muir,[2] and James Bonar in his article

---

1 Morrow, Theories, op. cit., passim.

2 Muir, op. cit., passim.

"The theory of Moral Sentiments by Adam Smith 1759".1 This method first suggested by John Millar, and Dugald Stewart, and now adhered to by most moralists and sociologists who have studied Smith, attempts to interrelate the total method of the Wealth of Nations with the total method of the Moral Sentiments. This pursuit derives from Smith's own well known conception of "Moral Philosophy" as the subject which combined Natural religion, ethics, political economy and jurisprudence.

In this traditional scheme of Smith's system, passions are but one part of the human character, and psychology is but one part of the total Smithian system of moral philosophy. The hallmark of this interpretation of Smith's system is that society, institutions and history altered individuals. Both man's sentiments and passions must change or find different modes of expression with changes of social relations in different times, places, and circumstances.2 Most important, we find that changes in property forms alter not only the state and social institutions, but these changes direct men's sentiments to different objects and cause alterations in the way our passions are expressed. According to this interpretation, because man is of necessity social, his passions and sentiments were implanted in

---

1 James Bonar "The Theory of Moral Sentiments by Adam Smith" op. cit., pp. 333-53.

2 TMS, V, "Of the Influence of Custom and Fashion upon the Sentiments of Moral Approbation and Disapprobation" pp. 279-307.

him to enable him to live and develop in society and to fulfill social goals that have been set in the nature of society by God.[1]

Fundamentally these two methods: the individualist and the social, are simply two ways of looking at the same social development Smith describes. Both are valid methods considered objectively whenever used for analyzing the two sides of man's social behaviour. And both these methods are valid when describing various aspects of Smith's system because Smith employed both methods himself.

Cropsey, Bitterman and Robbins describe Adam Smith's use of the individual method when attempting to show how specific economic institutions arise from certain human traits. The division of labour, for example, arises from the instinct to barter. At times Smith suggests that the whole economic order arises from the activity of individual self-interest, and from all of Nature's self preservative activities.

Pascal, Meek, Small and Morrow show Smith's use of the later social method when he describes the effects in the individuals' behaviour as a result of "change" in the nature of property". His treatment of social change and advancement are analyzed by them in specific terms as anticipations of our modern sociological

---

1 Divine Direction of Society is suggested by Smith in the TMS, p. 125 and in countless other passages. It is described in detail by Bitterman, op. cit., pp. 703-4, and T. E. Cliffe Leslie, Essays in Political and Moral Philosophy (London, 1879) Introduction. And Viner "ASLF" pp. 202-214.

method. Types of conduct approved at one time are totally disapproved of in another epoch, society, or class. Smith's spectrum of such modern social changes which transform individual senitments range from the disapproval of infanticide, to the "necessity" for every "credible man" to "wear a linen shirt."[1]

But precisely because Smith employed both these two methods: the individualist and the social, it is incomplete for his interpreters to analyze him as if he used only one of them. Cropsey's method attempts to make Smith's system a mechanical model of self-preservative drives, much as in Hobbes' system. In Cropsey, Bitterman and others holding the individualist view, very little admission is made that there are other decidedly different interpretations of Smith's sociological, or historical investigations of property. That is, Cropsey and several others treat the individual psychological system as the only one Smith advances. On the other hand, Pascal, Small and others considering Smith as a forerunner of modern sociology somewhat neglect the individualist drives that spring from universal human psychology rather than social forces.

Although G. R. Morrow did not recognize that individualist vs. social analysis was the basic division between the different interpreters of Smith, he did recognize better than most that Smith employed both these two methods. And Morrow perceptively

---

1 WN, II, p. 399.

concluded that the individualist method used by Smith was largely a residue from earlier centuries; whereas the effects of society upon individuals was:

> ... practically a new line of enquiry in eighteenth century thought. It looks for the origin of the moral judgement, not in an innate individual source of insight, but in social experience. The individual's moral consciousness with its judgements of approval and disapproval is a reflection, or a derivative, of the social consciousness; it grows through experience in society, and represents the demands of his fellow-men upon the individual. This theory, therefore, looks upon the individual not as an absolute and irreducible entity existing prior to social experience, but as a product of his social environment.[1]

Thus we find that these two sets of interpretations of Smith are based upon two methods of viewing man in society used by Smith himself.

Though Smith does not explicitly state that he was using these two methods he does, in his descriptions of his own work's scope and purpose, appear to recognize these different approaches; individualist and social.[2] Smith investigated, like the Greeks before him,

> Wherein consisted the happiness and perfection of a man, considered not only as an individual but as the member

---

1 G. R. Morrow, "Adam Smith: Moralist and Philosopher" Journal of Political Economy XXXV (1927), pp. 321-42. See esp. p. 340.

2 Lectures, p. 8.

> of a family, of a state, and of the great society of mankind.[1]

But a clearer statement that Smith recognized one aspect at least of these divergent approaches to men in society appears in his *Lectures*. And this comparative viewpoint is particularly relevant for this dissertation because he recognized that the study of property could be approached either in terms of each individual man's natural property rights, or in terms of the society's or state's property laws and property institutions. Smith says that some theorists:

> ... begin with considering government and then treat of property and rights. Others who have written on this subject begin with the latter and then consider the family and civil government. There are several advantages peculiar to each of these methods, although that of the civil law seems on the whole preferable.[2]

## II

Adam Smith taught philosophy for thirteen years (1751-63) at Glasgow University, lecturing particularly on moral philosophy. Following the traditional pattern, he encompasses ethics, religion, economics, and politics within the general subject of moral

---

1 *WN*, II, p. 293.

2 *Lectures*, p. 8.

philosophy[1] the former two subjects embracing the nature of virtue, the two latter subjects giving the objective exemplification of virtue.

Smith's Theory of Moral Sentiments (1759) develops his views on ethical virtue; his Lectures of Justice, Police Revenue and Arms (1763) develop his views on economics, law and justice: finally his Wealth of Nations (1776) integrated his theory of virtue with its exemplification in economics, law and justice.

The obvious relation between Smith's two major books has been noted by Jacob Viner among others[2] as an acknowledged fact.

---

1 For a brief discussion of the traditional formulation of Moral Philosophy at Smith's time see Dugald Stewart "Account" op. cit., xx-xxii. Compare this to the general views of the whole Scottish School. See Bryson, op. cit., pp. 3-5, 11-12, 17, 37, 112-3, 152, 173, 176-7.

2 Joseph Schumpeter, in his History of Economic Analysis, op. cit., p. 141. echoes a generally acknowledged opinion when he stated: "Both the Moral Sentiments and the Wealth of Nations are blocks cut out from a larger systematic whole." Meek, op. cit., p. 129 and Macfie, Individual and Society, op. cit., Ch. 7, pp. 59-82, "Adam Smith's Moral Sentiments as Foundation for his Wealth of Nations" express much the same opinion.

This relationship between Smith's moral philosophy and his principles of political economy has been a source of frequent controversy. The vital issues of this controversy have not been centred on whether there were interrelating principles or themes between Smith's moral and economic thought. Most authors (I will deal with J. Cropsey's Polity and Economy separately) would tend to agree with G. R. Morrow "That there was a unity of spirit and aim in Adam Smith's treatment of these separate divisions of moral philosophy (i.e. ethics, political economy and jurisprudence) cannot be doubted. Morrow, Theories, op. cit., p. 159. The controversy has centred instead on the drastically different methods Smith seems to recommend for the attainment of these aims in his ethical vs. his economic writings. In Moral Sentiments Smith recommends "self-interest" not only as the usual and most powerful motive for human improvement but as the motive which

> It is commonplace among the authorities on Adam Smith that it is impossible fully to understand the Wealth of Nations without recourse to the Theory of Moral Sentiments.1

Yet, even more important, Smith appears to have had an integrated set of philosophic principles employed in all his various writings.

In his History of Ancient Physics he says it is now accepted that:

> The Universe ... [is] ... a coherent system governed by general laws, and directed to general ends, viz. its own preservation and prosperity, and that of all the species that are in it.2

---

should actuate men in their economic relations. This striking dilemma which has troubled economists and moralists alike is fundamentally more apparent than real. For the sake of brevity I will cite Morrow's explanation for this: p. 166. "In fact, if those who believed there was a discrepancy between the Moral Sentiments and the Wealth of Nations had but taken the pains to consult the former work thoroughly, a great deal of this alleged discrepancy would have disappeared. It is true that in Moral Sentiments Adam Smith opposes the egoistic doctrine that man acts only from self-love, and exalts benevolence as the highest virtue. But there are other inferior virtues recognized, such as prudence, frugality, industry, self-reliance. These virtues must be restrained and regulated, bu justice, but when so regulated they are conducive to the welfare of the general public as well as of the individual. The important consideration is that these self-interested activities must be regulated by justice." p. 167. "In short, unregulated self-interest is no more advocated in the Wealth of Nations than it is in the Moral Sentiments, whereas in the latter work the moral value of the inferior virtues, when properly regulated, is fully recognized."

1 Viner "ASLF" p. 201.

2 EPS, p. 140, The History of Ancient Physics, EPS, op. cit., I, Introduction.

Since Smith makes a distinction between preservation and prosperity, we may assume that the universe must do more than survive to "prosper"; that is, the standards of "prosperity" must be other than "preservation".

"Prosperity," for Smith meant a universe preserving itself in a certain manner, according to natural moral laws which he discovered inherent in the universe:

> These important rules of morality are the commands and laws of the Deity, ...[1]

> In every part of the universe we observe means adjusted with the nicest artifice to the ends which they are intended to produce; and in the mechanism of a plant, or animal body, admire how every thing is contrived for advancing the two great purposes of nature, the support of the individual, and the propagation of the species.[2]

To understand Smith's full meaning for his phrase "the support of the individual" when he identifies it as one of "the two great purposes of nature," we must realize Nature's "support" meant far more than providing physical subsistence. It also meant setting qualities within human nature that would foster harmonious social development. As Smith says:

> It it [justice] is removed, the great, the immense fabric of human society, that fabric which, to raise and support, seems in this world, if I may say so, to have

---

1 TMS, p. 232.

2 TMS, p. 126.

> been the peculiar and darling care of nature, must in a moment crumble into atoms.[1]

Therefore, Nature cannot support the individual or society without justice. It is for this reason that Smith insists that men have been instilled by Nature with a natural sentiment to abide by "the most sacred laws of justice."[2]

Yet men are simultaneously instilled by nature, as are all animals at birth, with the instinct of self preservation. Self preservation and justice are two attributes which each man must harmonize for himself in all those actions where these two attributes would tend to conflict with one another. In property relations especially, Smith recognized this tendency of man's moral sentiments to guide him to actions his instinct for self preservation would warn against.

> Thus man is by nature directed to correct, in some measure, that distribution of things which she herself would otherwise have made. The rules which for this purpose she prompts him to follow, are different from those which she herself observes.[3]

Smith does not make clear whether natural distribution of wealth would be more or less equal than it is, though two points are

---

1 TMS, p. 125.

2 TMS, p. 121. "The most sacred laws of justice, therefore, [are] those whose violation seems to call loudest for vengeance and punishment ..."

3 TMS, p. 238. See Albion Small, Adam Smith and Modern Sociology (Chicage, 1907), for an analysis.

raised in his writing. First, Smith believed in a natural "subsistence-minimum theory of wages",1 which implied if it did not state, that nature could not tolerate, for long, the rate of wages to fall below subsistence needs. Second, Smith believed that "the natural progress of opulence" would in the future tend to make more equal the general distribution of wealth. It was perhaps because of these assumptions that Smith concluded:

> The rules which she [nature] follows are fit for her, those which he [man] follows for him: but both are calculated to promote the same great end, the order of the world, and the perfection and happiness of human nature.2

'Perfection and happiness of human nature,' were not semi-religious objective as they may seem in the above passage. Not only in his Theory of Moral Sentiments, but also in his Lectures, and in the Wealth of Nations, Smith pursued this "same great end." What did Smith consider to be "the happiness and perfection of a man?" As he states it himself:

> To feel much for others, and little for ourselves, that to restrain our selfish, and to indulge our benevolent affections, constitutes the perfection of human nature; ...3

---

1 WM, I, pp. 76, 83. And see Albion Small, Adam Smith and Modern Sociology (Chicago, 1907), p. 133. "The Beginnings of the classical subsistence-minimum Theory of wages, as contained in Ch. VIII of the Wealth of Nations."

2 TMS, p. 238-239.

3 TMS, p. 27.

III

Although Smith's professed intention was to describe what men's actual moral sentiments were, not what they should be, his entire book, The Theory of Moral Sentiments is concerned, to a significant extent, with how this ultimate goal of "the perfection of human nature" is to be achieved. The book concentrates on the interrelations of "Sympathy," "the impartial spectator", and "Self Command". These were the three factors which he believed were responsible for perfecting or improving men.

"Sympathy" is man's capacity for fellow feeling with others.[1] It is the most fundamental moral sentiment and leads to or forms the foundation for all others. Through Sympathy the individual transcends the limits of his own individuality. In theory he observes and participates in all respects where men have common qualities.[2]

The "impartial Spectator" was not a real but hypothetical observer who passes positive or negative judgements upon the actions of those around him. All men place themselves in such a position to judge strangers and later in this same "impartial spectator's" role they judge their friends, family and finally their own actions.[3] Although Smith explains that a "partial"

---

1 TMS, p. 5.

2 TMS, p.18.

3 TMS, pp. 162-4.

and "impartial Spectator" within each man vie for predominance, Smith would describe society's laws and morality as the product primarily of the "impartial spectator." That is, all social judgements of right and wrong, justice and injustice, derive from the decisions of a hypothetical "impartial spectator". By reversing the role of the "impartial spectator" in respect to others, and applying it to ourselves each individual can measure the justice or rightness of his own actions and passions.[1]

> We endeavour to examine our own conduct as we imagine any other fair and impartial spectator would examine it.[2]

But for the individual to consider himself and to determine his actions and passions primarily from the standpoint of the impartial rather than the partial spectator requires "self-command".[3] "Self-Command" is the capacity of the individual to control his selfish and antisocial passions and to direct his efforts towards socially beneficial objectives.[4] Self-command is, therefore, the disciplined path to social harmony and to true

---

1 <u>TMS</u>, p. 161. "We can never survey our own sentiments and motives, we can never form any judgement concerning them, unless we remove ourselves, as it were, from our own natural station, and endeavour to view them as at a certain distance from us. But we can do this in no other way than by endeavouring to view them with the eyes of other people, ..."

2 <u>TMS</u>, p. 162.

3 <u>TMS</u>, Part VI, Sec. III, pp. 349-385; see entire section "Of Self Command."

4 <u>TMS</u>, pp. 349-385.

self-interest. Only the reciprocal process of sympathy, impartial spectator, and self-command yield the virtuous man, one who has discovered his true nature and true self interest.

Among the property and social relations of his own time, however, Smith observed that men tended to view their own actions and possessions very selfishly, and tended to sympathize with the rich not the virtuous.

> This disposition to admire, and almost to worship, the rich and the powerful, and to despise, or at least, to neglect, persons of poor and mean condition, ... is ... the great and most universal cause of the corruption or our moral sentiments.1

Despite this fact that "the great mob of mankind"2 are inclined to be selfish, Smith does not despair of obtaining the virtuous man. For even the "partial spectator" represents through sympathy the conditions of others.3 The problem is how the partial spectator can be made impartial: and thereby make us aware of our natural sympathies. To do this Smith concludes how we naturally appear to ourselves, must be made to conform with how we naturally appear to others.4

---

1 TMS, p. 84.

2 TMS, p. 85. "The great mob of mankind are the admirers and worshippers, ... of wealth and greatness."

3 TMS, p. 120. " ... he dares not look mankind in the face, and avow that he acts according to" selfishness.

4 TMS, pp. 161-165.

This process of creating an impartial spectator within oneself is, according to Smith, nothing other than the acquisition of reason;[1] for it is reason, or conscience, which compels us to view ourselves as others view us.[2]

> If we see ourselves in the light in which others see us, or in which they would see us if they knew all, a reformation would generally be unavoidable.[3]

In theoretical morals Smith believed a complete understanding of our own harmful actions was all that was vitally necessary to ensure that "a reformation would generally be unavoidable." Therefore men's sympathy, impartial reasoning, and self command (in what Smith calls "the courage of mind") are the vital agents of their moral improvement.

## IV

Smith's property theory and moral theory are usually said to be interrelated because each recognized the individual's self interest. The following I hope will indicate that sympathy was another and perhaps more fundamental basis for the interrelations of property and morals in Smith's system.

---

1 TMS, p. 194. "It is reason, principle conscience."

2 TMS, pp. 121-2. "The violator of the more sacred laws of justice can never reflect on the sentiments which mankind must entertain with regard to him, without feeling all the agonies of shame, and horror, and consternation ... he becomes in some measure the object of his own hatred and abhorrence."

3 TMS, p. 223.

The idea of the sympathetic spectator was not confined by him to ethics. In the Lectures we read:

> Occupation [right of the first holder] seems to be well-founded when the spectator can go along with my possession of the object, and approve me when I defend my possession by force. If I have gathered some wild fruit, it will appear reasonable to the spectator, that I should dispose of it as I please.1

This sympathetic basis of property is not restricted to the primitive stages of society. "The Foundation of contract is the reasonable expectation which the person who promises raises in the person to whom he binds himself; ..."2 John Millar, Dugald Stewart and James Bonar point out that Smith's property theory has its foundations in public sympathy with any man's reasonable expectations of reward.3 For example Dugald Stewart says:

> Some later philosophers (later than Locke and Grotius) have founded the right of property on the general sympathy of mankind with the reasonable expectation which the occupant has formed of enjoying unmolested the object he has got possesison of, or of which he was the first discoverer; and on the indignation felt by the impartial spectator when he sees this reasonable expectation disappointed. This theory (which I

---

1 Lectures, p. 108.

2 Lectures, p. 7.

3 Smith derived this sympathetic basis of property rights from Hutcheson, see System, I, pp. 319-320. However, Hutcheson and Smith did not entirely agree in their conception of the sympathetic basis of property because Hutcheson attributed the origin of property to benevolence. Though Smith does not appear to have contradicted this, his views nevertheless, point to more complex psychological origins of property.

> have been assured from the best authority [John Millar] was adopted by Mr. Smith in his Lectures on Jurisprudence) seems to have been suggested by a passage in Dr. Hutcheson's Moral Philosophy.[1]

Stewart implies that Smith's sympathetic basis of property was directly in contrast to Locke's labour theory of property rights. But, as the preceding passage from the Lectures suggests, Smith's theory of the sympathetic foundation of property could be used to justify various property claims. The public's sympathy might just as well justify the labourer's ownership of those things with which he had mixed his labour, as it might on the other hand, justify a will that left money to a cat. Though there might be a tendency for public sympathy to uphold the customary property rights of social tradition and established state laws this did not necessarily mean that the "natural" property rights of unpaid apprentices (or of other groups) could not call forth the sympathy of the public. It must be stressed that this sympathetic basis of

---

1 This passage is from Stewart's Life of Adam Smith. A Bibliographical Memoir for the Edinborough Royal Society, 1811, p. 12, and is contained in Dugald Stewart's Active and Moral Powers, 2 Vols., in Works op. cit., II, p. 317. The quotation from Hutcheson is a shortened version of a footnote appearing in his System, Vol. I, Bk. II, ch. V, pp. 317-8. cf. p. 254.

An important parallel from this interpretation of Smith's property theory as based upon sympathy is furnished by G. R. Morrow's assertion that "It might almost be said that the doctrine of sympathy is a necessary presupposition of the doctrine of the natural order expounded in the Wealth of Nations. At least it seems probable that Adam Smith had this earlier theory in mind as a covering for the naked economic individualism which he expounds in the later work, "Adam Smith: Moralist and Philosopher" op. cit., p. 341.

property usually did not contradict nor entirely presuppose either of the two property theories - from original labour, or from social coventions - which were shown in the previous chapter to have been used by Smith for the justification of property rights. Public sympathy formed a foundation of reasonable expectations on which to evaluate various property claims; based on laws, customs or the "natural rights" of the labourer. Any of these justifications of property rights, Smith implied, could receive the positive sympathy of the public or of an impartial spectator depending upon the circumstances of any dispute.1

In the following pages we will examine one ramification of this sympathetic basis of property in Smith's thought. We will concentrate on the relationship between the drive to acquire material wealth and the drive for the acquisition of positive sympathy or approval. The vital common link between these two drives I contend to be the individual's desire for dignity or a permanent condition of social approval.

Men's possession of sympathy did not only provide a foundation for evaluating property claims on the basis of reasonable expectations. The individual's ability to sympathize with others and to elicit sympathy from others is the primary assumption of

---

1 Examples from the Wealth of Nations of claims to rightful property ownership which Smith implies are supported by public sympathy are the claims of apprentices WN, I, p. 136, of colonists WN, II, p. 95 and the claims of workers generally to an equitable share of social wealth WN, I, p. 88.

Smith's moral theory. Men seek the positive sympathy or "approbation" of others. This is a fundamental motivation for human behaviour.

> But to be that thing which deserves approbation, must always be an object of the highest ...1

As suggested earlier, men seek approval not only for their benevolent deeds but for their just obedience to laws and for their prudent management of their affairs. Men even desire approval for their selfish defence of their property rights and property claims to ownership of things in dispute.2

But totally selfish acts are less likely to receive approval. Thus, the relationship between men's desire for approval and their desire for material wealth, was a complex psychological interaction. Smith's views in his various works are not entirely consistent and indeed his manner of argument may have tended to imply a clear cut division between these two desires when, in fact, his total thought show the realtionship to be quite subtle. Smith repeatedly implies that men's desire for wealth springs solely from their natural self interest. "Give me that which I want, and you shall have this which you want,"3 Smith says is the basis of all material exchanges.

---

1 TMS, p. 171.

2 Lectures, p. 108.

3 WN, I, p. 18.

> It is not from the benevolence of the butcher, the brewer, or the baker, that we expect our dinner, but from their regard to their own interest.[1]

Throughout the Wealth of Nations self interest recurs in various arguments as the rational motivation for exchange and for the drive to accumulate wealth. Self interest is the rational explanation for engaging in almost all property relations. What is not always apparent in these many discussions of self interested individuals who pursue the enlargement of their material possessions is the relationship between this selfishness and the universal desire of individuals to receive the approval of other men. Although the benevolence of the butcher would be more strongly approved by an impartial spectator than his prudent self interest, in most ordinary cases we do not disapprove of him for selling rather than giving meat. In fact we approve his prudent property relations and we approve of that material wealth he has accumulated, and that social position of dignity and prosperity which he had achieved.[2]

Therefore, although Smith gives numerous indications that self-interest is men's rational motive for their material acquisitiveness, their more fundamental desire is to acquire sympathy

---

1 WN, I, p. 18.

2 TMS, pp. 70-83 "Of the Origin of Ambition and the Distinction of Ranks" and see Lectures pp. 9-10, "our sympathy with our superiors being greater than with our inferiors; we admire their happy situation, enter into it with pleasure and endeavour to promote it."

from other men for their economic situation and for their riches.[1] Men seek wealth and position primarily in order to obtain approval, the positive sympathy of their fellow men.[2]

> Nay, it is chiefly from this regard to the sentiments of mankind, that we pursue riches and avoid poverty.[3]

The permanent approval of other men is sought by individuals through their struggle to achieve dignity.[4] Dignity, or that condition of continuous social approbation, could be obtained by possessing a thoroughly virtuous character, or by possessing a position of public trust, or by the possession of a considerable amount of wealth.[5] At its minimal level the dignity of an ordinary individual requires at least an honest character, a decent employment, and a moderate standard of living.[6] The desire of ordinary men to achieve this minimal level of dignity drives them to maintain and at times to improve their moral conduct and their economic and social position. This desire for dignity or social approval forms the link between Smith's theory of moral improvement and his theory of actual social, economic,

---

1 Compare WN, I, p. 15 to TMS, p. 70.

2 TMS, p. 70.

3 TMS, p. 70.

4 TMS, p. 72.

5 TMS, p. 78.

6 TMS, pp. 76-7.

and political motivations or ordinary men.1 Dignity, as discussed by Smith, will therefore be considered in some detail.

The individual's drive to achieve dignity is allied to "the pursuit of virtue." And of men's desire for this social approval Smith says, "the love of it is the love of virtue."2 In all Smith's work the idea of dignity is a prime motive for improvement and a prime object of emulation and ambition:

> To deserve, to acquire, and to enjoy, the respect and admiration of mankind, are the great objects of ambition and emulation.3

Dignity was not only the ordinary man's goal or object for ethical improvement4 but his goal in economic matters as well. For without the dignity afforded by the minimal material standards of decency,

> Everything that could render either life or death respectable is taken from them.5

---

1 Smith's concept of dignity forms what I believe Dugald Stewart sought for as the "connection between his system of commercial politics (sic), and those speculations of his earlier years which he aimed more professedly at the advancement of human improvement and happiness." Stewart, "Account", p. liv.

2 TMS, p. 171.

3 TMS, p. 84.

4 TMS, p. 194. "It is not the love of our neighbour, it is not the love of mankind, which upon many occasions prompts us to the practice of those divine virtues. It is a stronger love, a more powerful affection, which generally takes place upon such occasions; the love of what is hounourable and noble, of the grandure, and dignity, and superiority of our own characters."

5 TMS, p. 176.

A belief in material as well as moral improvement seemed to Smith,

> A hope and expectation deeply rooted in human nature, which can alone support its lofty ideas of its own dignity.[1]

Nor is dignity, to any real extent, frowned upon by Smith as a goal for either moral, economic, or other behaviour.

> To desire it [dignity, or deserved approbation] where it is really due, is to desire no more than that a most essential act of justice should be done to us.[2]

The reason that the idea of dignity might be sometimes frowned upon by the general public is that they tend to confuse it with pride. Yet, to Smith, pride and dignity represent two distinct roads leading from man's fundamental Self Regard. Self Regard according to Smith has two forms: Self Esteem which leads to pride and the pursuit of luxury and power, and ultimately results in corruption and waste; and Self Respect which leads to dignity and the pursuit of adequate propserity and the complete use of natural and human wealth.

This scheme is of the utmost importance in understanding Smith's theory of property. Smith continually distinguishes pride and the pursuit of luxury from dignity and the pursuit of prosperity.

---

1 TMS, p. 187.

2 TMS, p. 171.

> Two different characters are presented to our emulation; the one of proud ambition and ostentatious avidity; the other, of humble modesty and equitable justice.[1]

At many points Smith makes these two pursuits[2] seem diametrically opposed to one another.[3] And in absolute or theoretical terms they are opposed: "Two different roads are presented to us," "Two different characters are presented," "Two different models, two different pictures, are held out to us, according to which we may fashion our own character and behaviour; ..."[4]

However, Smith also recognized that in the general public's view, the two pursuits frequently seem the same,[5] because:

> In the middling and inferior stations of life, the road to virtue and that to fortune, to such fortune, at least, as men in such stations can reasonably expect to acquire, are, happily, in most cases very nearly the same.[6]

Several points regarding Dignity's relation to property and human improvement emerge from this passage. First, if these labouring poor are actually by circumstances directed toward prosperity and virtue why did Smith feel the need to press for improvement in

---

1 TMS, p. 85.

2 TMS, p. 85.

3 TMS, pp. 84-88.

4 TMS, p. 85.

5 TMS, p. 85, "Intentive observers are very apt to mistake the one for the other."

6 TMS, p. 86.

their condition? The answer was simply that though circumstance directed the poor toward the dignified life, their living and working conditions sometimes denied them often even the minimal standards of food, clothing and shelter, namely the simplest personal standards of dignity. As mentioned earlier, Smith believed that a certain minimal dignity must be possessed by individuals before they can choose and pursue dignity as a goal. Once again, dignity was both a means and an end; a man must have a certain self-respect before he can pursue the good opinion of others.[1] And a man must have a certain minimum of material possessions before he will respect the property rights of others. The relation between dignity and property was to be continually re-emphasized in exactly these terms; certain minimal levels of property were necessary for men to achieve, or even pursue dignity as a goal.

Secondly, concerning dignity and the labouring man;

> The success of such people, too, almost always depends upon the favour and good opinion of their neighbours and equals; and without a tolerably regular conduct, these can very seldom be obtained.[2]

As this passage suggests, dignity required the individual to feel not superior (as pride usually would require) but equal to his fellows. Once again Smith's own belief in a certain equality of

---

1 WN, II, p. 309.

2 TMS, pp. 86-7.

human beings led him to conceive the best moral and econmic condition as that which made circumstance of social and economic life lead to a greater equality.1

Nevertheless, we find that Smith contrasted the labouring classes' simultaneous pursuit of prosperity, virtue, and equal dignity, with the propertied classes' pursuit of pride, luxury and inequality. Smith catalogues the corruption and wastefulness of the rich in the Wealth of Nations2 The Draft3 of the Wealth of Nations and in his Lectures4 and it is useful for our examination of dignity's relation to property to find corroboration in the Theory of Moral Sentiments for this distinction between the pursuits of the rich and the poor.

> Men in the inferior and middling stations of life, besides, can never be great enough to be above the law, which must generally overawe them into some sort of respect for, at least, the more important rules of justice.5

By inference, the effect of great wealth was to place the possessor in certain instances above the law and by their wealth could corrupt to some extent the administration and even the making of laws. By doing so they were destroying not only the

---

1 Schumpeter, op. cit., p. 186

2 WN, I, p. 433.

3 Draft, p. 326-7.

4 Lectures, p. 256-7.

5 TMS, p. 86.

rules of justice but they were also hampering the natural development of property relations and depriving individuals of those minimal standards of dignity which would enable them through legal property relations to pursue the dignified life.[1]

V

To demonstrate the relevance of Smith's Moral Senitments to specific economic theories in his Wealth of Nations, his interpreters have usually analyzed the "invisible hand" which is mentioned in each of Smith's major works.[2] I believe the use of this method has tended to beg many of the important questions about the relations between Smith's theories. I also believe this method puts his system of thought into a determinist perspective before even considering his theories.

The interrelations of the two works is best shown by analyzing three formal principles which are found in both works and which form the key supports to these books' separate arguments. These three principles are: individual human equality, the harmony of individual and public interest, and the absolute necessity for justice as the fundamental requirement in both moral and economic development.

---

1 TMS, Pt. I, sec. III, pp. 60-90 "Of the Effects of Prosperity.

2 TMS, pp. 264-5 and WN, I, p. 477.

First, Smith's presumption in the Theory of Moral Sentiments that all men have moral sentiments (and hence are able no matter how corrupt or degraded, to feel sympathy, love, guilt etc.) led him ultimately to assert conjecturally a belief in the natural similiarity of all individuals in their economic and political relations. Individuals could only see themselves in one another's position to feel and then judge the approval and disapproval of one another's acts if there was something equivalent in men's sentiments and sympathies. Moreover, a certain equality, Smith insisted, must be the basis of the laws of justice and the basis of contracts in all market exchanges.

Although there exist certain questions about the extent of Smith's belief in universal human equality, there is general unanimity on Smith's tendency to equalitarianism. Albion Small when commenting on Smith's equalitarianism goes as far as to say Smith's

> ... propositions, taken by themselves, are identical with clauses in the doctrines of nearly all the modern revolutionary philosophers. They are taken for granted by most of the extreme socialists.1

On the other hand, Schumpeter in a quite different way notes the effect Smith's equalitarianism had on those who followed.

> A judiciary diluted Reousseauism is also evident in the equalitarian tendency of his economic sociology. Human beings seemed to him to be much alike by nature, all reacting in the same simple

---

1 Small, Adam Smith and Modern Sociology, op. cit., p. 100.

> ways to very simple stimuli, differences being due mainly to different training and different environments. This is very important considering A. Smith's influence upon nineteenth century economics. His work was the channel through which eighteenth century ideas about human nature reached economists.[1]

And we find an interesting corroboration of this view not only in other secondary material, but when directly comparing Smith's most famous statement of the equality of men with a comment of Karl Marx. For example Smith says,

> The difference between the most dissimilar characters, between a philosopher and a common street porter, for example, seems to arise not so much from nature, as from habit, custom, and education.[2]

Marx in The Holy Family stressed that what necessarily connects theories such as Smith's "with communism and socialism," are "a common belief in the equality of intellectual endowment among men, the omnipotence of experience, habit, and education and the influence of environment on man."[3]

Smith's belief in the universal equality of individuals throughout his works furnishes the clearest example of the bonds between his ethics and economics. Equality forms the basis of Smith's moral theory of sympathies and of original property rights, namely labour or occupation by anyone. Equality is the

---

1 Schumpeter, op. cit., p. 186.

2 WN, I, pp. 19-20.

3 Karl Marx, The Holy Family (Moscow, 1956) pp. 175-6.

original basis of property exchange according to Smith's labour-time theory of value. Only if all individuals are naturally alike or to some extent equal does it follow that "equal quantities of labour, at all times and places, may be said to be of equal value."[1]

However, Smith's conception of the movement of society from the "rude" towards the "refined" condition was not static but an active progress motivated by the striving for dignity. This led the general public continually to raise their standards of prosperity and hence the general level of property distribution. Nevertheless, though his moral theory called for an increase in general equality, it also recognized the need for a distinction of ranks.[2] In theory these were not contradictory because of his idea that we must strive to emulate those few who are truly virtuous. Thus in theory he reconciled his desire for equality with his acceptance of inequality, by his explanation that inequality provided a goal or a spur for the general effort of the whole population towards improvement. In practice these two goals must conflict. But Smith does not seem to have fully appreciated this.

The second theme, in both the Theory of Moral Sentiments and Wealth of Nations is the reconciliation of the interests of the

---

1 WN, I, p. 37.

2 TMS, pp. 70-83.

individual and the interests of the society. This conception of the possibility and even the necessity for some social harmony of individuals and groups within the society has fascinated many of Smith's interpreters and has been the subject of detailed analysis by Lionel Robbins in The Theory of Economic Policy in English Classical Political Economy[1] and by Warren J. Samuels in The Classical Theory of Economic Policy.[2] And many other writers such as Viner,[3] Checkland,[4] Morrow,[5] and Bitterman,[6] have observed the interrelations of Smith's descriptions of moral harmony and economic harmony. For example, G. R. Morrow states;

> May I suggest also that this ethical theory is of great importance for understanding the doctrine of economic harmony between the interests of the individual and the interests of the public which we found maintained in the Wealth of Nations.[7]

Social conflicts will always exist, Smith admits, but they must, he asserts, be restrained within acceptable limits of harmony.

---

1 Robbins, op. cit., pp. 25-9, 55-7.

2 Samuels, op. cit., pp. 6-9.

3 Viner "ASLF" op. cit., pp. 198-232.

4 S. G. Checkland, "Prescriptions of the Classical Economist", Economica XX (1953) pp. 61-72. See esp. p. 71.

5 Morrow, "Adam Smith, Moralist and Philosopher" op. cit., p. 159.

6 Bitterman, op. cit., p. 491.

7 Morrow, "Adam Smith, Moralist aan Philosopher" op. cit., p. 159.

Buyers and sellers, labourers and employers, rich and poor all may have conflicting interests but both in each case are better off because of commercial exchanges and thus share an interest in harmony. Yet a debate still continues as to whether harmony is the result of natural or divine inspiration in man, or whether such harmony as we can expect among antagonistic social interests will occur because of social direction and institutions. Bitterman argues:

> If nature assured a harmony of interest there would have been no complaint about mercantilism, monopoly, guild regulations, and the monopolistic employment of labour.1

And yet Smith at many points explicitly speaks of a "natural harmony of interests". Perhaps Smith was echoing what Mark Blaug describes as "the shibboleths of time, a convenient weapon against mercantilist thinking."2 Yet natural harmony seems contradictory to Smith's descriptions of classes. This contradiction is more apparent than real since by "natural", Smith did not mean necessarily that such a harmony was at present or had in the past been in existence. Moreover, harmony for Smith could often be only partial and it was only in "a utopia or oceana" that he believed a real harmony of social, moral, and economic interests would be possible. Social harmony did not now exist as his

---

1 Bitterman, op. cit., p. 491.

2 Mark Blaug, Economic Theory in Retrospect (London, 1964), p. 52.

voluminous criticisms of existing society demonstrate.[1] He never argued that existing social "evils" were part of a divine harmony that men as yet could not understand. A partial harmony would only come in the future he believed if a number of important social policy alterations were put into effect.[2]

Third, in both Smith's two major works we find "Justice" is the fundamental requirement of either moral or economic development.

> If it [justice] is removed, the great, the immense fabric of human society ... must in a moment crumble into atoms.[3]

Smith asserts throughout his Theory of Moral Sentiments that men generally will not be moral in an unjust society. And in an unjust society, industry, vast commercial exchange, and generally prosperous property relations cannot take place. Consequently, in an unjust society the basis of morals and property was undermined and development made almost impossible.

On the other hand, in a society such as Smith's own there were many injustices, though the total society was not itself

---

1 Viner, "ASLF" op. cit. composed an extensive list of social disharmonies which Smith describes. The degree of harmony he thought possible in moral philosophy was far greater than that which he believed was possible in economic relations. Viner correctly concludes that these disharmonies recorded by Smith point to the impossibility to trusting in the natural harmony of interests. See pp. 198-215.

2 To be discussed in Ch. 9 and 10.

3 TMS, p. 125.

unjust. G. R. Morrow points out clearly Smith's belief that in such a society legal restrictions must be changed before economic or moral harmony can become possible.

> To realize the natural order in its fullness, it is necessary to remove these restrictions, and to restore the conditions of free competition, the system of natural liberty.[1]

In moral terms Smith asserts that *if* the injustices of the society could be removed and justice assured, then each individual's moral sentiments could alone ensure the improvement both of individuals and society. It should be obvious that this formulation of Smith's moral principle corresponds closely to his best known economic principle; that the invisible hand would take care of improving the general economy *if* legal monopolistic injustices did not exist.

In short, the free market is the one *ideal* condition[2] under which self-interest becomes self-command. The free market is the impartial spectator; the general, invisible but rational hand which rational producers for their self interest must obey.[3]

---

1 Morrow, "Adam Smith, Moralist or Philosopher" op. cit., p. 159.

2 Small, *Adam Smith and Modern Sociology*, op. cit., p. 74, discusses Smith's curious belief that his proposals for change were almost totally improbable of accomplishment, when they were almost without exception instituted within fifty years of his death.

3 Macfie, *Individual in Society*, op. cit., p. 104, that "The impartial spectator in fact makes no appearance in the *Wealth of Nations*. He there becomes the impersonal market."

According to Smith, the free market demands not only contractual justice, fairness, and prudence, but the possession of self-command in terms of strict discipline for all producers and purchasers; a personal self-command within each individual. Indeed, such self-command is the ultimate requirement for the survival of the free market.

VI

We are told in the Moral Sentiments that morality begins with society,[1] that the field of moral training is provided for a man in the family first, and then in society and the state, how the range though not the intensity, of his sense of duty expands[2] as he feels himself within the larger after the smaller circles.

Smith's morality begins and is firmly rooted in the great world of commercial exchanges "the great school of self-command, in the bustle and business of the world."[3] This does not mean that in the Moral Sentiments or the Wealth of Nations he approves of greed, nor that property desires are in any way the only drives men have, but Smith's is an "in this world" morality.[4]

---

1 TMS, pp. 124, 185, 199, 200.

2 TMS, p. 185.

3 TMS, p. 206.

4 He attempted to derive moral judgements not from what men ought to do according to any metaphysical law but from what men actually approve and disapprove of. Smith according to far more strictly in his Theory of Moral Sentiments than he did in his

In Moral Sentiments as in the Wealth of Nations Smith makes exactly the same assertion, that he expects men to act first in accordance with their self interest before thoughts of benevolence. Yet William D. Gramp has said of Smith's Economic Man, "However strong his acquisitive instincts are, his desire for approbation is stronger.[1] Moreover in neither books does self interest eliminate sympathy. The two are universal human sentiments which are experienced by all men. Nor, as is commonly thought, were sympathy and self interest totally exclusive passions such that when an individual felt one he could not feel the other. They were sentiments which often exerted simultaneously their influence upon individuals engaged in property relations. Sympathy meant being able to comprehend and enter into the situation of others, especially into their property and self-interested situation and sensing and then judging our approval or disapproval of their acts.

Smith's ultimate attitude to men's drive for property was neither praise or blame. His theory was far subtler than that. Though he is often thought to have celebrated the Wealth of Nations, he also called wealth and greatness "mere trinkets of frivolous utility." He describes "the poor man's son whom heaven

---

later work on economics where he allows frequent opinions and moral attacks to colour his analysis.

1 William D. Gamp, "Adam Smith and the Economic Man," Journal of Political Economy LVI (1948), pp. 315-336, esp. p. 319.

in its anger has visited with ambition" and who in order to get the blessings and honours of the rich submits to "more fatigue of body and more uneasiness of mind, than he could have suffered through the whole of his life from want of them,"[1] and finally Smith asks: "What can be added to the happiness of the man who is in health, who is out of debt, and has a clear conscience."

But through wealth is "a deception" or "illusion" compared with true happiness which resides in virtue, dignity and self-command, "It is this deception which rouses and keeps in continual motion the industry of mankind,"[2] and Smith then says it is in this practical business that morality develops. It is "the [world's] bustle and business" that have trained "the man of real constancy and firmness,"[3] who keeps his self control and is always mindful of his inward monitor."[4]

In summary: it is fundamentally the individual's paramount desire for the approval of other men which motivates him to virtuous acts and to property accumulation. And this approval or "approbation" which men desire springs from their ability to sympathize with the situation or acts of one another. Although Smith gave numerous indications that self interest was men's

---

1 TMS, pp. 259-60.

2 TMS, p. 263.

3 TMS, p. 206.

4 TMS, p. 206.

rational motive for their acquisition of wealth, their fundamental desire was to receive sympathy from other men for their material as well as their moral situation. They sought wealth to acquire approval. Ultimately they sought dignity because this would ensure the continuous approval of other men. Therefore "sympathy" rather than self interest was the basis of property in Smith's system. However, although great wealth provides the strongest security of approval, Smith asserts that luxury tends to lead men towards corruption and injustice. On the other hand although the hard work of the labouring classes usually leads to a certain prosperity and virtue, their poverty sometimes makes them lose hope or initiative. Consequently Smith concluded that only a certain degree of general equality and a rising prosperity among all classes can ensure the continuous health, morality and justice of social relations. Thus, for Smith, property relations provide the concrete setting for moral relations. As property changes through history so it causes changes in society, the state, and so also, in part, it changes men and their morals.

# CHAPTER V

## ORIGIN OF PROPERTY: CONJECTURE OR HISTORY

Smith conjectured that the first property of each man was his labour and yet at other times he studied the historic origins of property from evidence and tales of primitive cultures. Smith tended to blend these two methods of enquiry in each of his economic works. He conjectured four stages of progress in the history of property and manners. Yet much of the detail of these sketches was based on historic fact available in his time. Nevertheless, throughout the entire sketch we find that he assumed or conjectured a "progress of civilization" by which production and society were "improved". I intended to show that Smith was more concerned with the model of historic stages and with the "progress of improvement" than with describing the detailed factual evidence of past societies.

### I

Conjecture and historic analysis were two methods of enquiry used by members of the Scottish Historical School. Nowhere is the conflict of these two methods more in evidence than in their arguments concerning the origin of property. These two modes of enquiry and argument were used most especially by Smith (in somewhat awkward combination) when he analyzed the original condition of property, of society, and of government.

Whereas Smith was quite explicit in his Lectures that the origin of property was an "acquired right" from civil society, in the Wealth of Nations Smith describes men's natural labour as "the first property" "the original property" and "the great foundation of property". Bitterman[1] and others tend to emphasize the assertion from the Lectures that:

> It in reality serves no purpose to treat of the laws which would take place in a state of nature, or by what means succession to property was carried on, as there is no such state existing.[2]

Yet, Schumpeter, Schlatter, Douglass, and others have pointed out that the main thrust of the moral argument in the Wealth of Nations is that the Lockean theory of property originating in men's labour is correct.[3]

Smith describes at length a conjectural or totally hypothetical set of original property exchanges in the famous deer and beaver example.[4] But, at a later point we find Smith describing in detail what he believes to be factual historical property relations of savage hunting societies.[5] Smith himself does not appear to be disturbed or even conscious of this

---

1 Bitterman, op. cit., pp. 703-706.

2 Lectures, p. 2.

3 Schumpeter, op. cit., p. 310. Schlatter, op. cit., p. 184.

4 WN, I, p. 53.

5 WN, II, p. 213.

continual shift from conjectural to factual method which occurs throughout his entire Wealth of Nations.

Smith, as Schlatter points out, was not ostensibly interested in property rights and his mention of them is largely incidental to his technical economic argument, about the labour theory of exchange value, which as Schumpeter, Meek and many others have clearly stated is a separate issue from the labour theory of property. Yet, when Smith conjectured original exchanges of property, it was not solely to find simple equivalents in labour time. It was part of a larger system of economic principles concerning the motive to truck, barter and exchange, the principle of social development, and the basis of social equality.

It is useful to contrast briefly Smith's conjectural and historical methods of looking at the origin of property with other writers of his time.[1] Hutcheson had inclined primarily to Locke's conjectural theory of the origin of property and his historic material dealing with the facts of property's origin was slight, and entangled with conjecture. Furthermore, it was never as extensive as his later study of existing property.

Hume had strongly advocated the purely factual method of historical analysis and dismissed Locke's labour theory of the origin of property as unhistoric. Yet he never really went into

---

1 See Andrew Skinner, "Natural History in the Age of Adam Smith" Political Studies XV (1967) pp. 32-48. Compare this to Roy Pascal op. cit., p. 168, and R. L. Meek "The Scottish Contribution to Marxist Sociology" op. cit., pp. 88-9.

detail on the actual historic facts of primitive societies or their adoption of property.

It is partly because Hutcheson and Hume did not devote more than passing reference to factual property origins and development, that they are not included in the strictly defined "Scottish Historical School". Smith, in his detailed concern with the origin and progressive transformation of property and social and political forms, therefore, has far more in common with Ferguson, Millar and Robertson.1 Yet within this group there are several vital differences concerning both the importance attached to the origin of property, and the social framework and analytical method employed by these authors in describing this primitive history.

For example, Ferguson, unlike Millar, Smith and Robertson did not believe that the study of the origin's of property, government and society should be an interest on its own, or could be especially important, except as it informed us about the present mode of property or society.

> Whatever may have been the original state of our species, it is of more importance to know the conditions to which we ourselves should aspire, than that which our ancestors may be supposed to have left.2

---

1 On Smith and the idea of Progress see Duncan Forbes "Scientific Whiggism: Adam Smith and John Millar" op. cit., pp. 643-70.

2 Ferguson, History, op. cit., p. 10.

This did not mean that Ferguson devoted less space to original society and its property relations than Smith for in fact he probably devoted more. But Ferguson's discussion was not devoted to a conjectural form of supposed deer and beaver exchange, or to suppositions about early acquisitive instincts in men as logically derived from our present instincts and propensities. Ferguson attempted to describe the known facts of original society, which by varying methods he could document.

Thus for example, according to Smith, Ferguson, Millar and Robertson man is naturally sociable. Yet, whereas Smith derives this from man's "instinct to truck, barter and exchange," Ferguson argues:

> Both the earliest and the latest accounts collected from every quarter of the earth, represent mankind as assembled in troups and companies; ...[1]

Likewise whereas Smith (as Hume, Millar and Ferguson) dismisses the State of Nature considered traditionally "as there is no such state existing," he speaks at other times in great detail of man's "natural condition", of labour, subsistence, authority, and forms of "natural right" implying that he did accept the existence of a "State of Nature." Furthermore, he actually uses the term in the traditional manner at several points.[2] Ferguson on the other

---

1 History, p. 3.

2 Lectures, p. 1. "As states have no common sovereign and are with respect to one another in a state of nature, war is their only method of redressing injuries." And see TMS, p. 115. Compare

hand, derides those who discuss:

> The supposed departure of mankind from the state of their nature ... [who] ... allude to this ancient time; ... from which mankind have either degenerated, or on which they have greatly improved. On either supposition, the first state of our nature must have borne no resemblence to what men have exhibited in any subsequent period; ...[1]

Smith like Ferguson was prone to assert the same conclusions about primitive societies and property relations, though sometimes he adopted them from a different mode of argument. For example, Smith like his colleague would argue that a wild man alone in the woods is a totally uncharacteristic individual in a totally unusual situation. Men are social by nature. Smith, Robertson and Millar therefore, to the extent that they believed their investigations must not be into single men and their traits but men in society and social instincts could perhaps agree with Ferguson's conclusion that:

> If we are asked therefore, where the state of nature is to be found? We may answer, It is here; ... all situations are equally natural.[2]

Yet Smith could still at times assume the existence of a "State of Nature" for a particular conjectural argument.

---

this to Locke's Two Treatises pp. 294-5. "All princes and rulers of independent governments all through the world are in a state of nature."

1 History, op. cit., p. 1.

2 History, op. cit., p. 8.

Ferguson may have included Smith when he chided those who abandoned their factual method of describing society, when they came to depict original society by "many wild suppositions."

> In every other instance, however, the natural historian thinks himself obliged to collect facts, not to offer conjectures.[1]

In this very consciousness of two distinct methods Ferguson went beyond Smith. Smith tended even in his factual material to place social customs and particular events within four rigidly schematic, and distinct, stages of society. However, Ferguson later showed how these social forms were almost invariably blurred into one another. Duncan Forbes in his Introduction to Ferguson's <u>History</u> insists that Ferguson was among the first to abandon conjectural history of the origin of property and society,[3] though Montesquieu had to a lesser extent done this with his history of law.

John Millar attempted to employ a more strictly factual and documented history of original property and government than Smith. In far greater detail than Smith or Ferguson he examined the documentary evidence not only from travellers records among the American Indians as Smith and many others had done, but he made extensive use of the Bible and ancient writings as historic

---

1 <u>History</u>, ibid., p. 2.

2 See Duncan Forbes' Introduction to Adam Ferguson's <u>Essay on the History of Civil Society</u>, op. cit., vii-x.

3 <u>History</u>, op. cit., p. 147.

sources of factual records of the social arrangements of early civilization.

Nevertheless Ferguson, Millar and Hume all adopted the conjectural method when describing the origin of property from men's instincts for acquisition or for sympathy. For example Ferguson says:

> Property emerges when men discover that they can produce more on their own than in common work, such a man is urged as much by emulation and jealously, as by a sense of necessity.1

And Millar makes the same kind of conjectural digression when he comes to describe the reasons why property originates.

> In a rude age, where there is little industry, or desire for accumulation, neighbouring independent societies are apt to rob and plunder each other; but the members of the same society are attracted by a common interest, and are often strongly united in the bonds of friendship and affection, by mutual exertions of benevolence, or by accidental habits of sympathy.2

To some extent Ferguson's, Millar's and Smith's conjectures about the original property drives in men were less abstract than those of Hobbes and Locke who had based original property entirely on the universal instinct of men to their own self interest. Smith and Ferguson despute the argument which Hobbes and others had advanced that self interest was the first basis of that self-interest. Yet whereas Smith had based his disproof of primitive

---

1 History, op. cit., p. 147.

2 Millar, p. 387.

men's self interest on his conjectured "sympathies" in the earliest savage, Ferguson argued from historic records that men's attachment to society is strongest among primitive tribes where his material possessions and positions are least.1

Having briefly considered the origin of property in Hutcheson, Hume, Ferguson, and Millar we turn then to the factual and conjectural view of the origin of property which Smith himself presented.

## II

Echoing Locke's description of hunting and gathering in the "State of Nature" we find references to "Rude society" scattered throughout Smith's works. As Smith describes them these are:

> ... nations of hunters, the lowest and rudest state of society, such as we find it among the native tribes of North America.2

This statement is surprisingly similar to Locke's many references to America in his discussions of the original State of Nature. The most famous such passage is: "Thus in the beginning all the world was America ..."3

---

1 Smith's statement that the American Indians are an example of men in their rudest state has an awkward corollary for his strict four stage scheme of social development, since in the first pages of his Lectures he admits that these American Indian Tribes form one of the only exceptions to his scheme in that they hunt and have some small agriculture, without any thought of herding.

2 WN, II, p. 213.

3 Two Treatises, I, V, 49. p. 319.

During this earliest period, Nature so completely dominated man by imposing survival needs on him that Smith described man's condition saying:

> He is in continual danger: he is often exposed to the greatest extremities of hunger, and frequently dies of pure want.1

According to Smith nature provides some of the tools of the hunter as well as the fish and game he kills with them. Yet, even when discussing these remote periods of bare subsistence, Smith is anxious to hypothesize an objective rule for the earliest exhanges of property:

> In that early and rude state of society which precedes both the accumulation of stock and the appropriation of land, the proportion between the quantities of labour necessary for acquiring different objects seems to be the only circumstance which can afford any rule for exchanging them for one another. If among a nation of hunters, for example, it usually costs twice the labour to kill a beaver which it does to kill a deer, one beaver should naturally exchange for or be worth two deer, it is natural that what is usually the produce of two days or two hours labour, should be worth double of what is usually the produce of one day's or one Hour's labour.2

We see in this passage that Smith used suppositions and hypotheses rather than historical facts to examine the character of the rudest forms of property relations. This difference in method from Smith's more typical practice of theorizing from actual

---

1 TMS, p. 297.

2 WN, I, p. 53.

conditions of society to understand property relations existing during his own day[1] appears significant because of the way Smith uses his conclusions about Rude Society. Following the example of Locke, Smith uses his discussion of Rude Society to establish a justification for private property through the individual's mixture of his labour with those objects of nature which he appropriates and exchanges.

> The property which every man has in his own labour, as it is the original foundation of all other property, so it is the most sacred and inviolable.[2]

And again:

> In this state of things, [primitive Human Existence] the whole produce of labour belongs to the labourer; ...[3]

Henry J. Bitterman has in his article "Smith's Empiricism and the Law of Nature", for the most part dismissed the obvious parallels between Locke and Smith's description of the origin of property. Yet:

> The Smithian "early and rude state of society which precedes both the accumulation of stock and the approbation of land" resembles in its economic organization the state of nature of

---

1 Smith's famous example of the manufacture of pins is a useful contrast since although Smith does not deal with a specific factory or historic period the actual division of labour in the production of pins was not hypothesized from human nature or the shape of a particular pin but from observation and heresay of existing practice.

2 <u>WN</u>, I, p. 136.

3 <u>WN</u>, I, p. 54.

> Locke and Puffendorf but analytically is used quite differently. These writers did not probably regard their state of nature as historical or even prehistorical; it was less conjectural history than it was an analytical device for discussing the nature of human relations in the absence of government. They used this fiction as a way of reducing human nature to its simplest elements and so derived their theories of natural rights from this elemental human nature. Smith's early and rude state of society was obviously in part conjectural, but it corresponded with what was known of primitive cultures, and Smith illustrates his arguments by reference to known primitive peoples.[1]

To a certain extent Bitterman is quite right in this assessment. Smith's conjectures often correspond to historical facts known in his time. Although his famous "exchanges" of beaver and deer were conjectural his other descriptions of tribes of hunters were based on records, tales or other evidence of the simplest and most primitive type of society, where subsistence is obtained by means of hunting or gathering the things of nature.[2] The entire society is involved in these two activities,[3] and specialization in its different branches takes place only to a very limited degree.[4] Everyone in these societies is able to perform each specialized activity of tool making or weapon making when the

---

1 Bitterman, op. cit., p. 706.

2 Smith, WN, II, p. 213.

3 WN, II, p. 213.

4 WN, II, p. 19.

need arises.[1] The result is that savages have much the same skills because they do the same work.[2] "It is upon this account that a much greater uniformity of character is to be observed among savages than among civilized nations."[3] Savages consider themselves and they are equal in property in authority. Executive, legislative and judicial decision are usually taken by the society as a whole. However, the numbers in such societies are small; usually no more than a few families.[4] Although Smith at times describes their economic organization as providing adequate subsistence[5] is very insecure and that savages "frequently die of pure want."[6] Yet Smith, like Ferguson, insists that these savages do not struggle all their day for survival but have long periods of leisure in which they engage in athletic, religious, or artistic activities.

At times Smith says property in this most primitive hunting society is non-existent. For example he says of savages "they have no property". As I explained in detail in the chapter on

---

1 Draft, pp. 341-2.

2 Draft, pp. 341-2.

3 Draft, p. 342.

4 Lectures, pp. 14-15.

5 Lectures, p. 161.

6 TMS, p. 297, EPS, p. 32.

Locke, Smith does not remain consistent on this and at other times he says:

> Among nations of hunters as there is scarce any property, or at least none that exceeds the value of two or three days labour; ...1

Smith takes the origin of property from differing vantage points in time depending upon the argument he is putting forward.

Smith's description of private possessions among hunters is sometimes dismissed as not property at all since it is often pure subsistence which is not stored up but immediately consumed. Nothing is "established" by such tribes of a permanent nature; they are nomadic and once they have exhausted the wild life of an area they move on. When speaking in these terms Smith might be as liable to say they have "no property", "scarce any property" or "but the most necessary property". Such comments are best summed up by Smith when he says:

> Among savages property begins and ends with possession, and they seem scarce to have any idea of anything as their own which is not about their own bodies.2

Yet at other times we find Smith saying that these savages have tools and works or religious art, which last longer than two or three days. Such discrepancies could be easily overlooked with the comment that the total property of the entire society was so meagre that Smith was quite justified in saying they had none, or

---

1 WN, II, p. 231.

2 Lectures, p. 108-9.

merely subsistence, were it not that Smith blends these random historic comments with an entire conjectural discussion of the origin or private property exchange, and the basis of legal property rights from these groups of hunters.

It is because these discussion of original property exchange (by hunters of beaver and deer) have played such a well known role in Smith's economic theory, of exchange value, and labour-cost, that we find it difficult to accept his statements that historically property was not established among hunters but only later in the entirely separate historical stage of herding societies who possessed domesticated animals. It is also difficult once one is familiar with the deer-beaver example of private exchange of property to accept Smith's occasional dating of the origin of property from the communally owned food of hunting societies.[1]

The clearest example of the conjectural method Smith uses for discussing original property occurs when he considers property rights in terms of what "the spectator" would consider reasonable, and where he directly afterwards describes the conjectural basis for property laws of "occupation", during his own time.

> Occupation seems to be well founded when the spectator can go along with my possession of the object, and approve me when I defend my possession by force. If I have gathered some wild fruit it will appear reasonable to the spectator that I should dispose of it as I please.

---

1 Lectures, p. 109.

> The first thing that requires notice in occupation among hunters is what constitues it, and when it begins, whether it be on the discovery of the wild beast or after it is actually in possession. Lawyers have varied on this head, some give a part to the person who has formerly wounded a wild beast, though [he] have given up the chase, and others do not. All agree that it is a breach of property to break in on the chase of a wild beast which another has started, though some are of opinion that if another should wound the beast in its flight he is entitled to a share, as he rendered the taking of it more easy upon the whole.1

It is important to note that Smith took this conjectural argument directly from a continuing legal and philosophic discussion of conjectural issues.2

On the very next page from the above totally conjectural argument about spectators' concurrence with an individual's property rights and legal rights to beasts wounded or killed, Smith returns to factual historical description of actual property conditions without any indication that he realizes he is totally changing his argument.3

Among the important discrepancies between Smith's conjectural and historical interpretations of original property is the general

---

1 Lectures, p. 108.

2 More precisely Smith took this view and this discussion largely from Hutcheson's Introduction to Moral Philosophy, p. 154, who had in turn taken it almost directly from Locke's Civil Government section 30. Puffendorf in De Jure Naturae at Gentium op. cit., iv, cap. vi sec. 10 also may have been in Smith's mind when he wrote this passage.

3 Lectures, p. 109.

conception primitive men had of property acquisition. Smith sometimes said that primitive men's acquisitive drive to obtain material subsistence operated continually,[1] thus echoing the views of Hobbes and Locke. At other times Smith (like Ferguson and Millar) stated that primitive tribes far from spending every hour searching for subsistence, love their ease, leisure, and amusements, and appear to consider the menial work for subsistence, beneath their dignity. That property in the household or in the neighbourhood of the camp which is "owned" is possessed and arranged primarily by women. The gathering of fruit, berries and other food, the making of clothes, bedding, cooking utensils, and repair of huts and tools are all tasks performed by women. They represent the menial property relations of this society. It is significant that simultaneously with this female control of property, many primitive societies are socially arranged along matriarchal lines.[2]

What does Smith mean when he speaks of these societies as "prior to the establishment of property?" He does not mean that some necessary objects such as food, clothing and huts or household tools, or some luxuries such as ornamental or religious property, are absent, or that they are few in number. But he is saying that it is not primarily the possession of property which

---

1 <u>EPS</u>, p. 29.

2 Millar described, however, some patriarchial tribes and some that practiced polyandry.

accords status or honour; endurance and age forms the basis of social respect rather than property possessions. Property acquired without these confers, according to Smith, no honour at all. And that wealth which is bestowed upon an honourable man often is not retained for the individual hero or his family but immediately shared out at a feast, or given in treaty to another tribe, or gambled away in games of chance or feats of skill.1 That is, property though present in, and necessary for, these societies, is not according to Smith, Ferguson or Millar, the primary basis of honour or authority in these primitive tribes. These societies are "prior to the establishment of property" mainly because "establishment", for Smith, means not merely the existence, use or need of material objects but their primacy among all social acquisitions or pursuits. Smith though he only suggests it in passing would certainly have agreed with Ferguson's summary of savage society that:

> While one sex continues to value themselves chiefly on their courage, their talent for policy, and their warlike achievements, this species of property which is bestowed on the other, is in reality a mark of subjection; not, as some writers allege, of their having acquired an ascendant. It is the care and trouble of a subject with which the warrior

---

1 Gradually these many gifts to the chief "increase his fortune and consequently his authority." However the principles of giving are quite different from today. "In a civilization the man who gives the present is superior to the person who receives it, but in a barbarous nation the case is directly opposite." Lectures, p. 16.

> does not choose to be embarrassed. It is a servitude, and continual toil, where no honours are won; and they whose province it is, are in fact the slaves and helots of their country.[1]

Whether primitive savages struggled for meagre necessities which they exchanged in proportion to their labour time for other things which they needed, or, whether on the other hand, they cared little about property possession or exchange, and concerned themselves with courage more than wealth, Smith leaves undecided. This ambivalence stems from his conjectural and his factual presuppositions. When he followed Locke's conjectural method in attempting to form a basis for his own economic theories he emphasized continual struggle for subsistence and the importance of property exchange, whereas when he was concerned with a complete description of known facts he noted the records of travellers among savages which emphasized hunter's leisure, games, and disdain for menial property relations.[2]

---

1 History, p. 83.

2 History, 2, pp. 96-7. Ferguson after studying primitive tribes concludes that "the convenient and ornamental, in their several forms however rude, are studied in the same age with the necessary; and the same person who subsists from meal to meal on the precarious returns of the chase is, in the intervals of his necessity, no less studious of ornament in his person, his dress, and of his habitation than he was in earnest in procuring his food."

III

Smith established the practice which Millar followed and elaborated upon in his more detailed historical study, of conceiving four stages of social development.[1]

These stages of social development which Locke described were largely theoretical speculation in contrast with Smith's which were based more on historical fact. Although it is a matter of controversy whether Locke assumed two or three stages of social development[2] Smith assumed quite different historic periods altogether. He did not divide history into natural, social, and civil, or a state of nature and a state of civil society. As mentioned earlier he attempted to uphold the historic assumption that man is always social by nature. Smith distinguishes the following four stages of society: hunting,[3] herding,[4] agriculture,[5] and commerce.[6]

---

1 The reason Ferguson did not adopt Smith's scheme will be discussed in detail later.

2 For the intricacies of this dispute compare Peter Laslett's Introduction to _Two Treatises_, pp. 92-121 with Otto Gierke's _Natural Law_, op. cit., pp. 101-49.

3 _WN_, II, p. 213.

4 _WN_, II, pp. 213-4.

5 _WN_, II, p. 215.

6 _WN_, I, p. 27, II, p. 159.

Throughout Smith's Lectures and Wealth of Nations there are frequent references to such stages of society. Each stage he identified by men's particular relationship to their property during that period.

For instance, concerning hunters Smith remarks on "the precarious subsistence which the chase affords,"[1] but concerning herding Smith says: "Among Shepherds the idea of property is further extended."[2]

> The second period of society that of shepherds, admits of great inequality of fortune.[3]

And yet their mode of subsistence still totally controls their place of dwelling at any time:

> They can go on from one district, of which they have consumed the forage, to another which is yet entire; ...[4]

Next we find that - "property receives its greatest extension from agriculture."[5] But farmers

> ... have little foreign commerce, and no other manufacturers but those coarse and household ones which almost every private family prepares for its own uses; ...[6]

---

1 WN, II, p. 214.

2 Lectures, p. 109.

3 WN, II, p. 234.

4 WN, II, p. 214.

5 Lectures, p. 109.

6 WN, II, p. 215.

Nevertheless, though limited, property is permanent in land and houses.

> Agriculture, even in its rudest and lowest state, supposes a settlement; some sort of fixed habitation which cannot be abandoned without great loss.[1]

As will be explained in the following chapters, the 4th stage, commercial society, is based upon a near total property market in which all goods and services can be exchanged, and usually must be to keep the commercial market free and properly functioning.

Property changes in each of these social forms and it is its change which transforms one society into another. It is useful in a description of this transition from original property to give some detail of the property forms which followed.

Herding where subsistence is obtained largely from tamed animals[2] provides specialization only fractionally more extensive, and yields subsistence only slightly more secure than hunting, since many periods of "pure want" still occur.[3] But periods of leisure are more extensive among shepherding societies than among hunters.[4]

The animals of a herding society are the property of individuals and not of the society as a whole, though Smith does

---

1 WN, II, p. 216.

2 Lectures, pp. 15-16.

3 TMS, p. 297.

4 WN, II, p. 219.

not offer an explanation of how this developed from the communal ownership of most permanent property among hunters.[1] Perhaps animals become the property of individual herdsmen because they are necessary for the labour of herding, somewhat in the fashion that weapons (the possession of individual hunters) are necessary for hunting. There is great inequality of property and of authority which Smith describes as developing from a victorious tribe dividing the spoils of war among itself and adopting the conquered people into the tribe as slaves.[2]

> The inequality of fortune, making a distinction between the rich and the poor, gave the former much influence over the latter, for they who had no flocks or herds must have depended on those who had them, because they could not now gain a subsistence from hunting, as the rich had made the game, now become tame, their own property. They therefore who had appropriated a number of flocks and herds, necessarily came to have a great influence over the rest; ...[3]

From the first, the possession of wealth, according to Smith conveys more substantial and permanent authority than other sources of authority such as age or wisdom.[4] Property wealth is preserved in relatively few hands by the establishment of rigid government by the few in contrast to the loose justice and defence

---

1 Lectures, p. 15.

2 WN, II, p. 214.

3 Lectures, pp. 15-16.

4 Lectures, p. 9, 16.

which previously had been carried out by the hunting society as a whole.1

In Agricultural society, the third stage of development, food is supplied by cultivation, and there also exists "coarse arts", home manufacturers, a good deal of herding and some hunting.2 Specialization is very considerably extended into the basic trades of smiths, bakers, butchers, carpenters.3 The larger size of this society than most herding shepherd societies and the surplus over the absolute subsistence needs provides an "agricultural market" even in years of poor harvests. The primary result of this is greater property wealth than in previous stages of society. Periods of "pure want" rarely occur. Furthermore, this mode of economic organization gives rise to the "greatest extension" of property - namely property in land.4 The division of land forms the basis of the property, social and political relations of agricultural society. Smith distinguishes two patterns of land division which lead to drastically different forms of society. The first is divided among a few large land-owners and is usually feudal, the second is divided among a large number of small landowners and tends more towards a primitive

---

1 Lectures, p. 15.

2 WN, II, p. 215.

3 WN, I, p. 430.

4 Lectures, p. 109.

democracy. Though each leads eventually to town or city commercial society Smith insists that the greatest differences of social forms resulted from these two modes of land property.

The first kind of agricultural society[1] where land is owned by a few is by far the more prevalent form, and it is the origin from which modern European commercial societies developed. Smith therefore goes into far greater detail on the property divisions in the allodial and feudal types of agricultural society than in the more democratic type. Allodial society arose when the chiefs of the armies of hunters and herdsmen appropriated large tracts of land when the Roman Empire collapsed.[2] They lent these lands to their subjects to use to produce their necessities, but all the surplus production was the property of the lord who used it to support his retainers and for "rustic hospitality."[3] Both the cultivators and retainers were, therefore, economically dependent on the lord.[4]

The landlord held overwhelming authority and was himself the government for those living on his territories.[5] At first both justice and defence were in his hands but gradually he appointed

---

1 Lectures, P. 25 and WN, II, p. 75.

2 Lectures, p. 35, p. 225; WN, I, p. 407.

3 Lectures, pp. 35, 116.

4 Lectures, p. 34.

5 Lectures, pp. 35-6.

magistrates and military assistants who would respectively judge, or assemble for battle the retainers of the landlord.1 In practice Smith says those landlords provided only slight security, for many neighbouring landlords frequently came into conflict. This led those with smaller estates and fewer retainers to band themselves to a greater landlord for self-protection. These greater landlords eventually became kings when this form of land property ownership reached its ultimate feudal proportions. Yet still there existed many feudal barrons as well as the great landholders of the Catholic church, who continued to conflict among themselves. Thus, although land, property and authority were theoretically almost static under this feudal society, this did not prevent a constant shifting and realignment of feudal ownership and authority at the top of the heirarchy, while the base remained fairly constant.

The second form of agricultural society where the property holdings are all small and relatively equal is termed by Smith the "natural one".2 It is comparatively rare and the examples of the Greek republics are dealt with far more briefly than the Feudal example of the European middle ages. The "natural" agricultural society of landholdings is likely to come about by an agreement among cultivators rather than force since it establishes

---

1 Lectures, p. 36, WN, II, p. 216.

2 Lectures, pp. 22-3, 109.

a situation in which they are all economically independent and relatively equal in wealth. The few towns which develop provide protection, coarse arts and a market. Government is a broad aristocarcy or a narrow democracy among all those owning property. Since no single property owner is substantially wealthier than the others, authority is relatively equally distributed. Smith says Greek and Roman states were quite similar to the North American colonies where large scale landholdings were prevented by physical circumstances or by law.[1]

In both forms of agricultural society, "feudal" and "natural", justice is more exact, than under earlier societies, especially with regard to property. And the other similarities between the two agricultural forms of society includes the development of professional armies so that the whole society no longer goes to war;[2] the development of rough manufacturing in the towns, and the gradual independence of the towns from the countryside.[3] Yet the Feudal society creates dependence in all ranks of the people, whereas the "natural" agricultural society develops "independency."[4] Smith contrasts these effects by saying: "Nothing tends so much to corrupt mankind as dependency while

---

1 WN, II, pp. 83-5.

2 Lectures, p. 261; WN, II, p. 215-7.

3 Lectures, p. 40; WN, I, pp. 421-6.

4 Lectures, p. 42; WN, I, p. 437.

independency still increases the honesty of the people."

The fourth stage of social development is commerce and it will be dealt with in later chapters. For the moment we will simply summarize Smith's discussion by saying that the commercial market for all forms of exchangeable property developed from both forms of agricultural society, principally from the towns, seaports and river ports where there were rough manufacture, social independence, and commodity markets.

Smith's analysis of the four stages of the history of property, while it exemplifies much of the Scottish School's method, was not the only historical structure that was used by the group. Ferguson did not agree with Smith's four stages view of social development. From factual documentary evidence, Ferguson describes two groups - savages and barbarians - as examples of "mankind in their rudest state", existing simultaneously in the earliest periods of any continent. Ferguson makes a sharp division between the savage,

> ... who is not yet acquainted with property; and that of the barbarian, to whom it is, although not ascertained by laws, a principal object of care and desire.[1]

Since Ferguson showed that both groups existed in men's earliest condition he tends to confuse the clear distinctions Smith laid down for society's four stages. This occurs because Ferguson, the more factual investigator, found that the most primitive form of

---

1 History, p. 82.

society in some continents was hunting whereas, in others it was herding or shepherding. Although logically one might seem prior to the other Ferguson said no evidence of the earliest tribes proved this. In yet other continents Ferguson studies in detail "where savage nations, as in most parts of America, mix with the practice of hunting some species of rude agriculture." This difference between Smith's more schematic use of rude and advancing types of society with his clear distinctions and progression differs sharply from Ferguson's, who used far more historical comparison to show the nature of mixed societies of hunting and herding and farming, (and even commerce when the Indians trade with more advanced societies on a commercial basis.)1 It will be remembered that Smith described the agricultural plots of the American Indians as the one exception to his scheme of four stages, not as symptomatic of many peculiar

---

1 History, p. 81-82. "Of the nations who dwell in those, or any other of the less cultivated parts of the earth, some entrust their subsistence chiefly to hunting, fishing, or the natural produce of the soil. They have little attention to property, and scarcely any beginnings of subordination or government. Others having possessed themselves of herds, and depending for their provision on pasture, know what it is to be poor and rich. They know the relations of patron and client, of servant and master, and suffer themselves to be classed according to their measures of wealth. This distinction must create a material difference of character and may furnish two separate heads, under which to consider the history of mankind in their rudest state; that of the savage, who is not yet acquainted with property; and that of the barbarian, to whom it is, although not ascertained by laws, a principal object of care and desire." Ferguson's factual method admits no deer and beaver exchange. The catch, "being the purchase of numbers, who fish or hunt in a body, it accrues to the community, and is applied to immediate use, or becomes an

mixtures of property forms among different social periods.

Yet although Smith was more schematic and less factually historical than Ferguson, Ferguson tended to be less clear than Smith as to the reasons one society developed from another, or why for instance, savages without the acquisitive desires for property, ever developed such a desire. Though he could have been far more explicit on the motor of historical change from one society and form one form of property relations to another, Smith did use an analogy of the men shipwrecked on a deserted island, in order to probe the reason for social development. In this analogy, the pressure of population on the food supply is the principal reason for social advance from one stage to another. Smith's description is as follows:

> If a number of persons were shipwrecked on a desert island their first sustenance would be from the fruits which the soil naturally produced, and the wild beasts which they could kill. As these could not at all times be sufficient, they came at last to tame some of the wild beasts that they might always have them at hand. In process of timee even these would not be sufficient; and as they saw the earth naturally produce considerable quantities of vegetables of its own accord, they would think of cultivating it so that it might produce more of them. Hence agriculture, which requires a good deal of

---

accession to the stores of the public" ... "As the men hunt so the women labour together; and, after they have shared the toils of the seed-time they enjoy the fruits of the harvest in common". "Even the returns of the market, when they trade with foreigners, are brought home to the stock of the nation." History, pp. 82-3.

> refinement before it could become the prevailing employment of a country ... The age of commerce naturally succeeds that of agriculture. As men could now confine themselves to one species of labour, they would naturally exchange surplus of their own commodity for that of another of which they stood in need. According to these stages occupation must vary.[1]

In contrast to Smith we find that Ferguson is not at all clear on why societies change and develop and why "property is a matter of progress",[2] or why "It requires ... other particulars which are the effects of time."

In conclusion, prior to Smith historians had established facts and series of factual events. Smith and others of the Scottish period and that this made periods primarily distinguishable according to their mode of property, production, or mode of subsistence. Furthermore, they presumed an historic progression from primitive modes of property relations to advanced property which they termed the process of "Civilization."

Whereas the whole of the Scottish Historical School showed that property forms were the distinguishing characteristic of different historic periods, Smith was the primary member of that School to set forth a clear scheme of the way these property forms evolved in a series of stages. And he was the one who attempted to set out a materialist explanation for the motive force of

---

1 Lectures, p. 107.

2 History, p. 82.

historic change and development from one property stage to the next. Smith created a motor for historic development: the material needs and drives of men. As expressed within various periods these material needs and drives took the form of developing forms of property, production, distribution, and modes of subsistence. That is, unlike Ferguson, Smith not only distinguished historic periods from one another, but established the pressure of material needs and the advance of production as the motive force of social development.1

In setting out this scheme Smith was more conjectural and less factually historic than Ferguson. But just because of this clearer set of stages and clearer picture of the motive force of development Smith's was less an exposition of the actual property of various societies (as was Ferguson's treatment) and more an argument for seeing all of history in these material terms of property progression from barbarism to civilization. Millar recognized that Smith's theory of "the progress of civilization,"

---

1 Smith's theory of progress was not monolythic. He recognized periods of decay and stagnation in various societies. It was over the broad sweep of history that his theory of Progress was applicable not in each particular series of events. In political histories of states and regimes Smith even went so far as to assume a fixed period of maximum life expectancy. Each state would die. In his Lectures, p. 32, he speaks of "That fatal dissolution that awaits every state and constitution whatever." and in WN, I, p. 443 Smith says, "It is now more than two hundred years since the beginning of the reign of [Queen] Elizabeth, a period as long as the course of human properity usually endures." See Forbes, "Scientific Whiggism" op.cit., p. 650, for commentary on this passage.

was new and original and was a significant organizing principle of his thought.[1] Millar's Origin of the Distinction of Ranks thus sought to amplify Smith's sketch of historic stages and to systematically apply the concept of a law of progress.

---

1 Duncan Forbes "Scientific Whiggism: Adam Smith and John Millar", op. cit. See p. 646. "Millar described Smith as the 'Newton' of the history of Civil Society, because unlike Montesquieu, he had discovered, or systematically applied, the 'law' of progress." Forbes shows that his idea of progress was present even in Smith's first lectures in Edinburgh in 1749-51. Forbes, ibid., p. 648.

# CHAPTER VI

## ALIENATION OF PROPERTY: THE MARKET

Smith drew his conception of the market from the property relations of his time. However it would be more accurately described as a theoretical model of emerging rather than existing property relations. His detailed descriptions of five contemporary modes of acquiring property demonstrate that a residue of feudal laws still circumscribed the market of his time. Although in describing current property relations he focussed on exchange of land, labour and goods as saleable commodities, much domestic produce and many landed estates did not enter the market. In abstracting his theories from current experience Smith showed his interest to be not with a detailed history of labour, currency, or the accumulation of wealth, but with the effects of changing property relations upon men and society.

### I

Smith advanced two historic sketches of the development of commerical society. In Europe a complex pattern of developments led to the emergence of the commercial from the agricultural stage of society: in the interior of the American continent a simple growth of a town from the countryside led to a basic form of commecial society. In Europe the cause of this change Smith stated to be the new availability of foreign luxury goods.[1] Money spent on luxuries reduced the funds available for the support of retainers. This released large numbers from economic dependence on landlords and the church. Landowners tried to increase their incomes by greater production of grain and cattle or by selling off their lands.[2] Often they sold their tenant farmers longer and more secure leases, or virtual freeholds. Tenants became economically independent. They improved their land and increased agricultural surpluses and thus spurred the growth of towns and exports. In contrast, in interior townships of America most land from the first was held freehold and as farms grew and prospered so equally did the town they used for the market for their produce.

Consequently, in urban development Smith calls these two major patterns - "violent", and "natural". The "violent" pattern was predominant in Europe,[3] and so called because its cause of growth was the sale of foreign manufacturers which were only gradually replaced by manufacturers from the local town or port. Yet once established this form of commercial town still depended upon exports and imports of foreign countries.

---

1 Lectures, p. 42. WN, I, pp. 427-438.

2 WN, I, p. 439. Lectures, p. 43.

3 WN, I, pp. 429-30.

The second pattern of town development, termed "natural" did not depend on exports or imports as the initial basis of economic growth.1 It occurred in relatively isolated or inland areas.

Both these patterns of town development in an agricultural society led to a new productive and commerical economic organization of agriculture, together with greatly improved and specialized arts and manufacture. However, they did <u>not</u> both lead to the same general results in social class realtions.

Smith's two theories of the evolution of society explain the emergence of 18th century Scottish society in Kirkcaldy, Glasgow, and Edinburgh, and also of the inland towns of the highlands and remoter part of the lowlands. His description of commercial organization, institutions, and morals, are nevertheless stated in a sufficiently general form to encompass almost all commercial societies.

The property organization of commercial society is the basis of its social, political and moral characteristics. Division of labour in agriculture and especially industry means that there is increased efficiency,2 the machines invented are used to make labour productivity very high.3 All producers are interde-

---

1 <u>WN</u>, I, pp. 430-1.

2 <u>WN</u>, I, pp. 401-2. <u>Lectures</u>, pp. 161-3.

3 <u>WN</u>, I, pp. 15-6.

pendent, for others supply each man with the largest portion of his consumption of both necessities and conveniences.

During Smith's life, commercial markets were still close to the land and dependent on harvests and weather, and this was true in the tobacco and cotton trade as well as of local corn and cattle. The rising market and the productivity of land gradually fostered the great increase in capital and credit necessary to support the new industry which was usually for technical reasons closely allied with rural coal, wood, or water supplies.

There had been for centuries in Scotland and England, market towns and commercial cities. However, the great shift from an agricultural to a partially commercial-industrial society occurred during Smith's life. The transition was sporadic if studied from any narrow vantage point of any particular industry where the technical advance, harvests, or flux of capital or wars made progress appear to ebb and flow. But the broad historic view revealed that during the 18th century the entire economy experienced a gradual transition from a mainly agricultural society to one substantially dependent on industry as well as agriculture, and almost entirely devoted to commerce. There were many interrelated effects of agriculture on industry and industry upon agriculture but the basic fact was the steady increase of the commercial market in all areas of the economy.

Smith had certain definite views concerning the relation of the schematic or conjectural development of commerce from any agricultural society. These were universal conclusions applicable to all commercial development but resembling most closely the "natural" pattern already described. For example:

> The great commerce of every civilized society, is that carried on between the inhabitants of the town and those of the country.[1]

In his conjectural sketches of the way this commercial relationship must develop, Smith states:

> As subsistence is, in the nature of things, prior to conveniency and luxury, so the industry which procures the former, must necessarily be prior to that which ministers to the latter. The cultivation and improvement of the country, therefore, which affords subsistence, must, necessarily, be prior to the increase of the town, which furnishes only the means of conveniency and luxury. It is the surplus produce of the country only or what is over and above the maintenance of the cultivators, that constitutes the subsistence of the town, which can therefore increase only with the increase of this surplus produce.[2]

The town is established with artificers whose residence is not, like that of the farmer necessarily tied down to a remote spot. Thus naturally they settle together forming first a village then a town. Smith's description becomes less conjectural when discussing the development of towns but still retains the abstract mode of expression:

> The inhabitants of the town and those of the country are naturally the servants of one another. The town is a continual fair

---

1 WN, I, p. 401.

2 WN, I, p. 402.

> or market, to which the inhabitants of the country resort, in order to exchange their rude for manufactured produce. It is this commerce which supplies the inhabitants of the town both with the materials of their work, and the means of their subsistence.1

Smith studied the conditions of various markets. His extraordinarily diverse enquiry into existing markets led him to form opinions even on the justifications of smuggling and the benefits of competition among professors for students' fees. He was particularly concerned to discover whether markets and industry blossomed in areas such as Lancashire and the West Riding and later Scotland where the more restrictive provisions of the Elizabethan code of industrial legislation had not been put into practice. Everywhere Smith probed the condition and boundaries of the market to appraise its total development. His was not so much a history of the development of industry, agriculture, labour or currency, but rather an historic sketch of the growth of the total market. The broad principles were sketched conjecturally:

> When the market is very small, no person can have any encouragement to dedicate himself entirely to one employment, for want of the power to exchange all that surplus part of the produce of his own labour, which is over and above his own consumption, for such parts of the produce of other men's labour as he has occasion for.2

---

1 WN, I, pp. 403-4.

2 WN, I, p.21.

The details of market development were amplified by voluminous historical cases, as we have already indicated in the description of the "natural" vs. the "violent" form of development. In fact, although Smith's famous first and second chapters of the Wealth of Nations deal with the division of labour as the motor of productive expansion,[1] his third chapter specifically argues "that the division of labour is limited by the Extent of the Market." The market thus forms the focal point of Smith's theories of economic development as much as his more famous analysis of the division of labour.

Smith devoted research into the extent of the market and effects of its limitation on the division of labour in several social stages and the consequent limitations of property forms and productivity. In this chapter we are concerned only with the property market in the final stage of society, that of "commerce," or commercial society.

## II

What typifies the property relations of Smith's times[2] is sale. The "market" or "commercial society" he describes is one in

---

1 WN, I, p. 7. "The greatest improvement in the productive powers of labour, and the greater part of the skill, dexterity, and judgement with which it is any where directed, or applied, seem to have been the effects of the division of labour."

2 Previous societies had experienced private ownership without the total ability to sell land or labour or other commodities. Also, with the growth of joint stock companies, public works,

which almost every commodity can be exchanged for a price. The total ability and even the necessity to sell goods, services, land and currency exemplifies the newer property relations of his times even more than the prevalence of "private ownership" or "division of labour"1 or "factory production."2

Because "Market Society" was the general subject of his economic analysis it may be useful to look at his general concept of "sale" to see what he was concerned with when he described each individual as "a merchant". Historically, the "sale" of goods or whatever, was known throughout Smith's lifetime as "the alienation of property".3

---

corporate investment, monopolies and the lack of any substantial private ownership by the masses of the labouring classes, or control over the use of their foremost property, their labour power - all these developments tended to make the term "private ownership" a far less meaningful paradigm of existing property relations than for example "sale" or "the market".

1 Slave and Feudal societies had depended upon a variety of divisions of labour before the capitalist period, and Smith as shown in the previous chapter hypothesized the existence of the division of labour in the deer hunters and fishermen of the very first society.

2 Factory production did not account for even twenty percent of the labouring populations employment or of capital investment or of gross national income during the life of Smith.

3 The Encyclopedia of the Social Sciences (New York, 1930), p. 639, explains that, "Alienation of Property may be voluntary, resulting from the intended acts of the owner, or involuntary, through the acts of organized society in forcibly taking the property for the benefit of creditors or of one long in adverse possession or for the public use." The earliest known form of property was the community ownership of chattels, such as weapons, cattle and slaves, by the family, tribe or village. The community property was for community use not sale.

The "Alienation of Property" was a legal and philosophical term employed not only in all learned treatises and documents dealing with the exchange of property, but in wills, confiscations by the state, and even in tax enactments.

"Alienation of Property" in its primary usage in Smith meant sale; Smith was vitally concerned with the sale price of "exchange value" of all goods, services and lands. And so it was natural that alienation by sale should be his central focus. However, we must discover whether sale was the universal mode of property transfer or alienation in Smith's time or whether Smith

---

Alienation of property had its origin long before the Roman Empire, but it was during the codification of Roman Law that the institutional forms of alienating property were laid down in the form they were used to take through the middle ages and, in part, through the life of Smith.

Alienation of property was sanctioned in two forms by Roman Law, by burdensom ceremonial or by mere delivery. The Justinian Code transformed this division into "moveables and immoveables" which in turn gave way under Normal Law to the more complex divisions between "personality and reality". Yet essentially this same distinction of two forms of alienation sprang from the _Res mancipi_ and _res nec mancipi_ of original Roman Law, and did not change substantially till the 16th century. In 1535 the "Statute of Uses" simplified the formalities for the "conveyance of land" and in 1541 land was made alienable by will. Yet, in Smith's lifetime there was still a clear distinction between the laws relating to the alienation of land and those to moveables. For discussions of the theory of the alienation of property see: Schlatter, _Private Property_, op. cit., passim. C. B. Macpherson, _The Poitical Theory of Possessive Individualism_, (Oxford, 1960) passim. For the general historical background to the theory of the Alienation of property see Max Weber, _General Economic History_ (New York, 1961) esp. ch. 3. "Commerce and exchange in the Pre-Capitalist Age" and ch. 4. "The Origin of Modern Capitalism" also see Arthur Birnie, _An Economic History of Europe_, op. cit., esp. ch. IV "The Revolution in Commerce", pp. 46-61.

was conjecturing a total commercial market society which did not yet exist.

The battle for the right to alienate one's property (whether "personality" or "realty"; "moveables" or "immoveables"; labour, capital, or currency) had been fought over many centuries. The controversies had extended to alienations of all forms of property including land, labour, capital, goods and currency. The controversies had centred on "entails", "primogeniture", and "commonland"; and also on "indentures", "service labour", and "apprenticeship" restrictions; and on the famous statute of "usury". With the enclosure movement and the birth of freedom of trade in land as well as moveable goods and most labour, many legal and customary restrictions and prohibitions on alienating private property were slowly dying away. But though in Smith's time these restrictions had by no means fully disappeared, nevertheless, Smith felt it was just to describe the existing economy as a commercial market governed by "money exchanges."

Such general descriptions of society as a market were not new. Almost one hundred years before Smith, John Locke had stated that:

> Commerce, therefore, is the only way left
> to us, either for riches or subsistence ...[1]

And he had insisted that there was a money basis to that commercial society:

---

1 Locke, Considerations, op. cit., 16.

> And therefore ready money must be constantly exchanged for wares and labour or follow within a short time after.[1]

To a large extent Locke as Smith later was describing an emerging not an existing market since most land and domestic produce was not bought or sold. Yet Adam Smith generalized about market society in much the same fashion as Locke before him by insisting that when the division of labour is thoroughly established:

> Every man thus lives by exchanging, or becomes in some measure a merchant, and the society itself grows to be what is properly a commercial society.[2]

Smith was far more interested than Locke, in discovering the absolute measure of exchangable value or alienability or saleability of goods, land and labour. He viewed exchange as the first principle of the science of political economy. However, we must enquire to what extent exchange was the exclusive or prevailing mode of property transference and acquisition in Smith's time.

II

Adam Smith's Lectures contain almost a forty page section dealing with the private law of property, five methods of its acquisition, and different forms of contracts, quasi-contracts, "servitudes, mortgages, pledges and delinquency," in any of these property relations. These careful analyses of property law

---

1 Ibid., p. 33.

2 WN, I, p. 26.

setting out the existing practices and contrasting them with the earlier history, are only to be found in scattered references in the Wealth of Nations.[1] For the clearest account of Smith's views on property laws and conventions during his own time, the Lectures,[2] is the only complete analyses Smith provided. It is there stated that property as it exists under current conventions is but one division of private law. Though Smith was not to take so fully legalistic a view of property in his Wealth of Nations or indeed in the Draft of the Wealth of Nations written later in the year 1763 when these lectures were given, they do provide the best and in some cases the only clear description of Smith's conception of existing property. For example:

> Property is acquired five ways. First, by occupation, or taking possession of what formerly belonged to nobody. Second, by accession, when a man has a right to one thing in consequence of another, as of a horse's shoes along with the horse. Third, by prescription, which is a right to a thing belonging to another arising from long and uninterrupted possession. Fourth, by succession to our ancestors or any other person, whether by a will or without one. Fifth, by voluntary transference, when one man delivers over his right to another.[3]

---

1 Cannan shows this in his parallel chart of subjects dealt with in both the Lectures and the Wealth of Nations, to be found in the Lectures, pp. xxxv-xxxix.

2 Lectures, pp. 107-153.

3 Lectures, p. 107. Here Smith is dealing with how property is acquired by Private Law. He does not deal with theft or force nor with state confiscations or taxes which are part of Public Law. For theft see WN, II, p. 232. The Public Law of property will be dealt with in the chapter on the "objectives of Government" Ch.10.

Smith then goes on to devote separate sections to the discussion of each of these five methods of property acquisition. Though each of these five methods exist in Commercial society, it is obvious that voluntary acquisition is the method of acquiring property that best typifies commerce and it is useful in orienting our discussion of commercial property to sketch a clear picture of the tradition-bound society in which Smith saw the commercial system developing.

For example, Smith describes "occupation" as still in existence in his own time as a method of acquiring property: in the form of the hunt or chase and fishing and berry-picking, and wood-gathering from the common land.

> When it first became necessary to cultivate the earth, no person had any property in it, and the little plot which was dressed near their hovels would be common to the whole village, and the fruits would be equally divided among the individuals. There are remains of the common land property in our own country at this day. In many places there is a piece of ground belonging equally to several persons, and after harvest, cattle are, in many places, allowed to feed where they please.[1]

And later Smith describes how approbation is not permitted to take place by private individuals of parks or some "common lands" or waterways or seas or abandoned treasure still remaining in Britain. Hence, these are usually not part of the market for

---

1 Lectures, p. 109.

private property, and hence cannot be voluntarily or involuntarily transferred.1

The second way of acquiring property; accession, is quite generally in evidence wherever the transfer of land carries with it the ownership of that which that land possesses or is capable of possessing. "The most important accessions are in land property," says Smith:

> Land property is founded on division or an assignation by the society to a particular person of a right to sow and plant a certain piece of ground. In consequence of this right he must also have a right to whatever it produces, trees, fruit, minerals, etc. Alluvions made by any river naturally belong to the proprietor of the adjacent territory; but when the additions are very large, as is often the case in low countries, the government claims them, and the proprietor of the adjacent estate must purchase it before he possess it.2

Smith in this as in many other discussions of property law is credited by Cannan with drawing extensively upon Locke and the Natural Rights theorists.3

---

1 Lectures, p. 110.

2 Lectures, p. 110.

3 Compare Smith Lectures pp. 107-125 to Puffendorf De Jure Naturae at Gentium, lib., iv. cap. vii. p. 12, and iii 6, and Hutcheson's Introduction to Moral Philosophy which has an extensive chapter already described dealing with the different modes of alienating or acquiring property, as does his more famous System which we have also described; these are contained in Book II chapters v through viii entitled respectively "The private rights of men", p. 293, "The adventitious Rights, real and personal Property or Dominion, p. 309, "The means of acquiring

The third way of acquiring property is prescription. "It is founded on "the supposed attachment of the possessor to what he has long been possessed of and the supposed detachment of affection in the old possessor to what has long been out of his possession."1 Smith describes four requisites for a prescriptive right to property, which in brief are a bona fide claim, a title, charter or convention, uninterrupted possession and the sanity or acceptability of the person claiming. Smith concludes with a brief comparison of Roman and English law relating to prescription and state that "by the English law nothing can interrupt prescription but a claim of the old possessor." The importance of this is that neither the Parliament nor the town can intercede. However Smith does admit that "Kings seldom ever allow [any commoners] claims to prescribe;" where a short duration of possession is involved.

The fourth way of acquiring property is succession. It is either legal or testamentary.

> By legal succession is meant that the law should distribute the goods of the deceased to those [to] whom it is to be presumed the

---

property. How far it extends. In what subjects it resides", p. 324 and finally chapter 8 "Concerning derived property and the ways of alienating or transferring it", p. 340. Cannan also credits Smith's views on the five ways by which property is acquired to John Dalrymple, Essay towards a General History of Feudal Property in Great Britain (1758) pp. 33, 91.

1 Lectures, p. 111.

> person himself would have chosen that they should be given ...[1]

By testamentary is meant will or accepted document, in the modern sense which transfers ownership after death.

Smith provides several interesting reflections on the nature of the historic limitations of social property rights in varying periods when he says for instance,

> In a rude period a man had scarce the full property of his goods during his lifetime, and therefore it cannot be supposed that then he should have had a power to dispose of them after his death.[2]

Thus it was only in the mnore advanced stages of society that a man "had the full property of his goods" or that either form of succession became possible. Historically Smith insists that: "In all nations the relations of the dead person succeeded long before there was any such thing as a testament."[3]

Smith tends to disagree with Grotius and Puffendorf in certain details and in the historic progression of laws of succession.[4] Smith distinguishes the general social practices

---

1 Lectures, p. 113.

2 Lectures, p. 113.

3 Lectures, p. 113.

4 Compare Hugo Grotius De Iure Belli et Pacis, English trans. Francis W. Kelsey (Oxford, 1925) No. 3 of "Classics of International Law." lib. ii, cap. vii, p. 3. and Puffendorf, De Iure Naturae et Gentium, he chronicles the history of property accession and testament from the earliest to the most recent cultures.

regarding property succession from the actual laws of testament. He deals in general with the Roman and feudal property succession but in detail with their laws of testament. His argument concerning feudal entails and primogeniture will be considered later in this chapter. His general view was that whereas primogeniture was a bad social custom it was perhaps to some extent unavoidable, whereas entail were laws that could and must be changed if land and agriculture improvement were to take place throughout Britain.

> The greatest of all extensions of properties is that by entails. To give a man power over his property after his death is very considerable, but it is nothing to an extension of this power to the end of the world.[1]
>
> Upon the whole nothing can be more absurd than perpetual entails[2] ... The earth and the fullness of it belongs to every generation, and the preceding one can have no right to bind it up from posterity; such extension of property is quit unnatural ... Entails are disadvantageous to the improvement of the country, and those lands where they have never taken place are always best cultivated: heirs of entailed estates have it not in their view to cultivate lands, and often they are

---

1 Lectures, p. 122.

2 Smith in his Lectures, p. 123, asserts "Entails were first introduced into the modern law by the ecclesiastice, whose education made them acquainted with the Roman customs," indicating that Roman Law was the source of entails. However, in his Wealth of Nations, Bk. III, Ch. II of Vol. I, p. 388 Smith asserts that Roman law was not the source of entails.

> not able to do it. A man who buys land has this entirely in view, and in general the new purchasers are the best cultivators.[1]

"The fifth way of acquiring Property: Voluntary Transference," is the foundation of commercial market property relations. But, Smith described it as only one of five methods of property acquisition and these others tended to restrict the market in which the voluntary transference of property could exist within many feudal, or traditional laws or customs.

To a large extent Smith's discussion of voluntary transference is separated into legal and historical analyses and it is not interrelated to his total theory of property or economic theory. For example the legal analysis is typified by such statements as:

> In voluntary transference two things are required: first, a declaration of the intention both of the person who transfers, and of him to Whom it is transferred; second, the actual delivery of the thing.[2]

This in brief means that there is no right without possession and

---

1 Lectures, pp. 124. Smith expressed the identical views concerning entails in the Wealth of Nations BK. II, Ch. II, vol. I, p. 409 where he says, "Entails" are founded upon the most absurd of all suppositions, the supposition that every successive generation of men have not an equal right to the earth and to all that it possesses; but that the property of the present generation should be restrained and regulated according to the fancy of those who died perhaps 500 years ago."

2 Lectures, p. 125.

property cannot be transferred without tradition or delivery.1

Smith admits that transference of goods is distinct from that of land. Whereas the possession and delivery of goods are obvious or straightforward and have legally long been permitted, the transference of land has traditionally been more difficult, the delivery more symbolic than actual, and has often been legally prohibited. As Smith says,

> In transferring the property of lands and other large objects, what gives possession is not so easy to determine. As there cannot be an actual delivery, in our country a symbolical delivery is used; an ear or sheaf of corn signifies the whole field, a stone and turf, the estate to the centre of the earth, and the keys of the door, the house. By the Scotch law, if there be a transference of several estates, the purchaser must be infeft in each. By the English law infeftment in one serves for all when done in presence of the county court. In Scotland it must be done on the land: it is enough in England if it be done in view of it. Besides delivery a charter or writing, showing on what terms the transference was made, is also requisite for security. Till the custom was abolished by a late statute no vassal or possessor had a right of alienating his estate without the consent of the superior.2

I have given the full citation of this passage because it provides the full flavour of the residual feudal restrictions upon the alienation of property. This passage shows the importance of

---

1 Both these principles Smtih derived from Grotius (De Iure Belli at Pacis, lib. ii, cap. viii 25) which Hutcheson (System in his Bk. II chapter vii and viii) had reiterated.

2 Lectures, pp. 125-6.

symbolism and social heirarchy still associated with property transfer, or, in some cases, only recently abandoned. This is exemplified in his discussions of the reciprocal restraints upon tenant and lord preventing either from selling property: "If therefore either of them alienated any part of their estates without the other's consent, his right was forfeited."[1] Smith's familiarity with these residual feudal laws was obviously enhanced because they persisted in Scotland throughout most of his life. He indicates this himself when he says,

> The duty of vassals to their lords continued longer in Scotland than in England, which may be accounted for from the differences of their government, for that [of] England all alone favoured democracy, and that of Scotland aristocracy.[2]

Allied to these various property rights, Smith described several forms of "real rights" which affected and sometimes controlled the way in which actual property rights were distributed. These other real rights included servitudes or burdens which one man has on the property of another. These included the right to build or use a road to the nearest water, or town. Such servitudes or burdens could also include the right to feed a certain number of cows on another man's pasture, or to lean beams from a how a good number of these real rights descended from the Feudal law whereby "the

---

1 Lectures, p. 126.

2 Lectures, p. 126.

right of the vassal is founded on the charter of the superior."[1] Smith then devotes a section to pledges and mortgages which he treats in a rather legalistic fashion. He does not attempt anything more than a summary of current laws saying pledges refer to movable property and mortgages to immovable. It is not in his Lectures but in the Wealth of Nations that Smith notes the full extent of the restrictions upon mortgaging landed property during his lifetime, caused by the widespread persistence of the laws of entail.[2] This will be dealt with later in this chapter.

His section of "Exclusive Priveleges" is important for it suggests the confusion in Smith's mind between natural and civil rights to property. One of the foremost "exclusive priveleges" is the natural right to inheritance.[3] Yet earlier he said that "succession" was the "civil right to inherit property."[4] It would be easier to account for Smith's contradiction if he had made an attempt to distinguish original man's exclusive privelege to inheritance, from current inheritance by legal succession, or testament. But Smith does not do this. He does say that inheritance is originally natural, however heirs today still have a natural right of inheritance:

---

1 Lectures, p. 128.

2 WN, I, pp. 407-410.

3 Lectures, pp. 7, 129.

4 Lectures, p. 113.

> Among these [Exclusive Privileges] is the right of inheritance, which is not a creature of the civil law but arises from nature. The heir, previous to any other person, has a privelege of demanding what belonged to the deceased, and after he is admitted heir it is his real property.[1]

Smith held strong views on a variety of civil forms of inheritance such as entail and primogeniture,[2] and it is therefore puzzling that he should have at times been unclear as to whether the heir had a natural or a civil right to inheritance.[3] Smith may have taken over this confusion from Locke who makes exactly the same self contradiction. According to Locke inheritance is a natural right of children in the state of nature.[4] However in civil society although minors still have a natural right to inherit enough to maintain themselves "Law and custom determine the division of inheritance."[5]

It is also under this category of exclusive priveleges that Smith said the rights of all monopolists exist. Monopolies are exclusive privileges granted by the state, yet the question arises

---

1 Lectures, p. 129.

2 Smith condemned "Entails" saying they "restrained and regulated" present property "according to the fancy of those who died perhaps five hundred years ago." WN, I, p. 409.

3 Although Smith said men have a natural right to inherit in civil society he then says the law must first admit them to be heirs. Lectures, p. 129.

4 Two Treatises, Bk. I, sections 88-94.

5 Two Treatises, Bk. II, sections 65-73, esp. pp. 333-334.

from the above discussion of inheritance whether monopolies as well have not a pre-civil origin. For example the first hunter or the first trader or the first inventor of anything even today still claims an exclusive privilege, to monopoly, patent, or copyright. Smith says of such rights or exclusive privileges:

> These rights are for the most part creatures of the civil law, though some few of them are natural, as in a state of hunters even before the origin of civil government, if a man has started a hare and pursued her for some time, he has an exclusive privilege to hunt her, by which he can hinder many others to come in upon her with a fresh pack of hounds.[1]

Similar natural origins to monopolistic rights of the present day hunter, fisher, treasure finder, writer, inventor, or trader in new lands might be claimed on these same grounds of first occupant. This raises the question of whether "occupation" in present society which Smith designated as the first civil right can be clearly distinguished from the natural right to occupation. This would suggest the existence in Smith (and before him in Locke) of the recognition of possible natural rights wherever new lands, new markets, new products or new states are found, within present day civilization. Smith recognized that nations are to one another even today, in a condition of a state of nature[2] and thus property disputes between nations are concerned with property laws and rights which are ultimately outside the realm of any one

---

1 Lectures, p. 7.

2 Lectures, p. 1.

state's civil laws. In his lectures Smith therefore goes into considerable detail concerning these property disputes between nations to establish certain general rules for treatises, and declarations of war, and other justifications of military threats.[1]

Rights of contracts Smith does not include among the "real rights" but among "personal rights". He gives a general survey of both the legal definition of a contract and the history of contracts throughout antiquity and more recent times.

Smith describes the contracts formed under Roman and Feudal law. These were of four kinds: the mutuum, commodatum, depositum and pingus. He shows how these laid the foundation for present contracts.

> The <u>mutuum</u> is when I lend anything to be returned in value, as money. This soon sustained action.
>
> <u>Commodatum</u> is when the thing itself is to be restored, as a borrowed horse.
>
> <u>Depositum</u> is when a thing is committed to another's care but not to his use.
>
> <u>Pingus</u> is a security for debt.
>
> All these sustained action before the consensual contracts, which are also four, to wit, buying and selling, letting and hiring, partnership, and commission. In buying, if the contract be not fulfilled, you lose your earnest money. Letting and hiring once comprehended leases, day's wages, building, and almost everything with regard to society.[2]

---

1 <u>Lectures</u>, Part V, pp. 265-281.

2 <u>Lectures</u>, pp. 132-3.

Smith concludes this history with the remark that "nothing can be more different than the present and ancient state of contracts." In ancient times, "drinking blood and water mixed, bleeding one another", "and the most solemn ceremonies were scarce thought sufficient to secure the performance of a contract." "At present almost anything will make a contract obligatory."[1]

IV

To place Smith's foregoing theoretical discussion of legal property alienation (transfer and acquisition) in perspective I will describe the contemporary markets for land and goods, of which he spoke or with which he can be expected to have been familiar.

In eighteenth century Scotland much landed property never entered the market at all. Smith discusses the legal restrictions upon the sale or mortgage of land in some detail. He was highly critical of both primogeniture and entail and was well aware of how widespread were these practices in his own time. He said that:

> The right of primogeniture, however, still continues to be respected, and ... it is still likely to endure for many centuries. In every other respect, nothing can be more contrary to the real interest of a numerous family, than a right which in order to enrich one, beggars all the rest of the children.

---

1 Lectures, pp. 133-4.

> Entails are the natural consequence of the law of primogeniture. They were introduced to preserve a certain linial succession, of which the law of primogeniture first gave the idea, and to hinder ... alienation ...[1]

Smith repeatedly criticises entails. By them the present property is regulated and restrained by the whims and "fancy" of those who died "perhaps five hundred years" ago.[2] Entails are founded on "the most absurd of all suppositions", "that every successive generation of men have not an equal right to the earth, and to all that it possesses."[3] Nonetheless Smith recognized that:

> Entails, however, are still respected through the greater part of Europe ...[4]

And he adds another observation on the persistence of the laws of entail in the Scotland of his time:

> In Scotland more than one-fifth, perhaps more than one-third part of the whole lands of the country, are at present supposed to be under strict entail.[5]

He then analyzes in detail the harmful effects which this persistence of entails has caused in the cultivation and improvemetns of land and agriculture. Entails caused "great

---

1 WN, I, p. 408-9.

2 WN, I, p. 409.

3 WN, I, p. 409.

4 WN, I, p. 409.

5 WN, I, p. 410.

tracts of uncultivated land"[1] and precluded much land from being improved. The reasons that entails had this effect were because they denied the right to sell land to those who would be energetic cultivators and kept ownership in the hands of those who had little interest in or knowledge of agriculture or profitable management of lands. Entails also maintained various restrictions upon leaseholders and the terms of leases which owners could offer to increase their revenue. But most important, the laws of entail prevented owners from selling or mortgaging even a portion of their lands to finance agriculture on a profitable basis. Entails prevented improvements, for no propreitor could borrow money for them on the value of his land. It was only by the act of 1770 that encouragement was given to "the improvement of lands ... in Scotland held under Settlements of strict Entail." Proprietors were permitted to grant long leases, provided they enclosed, drained, planted, and constructed buildings. They were required to repay only one quarter of borrowed money and to leave the other three quarters for their successors to cope with.

The emergence of commerce in this period is best conveyed by studying the enclosure movement which gradually divided up the common land into private holdings. Enclosure led to the fencing in of the hill pastures, abolished the common rights of grazing, and cultivation and right to gather wood or draw water and right

---

1 WN, I, p. 410.

of way. Enclosure made most land into a saleable or at least a mortgageable commodity which had by residual feudal laws and entails, been prevented from entering the commercial market.[1] It led to the "improvements" of agricultural lands generally in terms of their productiveness, and most important, changed the estate from a unit of ownership and subsistence to a unit of production. In so doing the enclosure movement helped to introduce division of labour using larger amounts of capital and supplied markets more plentifully.[2]

By Scottish Law the only title to land use was a written one, and thus another result of enclosures was that the parish

---

1 The political and economic effects on England and Scotland in the 18th century of the enclosure movement have been studied in detail by many authors. The material discussed in this chapter relates specifically to Adam Smith and is drawn from the following articles and books. W. E. Tate, "Members of Parliament and the Proceedings upon Enclosure Bills", Economic History Review, Vol. XII, (1942) pp. 68-75. "Opposition to Parliamentary Enclosure in Eighteenth-Century England," Agricultural History, Vol. 19 (1946) pp. 137-42; "The Commons' Journals as Sources of Information concerning the Eighteenth-Century Enclosure Movement", Economic Journal, vol. LIV (1944), pp. 75-95; M. W. Beresford, "Commissioners of Enclosure", Economic History Review, Vol. XVI (1944) number 2, pp. 130-40. Henry Hamilton Economic History of Scotland op. cit. pp. 16, 42-3, 56-65, 71-82, 84, 89, 95, 133 and T.S. Ashton's Industrial Revolution p. 20 and his An Economic History of England: The 18th Century, pp. 38-40. Daniel Defoe, A Tour Through England and Wales (Everyman Ed.), 2 Vols. (London, 1948) Vol. 2, p. 89. William Marshal The Landed Property of England (London, 1804) pp. 358-67 and William Marshal, On the Appropriation and Enclosure of Commonable and Intermixed Lands (London, 1801), and H.J. Habakkuk, "English Landownership, 1680-1740" Economic History Review, Vol. X, (1957) pp. 1-17.

2 T. S. Ashton's An Economic History, p. 37.

poor and many poor tenants and subtenants and cottagers were removed or "cleared" becoming respectively farm labourers, fencers; or moved to the towns or new industrial areas.

The establishment of compact holdings in place of the old "runrig" system, the physical enclosures of fields and the new crops of grasses, turnips, and potatoes destroyed the old community, based on cooperative work of tenants of a township and replaced it by the isolated farm. Efficiency and productivity increased, and rising prices of the second half of the 18th century after fifty years of relatively static prices, brought increased incomes to agriculture especially because this accompanied a fall in real costs of capital, equipment, seed, and transport. Consequently, landowners assumed that rents should rise at each reletting.

Nevertheless, there was great opposition to enclosure of the "commoties" or common pasture, as well as to the common agricultural plots,[1] common roads, streams, and some kelp and fishing shores. At least three statements of enclosure policy had been passed by the Scottish Parliament before the Union of Parliaments in 1707.[2] These were not enclosure acts in England

---

1 T. Johnston, History of the Working Classes in Scotland (Glasgow, 1921) pp. 159-60, 183-8.

2 See M. W. Markwick, Scotland in Modern Times (London, 1964) p. 4. For a contrasting view of the significance of enclosures in Scotland see Hamilton, Economic History of Scotland op. cit., pp. 16, 42, 43, 56, 57, 58, 59, 60, 61, 62, 64-5, 71, 72-4, 78-84, 89,95, 133.

and did not change land property much until well into the 18th century.[1] In Scotland unlike England it was not necessary as it was in England to have private acts of enclosure passed through parliament because the rights of owners were more clearly defined. The rights of occupation, custom or tradition were less taken account of in Scottish judicial decisions.[2] Only a written statute or document was legal. (This was primarily because Scottish Law had long been influenced by the continental French and Dutch legal system and education.) The Justice of the Peace and later the Sheriff was given authority to assign plots of land from the common. And legally that was the final word on property ownership and distribution. As Sir John Sinclair wrote in 1814 of this practice: "In no country in Europe are the rights of proprietors as well defined, and so carefully protected."[3]

However, "Division" and "Enclosure" were separate in Scotland because of the expense of fencing and the antagonism physical enclosures provoked.[4] As early as 1695 an act was

---

1 Marwick, ibid., p. 4.

2 Malcolm Gray, The Highland Economy 1750-1850 op.cit., pp. 95-7, 69, 70. Gray deals in detail with the two major reasons for evicting tenants and squatters in the highlands (for sheep-grazing and for improved cultivation).

3 Hamilton, Ec. Hist. of Scotland, op. cit., p. 57.

4 Gray, The Highland Economy, op. cit., p. 78.

passed providing for the "prevention of the discords that arise about commoties,"[1] well into the eighteenth century it was usual for tenants to make "slaps" in dykes, walls and fences and purposely let their animals restore rights of way and grazing rights.[2] Tenants' opposition was against the division of the common and the consequent distribution of common rights to pasturage, wood gathering, passage, and cultivation.[3] Yet, it also was against the fences and new agricultural methods of which enclosure was but a part. Leases often contained a clause binding the tenant to build fences and to ditch the enclosure, and imposed new methods of crop rotations.[4] Fertilizer and rootcrops gradually enriched the soil and enlarged the crop and cattle yields and led to a general rise in living standards. However tenant and cottager only gradually discovered these changes were real improvements, and in the interim there was much opposition to these new property relations and new agricultural methods.

Smith however, was an advocate both of enclosures and of the new agricultural methods and thus tended to concentrate on the

---

1 Marwick, op. cit., p. 4. And Hamilton Ec. Hist. of Scotland, op. cit., p. 58.

2 Gray, The Highland Economy, op. cit. pp.95-7 Hamilton, ibid.,p. 58.

3 Gray, The Highland Economy, ibid., pp. 69-70.

4 Hamilton, Ec. Hist. of Scotland, p. 63.

productive benefits of them rather than the property disputes they provoked. For example:

> The present high rent of enclosed land in Scotland seems owing to the scarcity of enclosure and will probably last no longer than that scarcity.1

Nonetheless the pattern of landownership continued in Scotland, as it had in England to result in the increase of larger tenant landholdings. Small freeholders sold out because of either coercion, or resignation.2 They could not compete in the market with the larger tenant farmers, and could barely subsist if they did not take part in the market.

Smith treats enclosure and the expected improvements from the new agricultural methods as the accepted general opinion of his time.

> The use of the artificial grasses, of turnips, carrots, cabbages and other expedients which have been fallen upon to make an equal quantity of land feed a greater number of cattle than when in natural grass, should somewhat reduce, it might be expected, the superiority

---

1 WN, I, p. 168.

2 Gray, The Highland Economy, op. cit., pp. 15-7. Gray also argues pp. 69-70 that the situation of poor tenant farmers was even worse than that of these small free holders. "Evicted tenants ... were many" and thus "A ruthless consolidation passed along this strip, roughly from South to North, leaving a new capitalist farming order."

> of butcher's meat naturally has over that of bread. It seems accordingly to have done so; and there is some reason for believing that, at least in the London market, the price of butcher's meat in proportion to the price of bread, is a good deal lower in the present times than it was in the beginning of the last century.[1]

Smith then goes on to examine in great detail the history of the price of butcher's meat with the price of bread in earlier times, in order to reinforce his argument that these new agricultural methods were indeed a substantial improvement. In this entire discussion Smith was echoing current opinions of the productive benefits of the new property management and distribution.

Smith's detailed discussion of the rent of kelp[2] seashores is but a further example of enclosure and the extension of commerce which he witnessed during his own time, and which, like the land enclosures, led to controversies over property theory and property rights. Smith's famous conclusion that: "The rent of land, therefore, considered as the price paid for the use of land,

---

1 WN, I, pp. 168-9.

2 Kelp, an extract from seaweed, was important in 18th century Scottish manufacturers of soap and glass. See Hamilton Ec. Hist. of Scotland op. cit., pp. 6, 11, 78, 140, 135-6. Gray, The Highland Economy, op. cit., considers many aspects of the kelp industry during the 18th century. See pp. 124-58 on the rise and fall of the kelp industry.

is naturally a monopoly price," is directly preceded by the example of the rent from kelp shores which demonstrates that rent is not related to what the landlord may have laid out upon the improvement of the land or sea rocks upon which the seaweed grows, but rent is related to what the tenant can pay. The landlord:

> ... sometimes demands rent for what is altogether incapable of human improvement. Kelp is a species of seaweed, which, when burnt, yields an alkaline salt, useful for making glass, soap, and for several other purposes. It grows in several parts of Great Britain, particularly in Scotland, upon such rocks only as lie within the high water mark, which are twice every day covered with the sea, and of which the produce, therefore, was never augmented by human industry. The landlord however, whose estate is bounded by a kelp shore of this kind, demands a rent for it as much as for his corn fields.[1]

Smith then goes on to describe a further extension of property rights practised in his time whereby portions of the sea known to be abundant in fish were rented by those whose properties bordered the sea at these points.

> The sea in the neighborhood of the islands of Shetland is more than commonly abundant in fish, which make a great part of the subsistence of their inhabitants, but in order to make a profit by the produce of the water, they must have a habitation upon the neighbouring land. The rent of the landlord is in proportion, not to what the farmer can make by the land, but to what he can make both by the land and by the water.[2]

---

1 WN, II, p. 162.

2 WN, I, p. 162.

We turn from the market in land property either for sale or rent to the existing conditions of the market for goods property or trade. As in the foregoing information concerning land, Smith documented the origin and existing condition of town markets not by conjectural arguments, but by citations from the famous Doomsday Book, and other records of the times. He frequently makes reference to Robert Brady's Historical Treatise of Cities and Burgs or Boroughs,[1] and he also makes use of more general histories, such as The History of England by his friend, David Hume.

V

Aside from land entails and laws which restricted the sale of moveable goods there was also a far more important limitation of the market. Most Scottish families were forced by poverty or habituated by custom to produce their own food, clothes, tools, and furniture. Not only in Scotland says Smith but,

> In every large country, both the clothing and ousehold of the far greater part of the people re the produce of their own industry.[2]

---

1 Robert Brady, Historical Treatise of Cities and Burgs of Boroughs, second ed. (London, 1711)

2 WN, I, pp. 428-9.

Thus the great 18th century expansion of the market did not by any means indicate that all goods or land had entered the market for sale.[1] It was only the potential marketability of property which had become generally appreciated.

What little commerce most farmers, shepherds, fishermen and rural labourers actually engaged in was carried out with the travelling pedlars. The sale of property in goods, or "commerce", according to Marwick, Hamilton and Ashton was very much an itinerant trade. Marwick stresses that most goods were produced and consumed by members of the family without resort to purchase or sale. But "there was an increased resort to travelling weavers and taylors."[2]

Aston states:

> Internal trade was conducted by merchants most of whom specialized in a narrow range of products. Some themselves travelled about the country, but many employed "riders-out" to secure orders and collect payment from customers.[3]

Where townes developed as markets for local trade only, Smith asserts they could grow only to a moderate size which was always directly dependent on the produce of the surrounding country. Where towns and cities developed as ports for domestic and foreign

---

1 Marwick, op. cit., p.7.

2 Marwick, ibid., p. 7.

3 Ashton, Industrial Revolution, op. cit., p. 46.

goods they had not such limitations by the productivity of the surrounding countryside and could grow rich though their area be poor and the area from which they drew foreign goods be poor as well.1 This pattern of commercial growth in or near port towns epitomized Smith's experience in first Kirkcaldy, then Glasgow, Edinburgh and London. The trade in each of these areas has already been discussed.2 Each greatly expanded through the period of Smith's life, both because of foreign trade with the Baltic in the case of Kirkcaldy and Edinburgh, and the American plantations in the case of Glasgow and London, and because as sea or river ports (or near ports) they represented the principal focus of communcation, transport, and trade within the country. As Hamilton and others make clear, the Scottish foreign trade was far more dependent (by 1760) an America than was Britain generally. Glasgow was overwhelmed by the influence of the American Tobacco trade which accounted for 80 per cent of Scottish imports from America. Thus, Smith's strong connections with Kirkcaldy and Edinburgh, where trade was primarily with the continent, helped to give him a balanced picture of British trade. Ashton reminds us that,

> Historians have tended to pay undue attention to the commerce with distant lands. The overwhelming bulk of the import trade wash with

---

1 WN, I, p. 427.

2 See Ch. II.

> the Continent and in particular with the countries nearest to Britain.1

We can see Smith's appreciation of this in his comments about wood, flax, and hemp from Baltic countries, and tobacco and manufactures sold to them.2 Certainly the significance of trade to the expansion of Kirkcaldy, and Glasgow and London made Smith well aware of the actual experience of towns "situated near either the sea coast or the banks of a navigable river which are not necessarily confined to derive [wealth] from the country in their neighbourhood."3 Yet in towns there were also many restrictions on the market and the saleability of land and goods. This was partially because there were so many domestically made objects and because many feudal practices of service and legal restrictions upon sale continued in custom even as they were legally being destroyed. There were many restrictions on who could sell and what, when and how they could sell. The apprenticeship restrictions, statute labour and services to the millwright, the laird, the town etc. and the voluntary slavery of miners were symptomatic of the limitations upon the sphere of the actual

---

1 Ashton, Industrial Revolution, p. 47.

2 WN, I, pp. 25, 182, 386; II, pp. 117, 142.

3 WN, I, p. 427.

market for all goods, lands as well as services.[1] The market for goods was also restricted from its full development in the many ways Smith described; (i.e. by monopolies, prohibitions, and taxes, which will be discussed in the later chapter on existing government.) Nevertheless, there was a considerable local, domestic and foreign commercial market in towns and cities during Smith's life. "The home trade", wrote David Macpherson, a contemporary,[2] "is with good reason believed to be a vast deal greater in value than the whole of the foreign trade, the people of Great Britain being the best customers to the manufacturers and traders of Great Britain," and he adds in a footnote that "it has been calculated, though I know not upon what grounds, or whether it is at all calculable, that the home consumption of this country is two-and-thirty times as much as the exports to foreign countries."

Commerce in Smith's society even in towns was not continual as he describes it as being. The markets were occasional. The famous fairs of Cambridge, Norwich, Northampton, were in the 18th century still national events where traders and individuals gathered once a year. Yet as population in England and Scotland

---

1 These will be discussed in detail in the following chapter dealing with the individual in market society.

2 David Macpherson, Annals of Commerce, 4 Vols. (London, 1805), Vol. III, p. 340.

increased and became centralized in towns, or on the river banks, or seacoast, the practice of weekly markets in hundreds of towns over the major function of the previous yearly fair.1 According to Hamilton and Ashton these markets tended to specialize increasingly in agricultural or semi-agricultural products, and took the form of street stalls till gradually great halls were built to house the market.

Glasgow, like other large cities, was not only a market but an individual centre, and raw goods such as wheat and cattle which entered the city markets often left to be resold to the provinces as flour and leather. While "packmen" carried a meagre collection of wares through the rural countryside, numerous traders moved from one market to another, who bought and sold anything wherever a profit seemed worthwhile. In addition to these traders there were specialist dealers of "factors" in each particular commodity.

Trading professions had for long been frowned upon because a strong tradition of public feeling, and some laws, had made it wrong to resell goods at a higher price which one had not changed in form. And there was simultaneously a tradition that the same person could not perform the raising, butchering and selling of cattle, or the growing of grain, distilling, and selling of spirits. Though both these and other similar commercial traditions were breaking down in the 18th century they did so

---

1 Marwick, Scotland in Modern Times op. cit., p. 7. Weekly markets in the burghs for the disposal of agricultural produce from the locality continued and a wide range of commodities was made available at the annual fair."

gradually and at different rates throughout the country. Charles Townshend (the Minister to whom Smith was an advisor) reiterated the traditional views that "no one who fats cattle shall follow the business of a butcher". However, throughout the 18th century these traditions gradually disintergrated to the extent that most new trades operated outside the traditional channels and as Smith so aptly put it, the various trades and professions became "confounded." The same man might call himself a manufacturer or a merchant; a planter or a factor. In the markets there developed jobbers or speculators who never saw the goods they sold or bought because they dealt with either samples or sold stock at long distance from the market and transferred it directly to the retailer or consumer. In conjunction with these practices of dealing and jobbing there developed the notorious trading "combinations" which Smith described in detail.[1] In coal, cheese, grain, and many other commodities such combinations determined not only the price of goods and stock but determined what percentage of the market each would get and even which days various members of the combination could sell what amount of their produce.

---

1 WN, I, p. 74.

## IV

The causes why the prices of various goods rose or fell was among Smith's most important concerns.[1] Smith's general enquiries into the subject are well known.[2] But he was primarily interested in how far the variations in the price of provisions affected, for example labour and industry, not simply with studying changing prices as an end in itself.[3] He concludes:

> The wages of labour do not in Great Britain fluctuate with the price of provisions. These vary everywhere from year to year, frequently from month to month. But in many places the money price of labour remains uniformly the same sometimes for half a century together.[4]

Nevertheless, he asserts in a later passage that,

> We must not, upon this account, imagine that the price of provisions has no influence upon that of labour.[5]

High prices of necessaries must eventually raise wages.[6] This he had witnessed in Scotland throughout his life-first in years of famine and bad harvests and then after 1750 as a general pattern.

---

1 WN, I, ch. V, pp. 34-52, ch. VI, pp. 53-61, ch. VII, pp. 62-71.

2 See esp. WN, I, ch. V "Of the Real and Nominal price of Commodities"

3 WN, I, pp. 83, 92, 95.

4 WN, I, p. 83.

5 WN, I, p. 95.

6 WN, I, p. 95.

Smith's next enquiry was into whether the prices of property in goods were cheaper in the cities or in the country villages.[1] He concluded that,

> Though the profits of stock both in the wholesale and retail trade are generally less in the capital than in small towns and country villages, yet great fortunes are frequently acquired from small beginnings in the former, and scarce ever in the latter. In small towns and country villages, on account of the narrowness of the market, trade cannot always be extended as stock extends.[2]

Once again it was the extent of the market which was of paramount interest to Smith, not the level of prices and profits.

Smith's ultimate conclusion about prices of goods was that they were better regulated by competition in a free market than by law.[3] Yet once again Smith did not argue this point from conjecture as he sometimes implied, but took historic examples from when "In ancient times too it was usual to attempt to regulate the profits of merchants and other dealers, by rating the price both of provisions and other goods."[4]

Smith traced this practice down through the "assize of bread" which still continued in force in his own time and he took concrete examples to disprove the argument that fixing prices of

---

1 WN, I, p. 126.

2 WN, I, p. 126.

3 WN, I, p. 159.

4 WN, I, pp. 159-60.

goods by law was more beneficial to wages or to the general economy than competition. The assize of bread established by George II which could not be put in practice in Scotland, (because of a defect in the law), Smith showed to have "occasioned no sensible inconveniency, and the establishment of one in the few places where it has yet taken place, has produced no sensible advantages."[1]

Smith's catalogue of restrictions upon trade both domestic and international, however, led him to insist that such competition in many trades as then existed was quite limited and insufficient. He then set down in his Book Four the principle of the Mercantile system of restraints upon importation and promotion of exports which he argued had grave disadvantages to the entire economy. The principal disadvantage was once again the limits to the market, which again hindered progress and welfare.

At the same time that new land and new produce from land and industry was entering the market, there was taking place a considerable increase of capital. The growth of capital, credit and the medium of currency expanded all aspects of the market. Conjointly, the government's interest rate dropped from six per cent at the beginning of 1700 to five per cent in 1714, to four per cent in 1727 and finally in 1757, Pelham reduced the interest

---

1 WN, I, p. 159.

rate to three per cent. Hamilton examines in detail the resulting capital accumulation in Scotland throughout the century.[1] He shows that the development of cattle and grain after the Act of Union brought only small and temporary capital loans from the London Market compared to the vast capital investment in Scotland's foreign trade after 1750. It was only after this period that heavy capital investment occurred in Scottish mines, harbours, roads, canals and the new section of Edinburgh.[2]

Smith, as we will show in a later chapter, was primarily interested in the interest rate as a determinant of capital investment. He was vitally concerned that the level of investment should continue to increase for the improvement of the general welfare. And he even favoured fixing a low interest rate to spur industry and to prevent funds being loaned only to unthrifty, profligate, or rich borrowers.

Smith was not the first to observe that such adjustments of the interest rate vary with the rate of profit[3] nor the first to give a historical view of the alterations of interest rates in England or in other countries. Locke had devoted his _Considerations_ and _Further Considerations_ to the question of

---

1 Hamilton, _Ec. Hist. of Scotland_, Ch. IX-XII.

2 Hamilton, _Ec. Hist. of Scotland_, p. 330.

3 _WN_, I, p. 99.

interest rates. And as early as 1669 Josiah Child remarked that

> ... all countries are at this day richer or poorer in an exact proportion to what they pay, and have always paid, for the interest of money.

Child concluded that ":the bringing down of interest from 6 to 4 or 3 per cent will necessarily double the Capital stock of the nation."1 Smith recorded and applauded the fact that the rate of economic advance which increased after 1750 was largely due to precisely this cheapness of capital allied with the steady expansion of trade and, of course, the growth of industry. Once again Smith's concern was with the effect of different interest rates on the rate of social improvement or decline, not the study of interest rates or capital investment for their own sake in different historic periods.

Smith did not draw his abstract theoretical model of the market strictly from property relations of his time. It was more a model of emerging than existing property relations. His detailed description of five contemporary ways of legally acquiring property demonstrate that the residue of feudal laws still circumscribed the market of his time. Although his central focus in his theoretical analysis of political economy was on the sale or alienation of goods, most domestic goods and landed estates did not enter the market. Nevertheless throughout the 18th century land and goods were becoming more freely alienated

---

1 Josiah Child, New Discourses of Trade (London, 1693).

and the permanent city market districts were steadily replacing the itinerant pedlar and the yearly, monthly or weekly fair, as the general mode of commerce. Smith's primary concern in his detailed studies of the prices of goods, land and interest rates was not with an exposition of historic facts or a comprehensive narrative but with the discovery of different effects upon men and society of different prices and markets. Whether these benefit men and society or harm them was the question he focused upon. In the following chapter this will be shown to be even more true of Smith's considerations of wages, profit and rent, and of their general effects upon individuals.

# CHAPTER VII

## ALIENATION OF PROPERTY: THE EFFECT OF INDIVIDUALS

Two diametrically opposed effects of commerce are described by Smith. Firstly, it established useful routines for working behaviour and institutions and for market standards of exchange. But at the same time commercial society intensified the harmful effects of class conflict, and of extreme division of labour on industrial workers of all kinds. In this chapter we will consider these contrasting effects of commerce upon individuals and review Smith's explanation for them.

### I

Smith presents a schematic commercial society composed of equally independent individual merchants. He also outlines the existing class structure in which individuals' desires were submerged within economic group interests. Although each man may be a merchant, _what_ a man has to sell in this commercial society determines his interests and his position in the broad class structure. This differentiates one class of individuals who sell their labour and have no other property to sell, from the landlord and capital owner who can sell or rent their capital or landed property to purchase the labour of others.

In his abstract social scheme Smith says almost all men are totally dependent on others for their supplies in commercial society. Yet most men are "personally independent"; that is, they do not depend on one single other individual for their subsistence, but on many.[1] In Smith's factual description menial servants are the only completely economically-dependent group of labourers in commercial society. Wage labourers are dependent to some degree, but not in the same way as a feudal serf. Smith's schematic description of the commercial individual is only incidentally mentioned in connection with his historical class analysis. Usually the two methods are employed for strictly separate purposes and in entirely different contexts.

A commercial society is divided into a large number of different groups[2] which share not only common economic interests

---

1 WNI, p. 438. "Each tradesman or artificer derives his subsistence from the employment, not of one, but of a hundred or a thousand different customers. Though in some measure obliged to them all, therefore, he is not absolutely dependent upon any one of them."

2 TMS, p. 338. "Every independent state is divided into many different orders and societies, each of which has its own particular powers, privileges and immunities. Every individual is naturally more attached to his own particular order or society than to any other ...

"Upon the manner in which any state is divided into the different orders and societies which compose it, and upon the particular distribution which has been made of their respective powers, privileges, and immunities, depends what is called, the constitution of that particular state."

but also similar morals, characters and social rank.[1] Group members sympathise more easily and completely with each other. The social status of a group depends on other people's evaluation of it, and this in turn reflects mainly its wealth and power.[2]

Commercial society consists of three main groups: landowners, merchants, and labouring poor.[3] But Smith provides a much more detailed breakdown of its constituent groups which I have listed in a footnote below for the sake of brevity.[4] The three main classes, in Britain during Smith's life formed a social scale or hierarchical structure. But in contrast to France[5]

---

1 TMS, pp. 292-4. For a general analysis of Smith's discussion of classes see Albion Small's Adam Smith and Modern Sociology, op. cit. and also Albert Salomon "Adam Smith as Sociologist", Social Research XII (1945), pp. 22-42.

2 TMS, I, III, esp. p.88ff.

3 WN I, p. 276.

4 There are three main income levels: first, that of men of great wealth, and power. This includes the aristocracy and wealthy merchants. TMS, p. 88. The middle income level includes four groups of men who are usually completely independent economically and often owners of some property. Lectures, p. 232. They are, in order of social rank, men of letters and professional men - clergymen, professors, doctors; and lawyers; WN II, p. 334, small merchants like shopkeeper; WN I, pp. 382-3, craftsmen and the members of various guilds, WN I, p. 138, and finally yeomen, farmers with leases which are virtually freeholds, WN I, p. 415. In the third income level are men without property or skills who make up the largest part of the population, WN I, p. 88, WN II, pp. 302-3, unskilled urban labourers and farm labourers, WN I, pp. 12-3 who are roughly equal in social rank, and menial servants and beggars who are inferior, Lectures, p. 104; WN I, pp. 18-9.

5 Ashton, An Economic History, op. cit.,p. 20.

and to other continental countries, there was considerable intermingling and great fluidity within classes and a degree of mobility up and down the class structure[1] According to Ashton:

> These class gradations were rungs of a ladder on which many climbed and descended ... the rungs were many and closely spaced making it easy for ability to be equated with task.[2]

Ashton goes rather far in his assertion of the fluidity of classes in 18th century England.[3] He appears to equate the extreme intra-class mobility within each strata which did exist, with extreme inter-class mobility between rich and poor which was relatively limited. J.H. Plumb in The First Four Georges asserts that "The majority had a profound sense of the laws of subordination."[4] And later he spells this out:

> Free and mobile as the English Society was, compared with other European countries, it was nevertheles very rigid by modern standards. The theme of many people's lives was fixed by birth. They stayed in the village in which they were born and pursued

1 G.M. Trevelyan, History of England, op. cit., p. 514, expresses the general consensus of opinion on 18th century classes when he says "though the highest and lowest were far apart there were infinite gradations and no rigid class barriers as on the continent." For the views of some authors who believed classes were firmly separated see Lewis Namier, England in the Age of the American Revolution (London, 1930), Introduction and J.H. Plumb, The First Four Georges (London, 1956), pp. 22-25. For a contradictory opinion see Ashton, An Economic History, ibid., p. 20.

2 Ashton, An Economic History, p. 23.

3 Ibid., p. 20.

> those avocations in which their fathers and grandfathers had been employed.[1]

In Scotland, among the highland crofters and fishermen there continued the same social class relations that had persisted for centuries throughout much of northern Scotland. Only in the lowlands and particularly in the cities of Edinburgh and Glasgow was there really significant fluidity within classes and some upward mobility. In all the ancient walled towns such as Edinburgh rich and poor shared the same staircase in their tall tenement apartments. The Judge or rich merchant was distinguished by inhabiting the middle, not the upper or lower floors. These notoriously unpleasant tenements caused a similarity of social experience in this period which disappeared when the New City of Edinburgh was built and the rich en masse left the "old city" to the poor. In Glasgow the considerable growth of the city in population and wealth during the eighteenth century of necessity caused an extraordinary intermingling of classes. The good parish schools too may have led to a certain blending of strata within the middle class especially. And of course class fludity accompained the tremendously rapid transformation of Scotland from a stagnant rural backwater to a thriving commercial economy in the space of scarcely one generation in the 18th century.[2]

---

1 *Ibid.*, p. 25.

2 1720-1770 is taken by Hamilton to be the period of greatest Scottish economic development. See Henry Hamilton, "Economic

In Smith's works there is a recognition of considerable mobility within classes and to some extent between classes in his extensive descriptions of tasks and professions as "confounded". By calling many tasks "confounded" Smith meant that the primitive state of industry, manufacturing, and merchant trading was such that the same man often performed many of the different roles and tasks which in more advanced commerce are separated and singular. In Scotland, a man of mixed profession[1] was even more common than in England,[2] for poverty had required that each man hold more than one job. Few shepherds or farmers could subsist without fishing or gathering kelp. And most tradsmen, manufacturers, and merchants kept a small garden and some animals. Furthermore, according to Smith the majority of a Scotsman's furniture, clothing, tools and food were still of his family's own creation.[3]

Even though class activities were "confounded" in the 18th

---

Growth in Scotland 1720-1770":, Scottish Journal of Political Economy VI (1959), see esp. pp.86-7.

1 WN, pp. 60, 130, 432-3. Smith repeatedly mentions examples.

2 Marwick, op. cit., p. 7.

3 WN, I, pp. 428-9.

century (by the accounts of Gray,[1] Marwick,[2] the Webbs,[3] Ashton[4] and Smith himself[5]) it is noteworthy that Smith defined class structure with considerable clarity. Individuals he divided into three classes; those who derived their living from capital, land, or labour.

If this class division now seems obvious Ronald L. Meek's article "Adam Smith and the Classical Concept of Profit" helps to remind us that it was not obvious then. Indeed Meek goes so far as to claim that:

> Adam Smith seems to have been, if not the first to discern the existence of this pattern in the

---

1 Gray, The Highland Economy, op.cit., has various sections on "tacksmen", "as farmers, pp. 26-7, 194-5; as improvers, pp. 78, 86;' "as merchants", pp. 17, 110, as sheep farmers, pp. 92, 94 and "as kelp owners", pp. 130-1. Gray also has sections on fishing and farming combined, pp. 118-19, 145, 214-6. On merchants as farmers, p. 194, as capital accumulators and as fisherman, pp. 18, 164, 221.

2 Marwick, ibid., p. 7.

3 Sidney and Beatrice Webb, History of Trade Unionism (London 1950), pp. 29-40.

4 T.S. Ashton, An Economic History, pp. 20-22.

5 WN, pp. 55, 60, 130. Smith shows how lowland farmers and Glasgow merchants combined all three class activities and possessed all three forms of property; land, labour and capital. Such a man "cultivated some of his own garden with his own hands", improved his lands by investments of capital, and rented large tracts to tenants. Rent is often confounded with wages in various forms in the case of small farmers; or wages with profit in the case of small manufacturers.

> society around him, at least the first to appreciate its enormous significance.[1]

Smith was the first to establish profit on capital as a general category of class income which accrued to all who used "stock" in the employment of "productive" wage-labour[2] and which was qualitatively distinct both from the rent of land and from the wages of labour.[3] As Meek points out,

> Smith's division of society into landlords, labourers and capitalists would appear to presuppose quite a considerable infiltration of capital and capitalist methods of organisation into agriculture and manufacture, yet if we look at Britain, and still more if we look at Scotland, at the time when Smith's basic ideas were formed, we are forced to the conclusion that this process of infiltration had not then proceeded far enough to render Smith's basic pattern plausible as a delineation of the general state of affairs in these countries.[4]

---

1 Ronald L. Meek, "Adam Smith and the Classical Concept of Profit." Scottish Journal of Political Economy I (1954), pp. 138-153. p. 138.

2 Meek shows how to Smith's; predecessors, generally speaking, profit had appeared as "profit upon alienation" - i.e. as the gain from buying things cheap and selling them dear. To Smith, on the other hand, profit began to appear as an income uniquely associated with the use of capital in the employment of wage-labour added to the original value of the raw materials upon which they worked.

3 Smith's view of capitalists as a distinct class was not even fully present in the Glasgow lectures though by the later part of 1763 when he wrote the "Draft" of the Wealth of Nations we find his first clear statement of the tripartite division of social classes.

4 Meek, "Adam Smith and the Classical Theory of Profit", p. 142.

Smith was thus precient in his analysis of classes and more so than others at the time.

II

Smith's comments on class are scattered throughout his works and have been the subject of frequent analysis.[1] He is held largely to blame for the confusion in his discussions of classes about both what he meant and what he left unsaid. And it is true that Smith provided some ambiguous class theories and principles from which his different interpreters can sometimes justly lay claim to their separate interpretations.[2]

It can be assumed that from the ambiguities or tensions of Smith's fundamental theory of property, follow logically some of his indecisions about classes and about constituent forms of property in wages, rent and profit. Smith had several theories of wages:[3] a supply and demand theory, a subsistence minimum

---

1 These have included Albert Salomon, "Adam Smith as Sociologist", Social Research XII (1945), pp. 22-42, Gladys Bryson, "Sociology and Moral Philosophy", Sociological Review, Vol. 24 (April 1932); F.H. Giddings, The Principles of Sociology (New York, 1896), preface, and Studies in the Theory of Human Society (New York, 1922); Albion W. Small, Origins of Sociology (Chicago, 1924), ch. 1, and Adam Smith and Modern Sociology, op. cit.

2 See examples in Albion Small, Adam Smith and Modern Sociology, op. cit., p. 110.

3 For Wages see WN I (general discussion), pp. 72-97. For supply and demand see pp. 77, 83, 111. For exploitation see p. 74. For subsistence minimum see pp. 76, 83. For analysis of these

theory, his exploitation theory, and a "reserve claimant": theory. At different points in the Wealth of Nations Smith held various theories of rent;1 a supply and demand theory, an exploitation theory and a differential theory. And finally, he put forward several theories of profits;2 again a supply and demand theory, an exploitation theory, and his compromise justifications of some profits as actually the wages of labour, others as payments for effort of direction and supervision, and others as payments for risk of capital, and others simply as interest for the safe use of capital invested for periods of time.

These theories of wages, profit and rent often contradicted each other. And so consequently, did his views on classes. If profit was usually a "fair and reasonable reward" for risk, how could it also be exploitation? If rent was always monopoly exploitation, how could it be based on a differential from worthless to valuable lands? Could different levels of rent be

---

wage theories see Schumpeter, History of Economic Analysis, op.cit., pp. 111, 189-90, 268-70.

1 For Rent see WN I exploitation theory, p. 162, (differential theory) p. 164, (supply and demand theory) pp. 62-63. For an analysis of Smith's different theories of rent see Schumpeter, ibid., pp. 190-91, 264-5, 268.

2 See WN I (general theory of profits) pp. 98-110, for supply and demand theory, pp. 62-63, 66, exploitation theory of profits, pp. 74, 68-70, others p. 108, p. 60 ":confoundings":. For analyses of these different theories of profit see Schumpeter, ibid., pp. 190-1, 268, 331-4.

explained by a supply and demand theory if rent was always a monopoly price? Likewise if wages were governed by supply and demand only, there was no logical reason why they could not in the short run fall below subsistence minimum levels. If minimal wages always resulted from exploitation of the labourers by the masters' control of contracts, could wages also simultaneously rise and fall with supply and demand for labour?

In each case these alternative theories present a positive and a normative conception of wages, profits, and rents. In each case Smith's ambivalence regarding wages, profit and rent reflects his deeper seated indecision about the justice or rights to that property from which those three incomes are derived. That is, Smith provides very equivocal justifications of the ownership of capital, land, and the proper rewards of labour.[1] The positive theories of supply and demand do not consider the justice of rent, profit and wages, they simply state the income levels to be expected from adjustment of different variables in the economy. The normative theories Smith presents are, in each case, suggestions that property relations are based on exploitation of the

---

1 These equivocal justifications of the ownership of capital, land and labour are at times allied to ambiguities in Smith as to the meaning of these terms and their various usages. See S. Holender, ":Some Technological Relationships in the Wealth of Nations and in Ricardo's Principles", Canadian Journal of Political Science, 32 (1960) pp. 184-201. Holender shows Smith's ambiguities of "capital" esp. Later in this chapter I deal with Smith's ambiguous views of "labour".

propertyless by the propertied classes.

His positive discussions of property were based strictly on conventions of society as the justification and origin of ownership. That is, those who by whatever means had acquired property which the state now recognised as legally theirs, were the owners, and the only owners that positive theory would consider in its analysis. On the other hand, Smith's normative theories of exploitation, each related to property as justified by labour. They described income as earned by effort, or risk, whether by labourers, managers, or landowners. These normative theories of exploitation imply that rewards gained other than by effort of risk are unjust. Other implications from this argument were that the conventions of society by which individuals possessed and justified property, were class controlled social conventions and class controlled governments who made the laws which upheld these conventions.

Smith was ambivalent in combining these positive and normative discussions of rewards. As has been mentioned earlier he described many cases in which profits of master manufacturers and landlords were in fact "real wages" for actual labour they performed alongside their workers, or for efforts of directing their business. In justifying a scale of rewards he implied at times, a similar equation of the physical risk to life which labourers endured in some employments, to the capital risked by investors and landlord improvers. At times he also implied that labourers possessed a property in themselves and their labour similar to that possessed by the owner of capital or land. This has been taken by E.G. West to be another of Smith's justifications of the existing distribution of rewards.[1] However Joseph Schumpeter,[2] Richard Schlatter[3] and others have noted Smith's statements that capital and rent were "deductions" from labour,[4] and his suggestions that these deductions were appropriated by two classes who for the most part did not labour.[5] Smith did imply that rent, interest and profits involved little effort and often only slight risk and so were at times perhaps not fully justified rewards.[6]

Thus Smith provided two views of classes: first, as in conflict - the rich landlords and employers exploiting, and the poor labourers being exploited; and second, he viewed classes in partnership - as productive groups performing constructive economic functions: working, directing or risking life, land or capital.

---

1 E.G. West, "Adam Smith's Two Views on the Division of Labour", Economica, 31 (1964), pp. 23-32.

2 Schumpeter, op. cit., p. 190.

3 Schlatter, op. cit., pp. 182-5.

4 WN, I, p. 73.

5 Draft, pp. 326-8.

6 Draft, pp. 326-8 esp. p. 327, where Smith speaks of those few "who don't labour at all, and who yet either by violence or by the orderly opposition of the law employ a greater part of the labour of the society."

The first view described classes as divided between the propertied and the propertyless, the second viewed all three classes as possessors of different forms of property or scarce resources who entered into productive relations and contracts based not on exploitation but on the conditions of supply and demand at that moment.

Why did Smith hold these two views of classes? The first view tended to be based on factual and historical conditions of the distribution of wealth among classes; the second tended more often to be based on the abstract productive functions of different groups holding different kinds of scarce resources. But what conditions of the classes of his time did Smith witness in ordinary trades and farms which could have led him to these two seemingly contradictory views of classes? Were the actual conditions of classes the result of exploitation or the result of developments of supply and demand in the rapidly expanding Britain of the 18th century?

III

Information on Scottish incomes, productivity, classes, living conditions and working conditions are all somewhat meagre in the early 18th century.1 Prices and wages to a large extent

---

1 Hamilton, "Growth", op.cit., pp. 86-7. "The statistical material available is irregular and incomplete." See also Hamilton's Ec. Hist. of Scotland, p. 343. "Information on wage

stayed the same in many industries and especially in agriculture for most of the first half of the century except when in droughts or times of bad harvests the prices could double and starvations became a real threat. Prices rose sharply in the later half of the century and some wages rose as well.1

The staple diet of bread and milk with occasional fish was often only marginally improved with the introduction of the potato and tea.2 Working hours in both agriculture and the new industries were invariably 12 hours or more.3 The wages on farms frequently throughout the century stayed at two to fourpence a day plus food,4 and even on improved farms near the towns when wages reached sixpence they were less than half of

---

rates, particularly in the early eighteenth century, is extremely scanty." See also Jacob Viner, "Guide", p. 110 where he says "there does not appear to be a comprehensive study either of the history or the economics of serfdom of the Scottish mines" and Viner says (ibid., p. 93) "No history of the British society (for Extending Fisheries and Improving the Seacoasts of this Kingdom) seems ever to have been written".

1 Hamilton, "Growth", ibid., p. 86, "such information as is available indicates increased production". p. 87. "It is impossible to estimate the national income of Scotland at this time but the above table suggests that it was growing and indeed, growing faster than population, so that income per head was increasing. The improvement in the standard of living is commented on in many contemporary writers.

2 Hamilton. "Growth", ibid., pp. 86-7.

3 Thomas Johnson, History of the Working Classes in Scotland, op. cit., pp. 321, 349.

4 Johnston, ibid., pp. 349-356.

the rate in some of the new industries.[1] However, wages in the new factories were even less certain than in agriculture and often were paid in "kind" or "truck" or "bills" rather than cash.[2] The shortage of coin made labourers constantly in debt to those who supplied them with food and other necessaries.[3] When workers were finally paid cash or goods they could hardly keep any of it.[4] Only about the last quarter of the century with the growth of the friendly societies and building societies[5] was there real improvement in workers' savings.

---

1 Hamilton, Ec. Hist. of Scotland, op. cit., pp. 12, 343-374.

2 See Hamilton, ibid., p. 93, and Gray, Highland Economy, op. cit., p. 184.

3 Hamilton, ibid., p. 93; WN I, pp. 314-5; Gray, ibid., pp. 184-5.

4 The pinmakers whom Smith had described in detail formed a corporation or friendly society in the last part of the 18th century in London and stated their conditions as follows: "This company consists for the most part of poor and indigent people, who have neither credit nor money to purchase wyre of the merchant at the best hand, but are forced for want thereof to buy only small parcels of the second or third buyer as they have occasion to use it, and to sell off the pins they make of the same from week to week, as soon as they are made, for ready money to feed themselves, their wives and children, whom they are constrained to employ to go up and down every Saturday night from shop to shop to offer their pins for sale, otherwise they cannot have money to buy bread ... [Employers] have by degrees so beaten down the price of pins that the workman is not able to live off his work ... and betake themselves to be porters, tankard bearers, and other day labourers, ... and many of their children do daily become parish charges." Tracts Relating to Trade. Manuscript 13 p. 816. This volume of papers is filed in the British Museum. Cited also by Webb, op.cit., p. 42.

5 Thomas Johnson, History of the Scotland Working Classes, op.cit., pp. 12, 343-374.

From 1750, however, there was obvious progress in production and some areas of distributed produce.[1] The wage relation became more regular, cash replaced truck,[2] and the commercialisation of all the myriad sorts of employment became more commonly the accepted pattern.[3]

By an act of 1617 Justices of the Peace were authorised to fix wages of all workmen, labourers, and servants; to imprison those who refused to work at these rates and to enforce observance on the part of the masters. To what extent these were applied is not fully known.[4]

However, those records available show that landlords used their powers as Justices of the Peace to enforce engagements and control wages. These practices prevented the movement of labour and kept rural wages at the same meagre rate.[5] Undoubtably this was a reason for much emigration to the towns and for the gradual undermining of these restrictions in the countryside as they became depopulated. Yet the conditions in industrial trades,

---

1 Hamilton, "Growth", op.cit., p. 86. "In the course of little more than a generation, Scotland had established a vigorous and highly developed economy."

2 See Gray, op.cit., ch. III, Sec. 3 "Money Income Growth and Redistribution." pp. 141-155.

3 Hamilton, Ec. Hist. of Scotland, op.cit., p. 343, Gray, ibid., pp. 141-155.

4 Hamilton, ibid., p. 344.

5 Hamilton, ibid., p. 344.

fishing and mining will provide examples of the restrictions upon wages and movement of labour generally.1

The fishing industry differed from both agriculture and trade or factory employment in that its labourers were independent, but by itself it provided rarely even susbsistence and was usually combined with sheepherding.2 "Crofter-fishermen" in groups of three or four families could outfit a small boat and after sharing the hazards of the rocky coast could divide a meagre catch. There were not wage earners.3 In the Firth of Clyde and Firth of Forth there were paid fishermen and larger boats but as Smith explained in detail the catch was rarely sufficient to justify the industry and frequently boats set out to obtain the bounty which the government paid to encourage fishing, rather than the fish themselves.4 The bounty payments for a while gave the industry a successful appearance. But though more prosperous than the crofters such bigger fishing boats were still the concern of

---

1 The peculiar conditions of evictions and emigration in the Highlands are treated in Gray, op.cit., pp. 78, 69-70 and by R.H. Campbell in "The Highland Economy 1750-1850", Scottish Journal of Political Economy VI (1959), p. 61.

2 Gray, ibid., pp. 107-24, 158-70, Hamilton, Ec. Hist. of Scotland, op.cit., p. 113, Marwick, op.cit., pp. 8-9.

3 Gray, ibid., p. 108.

4 Smith's extensive fishing industry observations are scattered throughout the chapter "On Bounties" especially. In this chapter fishing bounties are shown to have actively harmed the fish industry.

several families who frequently, though supplying Glasgow or Edinburgh, found the need to keep a patch of land and some animals to make a living.1

Scottish miners had perhaps the most dreadful of working conditions during the 18th century although they earned more than in other trades.2 They were not merely isolated from any town and in continual danger because of the primitiveness of their equipment and shafts but they were bound by a form of serfdom. This meant that they could not leave to seek other employment and they were bought and sold with the mine itself. The coal, iron, and salt mines had the most appalling history of this period. Penal and poor laws all served to reinforce the taking of vagabounds and their families and forcing them to work in the mines. Once a child of whatever age had set foot in the mines he was bound by ancient statutes to lifelong contract. Miners and their families were despised by other communities and forced to stay together. They were denied most legal rights including Habeas Corpus, and often refused burial in the local cemetery. Adam Smith however noted their position with little irony when he said:

---

1 Hamilton, Ec. Hist. of Scotland, op.cit., pp. 113-127. Johnston, op.cit., p. 77.

2 Thomas Johnson, ibid., pp. 79-83; Smith, WN I, pp. 116-7; Hamilton, ibid., pp. 187, 367-72.

> They have indeed privileges which slaves have not. Their property after maintenance is their own, they cannot be sold but along with the work, they enjoy marriage and religion,...1

He later reflected that Scottish miners frequently fled to Newcastle for less than half their former wages in order to become free.2

Wives and children who were listed in colliery inventories like machinery, carried coal in baskets on their heads from the coal face to the surface. It was not until the Emancipation Bill of 1774 that any real change took place in the miners' conditions and even then it met with fierce protest from mine owners.3

Smith's treatment of apprenticeship, servitude, compulsory service, and voluntary slavery4 demonstrate the antique pecu-

---

1 Lectures, p. 99.

2 Lectures, p. 100.

3 Though the easy passage of the bill through the Commons might be thought an indication of parliamentary; sympathy for miners, even a casual reading of the bill will show that its real cause was the economic motivation to get more miners into this potentially rapidly expanding industry and into the newly discovered mines which "remain unwrought, and many are not sufficiently wrought, nor are there a sufficient number of salters for the salt-works, to the great loss of the Owners and Disadvantage to the Public." See Preamble to the Act 15 George III, c. 28.
Yet there also perhaps was a general moral antipathy to miners' servitude and to slavery in general as suggested by the humanitarian groups which sprang up in the last half of the century. A formal government policy against negro slavery in England was stated by Lord Mansfield in 1772 and this probably reflected a large portion of liberal opinion.

4 Though the laws of slavery differed from one age and country to another Smith gave a general description of their condition as

liarities of existing labour practices.1

The Statute Labour of Smith's time was a set legal requirement of work each year demanded from each labourer in rurual areas, to the town council or lord, for the roads, or the maintenance of walls, dams and public works or sometimes private works such as mills. There were definite remnants of Feudal legal property arrangements in this payment in "service" work days required by the council legally for the maintenance of roads. Adam Smith, when he defended statute labour of his times was only doing so to contrast local British practice with France where "the exaction is frequently the most cruel and oppressive."2 Statute Labour was, however, but one form of the more general and oppressive kinds of obligations exacted from rural labourers by their masters, their landlord, their millwright, council, laird and church. And all these Smith criticised as unjust. The multiplicity of days of service required of the labourer had

---

follows: WN , p. 411: "[The slaves] were not, however, capable of acquiring property. Whatever they acquired was acquired to their master, and he could take it from them at pleasure. Whatever cultivation and improvement could be carried on by means of such slaves, was properly carried on by their master. It was at his expense. The seed, the cattle, and the instruments of husbandry were all his. It was for his benefit. Such slaves could acquire nothing but their daily maintenance."

1 See Thomas Johnston, op.cit., "Forced Labourers", pp. 72-84.

2 In Scotland and England however, Smith said, "it is scarce ever exacted with any circumstance of cruelty or oppression". WN II, p. 253.

diminished from the number stipulated in Feudal times[1] but it was still considerable.[2] And this situation was not only widespread in 1750 but common after Smith's death.[3]

IV

In towns like Edinburgh and Glasgow the traditional guilds had achieved almost exclusive control over wages. Unlike unions today, the "master" craftsmen who controlled the guilds were not just fellow employees but were "masters" or often owners of their

---

1 Smith discusses the famous Statute of Labourers enacted in 1350 by Edward III which ordained that all servants and labourers should for the future be contented with the same wages and liveries which they had been accustomed to receive. Such legal Statutes for labourers eventually led to the legal remnants of such Feudal practices which Smith in all their many forms described as persisting in his times.

2 A letter in the Aberdeen Journal in 1750 from a tenant farmer describing these many obligations to the various local establishments makes a considerable list of days service. "In the summer, the only Season for Improvement, I am toiling, casting, winning and leading leet Peats, out of a worn out Moss; my servants and I are compelled to labour six days picking Straws and Stones out of the Highway, we are as many Days making hay for the Laird, shearing and loading his Corn, I must plow too and harrow, both from him and the Minister, my Men and my Horses are every now and then trotting to Aberdeen as Carriers, as often I am warned by his Officer; and when I am at Liberty, I must cast muck-feal, and lead it from a great Distance, or be repairing my Houses, which [need] perpetual mending, and which I am bound to leave in good condition; I am often forced to lead Lime and Slates from a great Way off, not only for the Laird, but for his Neighbours, at his desire; and when the Kirk or Manse want Preparations, I never want work either, at one or other of these Works all Summer over." Quoted by Hamilton, Ec. Hist. of Scotland, op.cit., p. 52.

3 Hamilton, ibid., p. 52.

shop or trade. Hence it was they who governed the wages and apprenticeship restrictions on those entering any profession. According to Hamilton, "The clash of interests between employer and employed was much in evidence[1] As Adam Smith repeatedly indicates:

> What are the common wages of Labour, depends everywhere upon the contract usually made between those two parties, whose interests by no means the same, the workers desire to get as much, the Masters to give as little as possible.[2]

The conflicts in trades in industry especially between employer and employees occurred throughout the century in both Scotland and England as Smith and every chronicler of the period make clear.[3]

Tailors, weavers, masons, shoemakers and many other trades experienced similar unrest or riots because of working conditions and inability to bargain with employers for higher wages. The famous apprenticeship restrictions attempted to control wages, and working conditions. They were allied to the "Settlement

---

1 Hamilton, Ec. Hist. of Scotland, ibid., p. 346.

2 WN I, p. 74.

3 WN I, p. 74; Plumb, Four Georges, ibid., p. 14; Thompson, op.cit., p. 60. See Johnson, op.cit., Chapter IV "Forced Labourers" and especially p. 75. When wage disputes arose, as they did frequently, the decision was left to the Justice of the Peace of the county or the town who ordered labourers or "journeymen" who resisted the parliamentary edicts "to be bound to go and work with any master who offers to employ him, and give him any sum not exceeding one shilling per day; that no master ... shall give higher wages." Hamilton, Ec. Hist. of Scotland., op.cit., p. 346.

Restriction" which prevented movement into and out of the various trades. Apprentices supplied a large fund of free labour,[1] andenabled masters to keep tight control of the trades labour market and hence of profits and prices.[2] Apprenticeship restrictions were weakening and in new industries especially there were far laxer rules governing legal qualifications for workers, dealers, and employers.[3] But although new industries were less strict in their adherence to age old laws and sprang up often in towns, cities, and villages where the Elizabethan code of laws governing employment had not existed or been enforced; nevertheless the majority of industry was still governed by these archaic statutes. Apprentices for instance, were virtually indentured for seven years.[4] They were maintained by their families who either paid their master for training or apprenticed the child for more than the seven year minimum.[5] And all the apprentices' produce belonged to the master.[6] Smith fully condemned the entire practice as unjust in prohibiting wages to what actually were

---

1 WN I, p. 114.

2 WN I, p. 114, also Johnston, op.cit., p. 75.

3 Hamilton, Ec. Hist. of Scotland, op.cit., p. 345. Ashton, An Economic History, op.cit., pp. 223-4, 229.

4 WN I, p. 114.

5 WN I, p. 114.

6 WN I, p. 114.

skilled labourers. But also it was inefficient because (like slaves) apprentices without payment for their efforts, desired to be idle as much as possible.1

The life of the rural and urban labouring common people in the 18th century was dependent on harvests. The bad harvest of 1739 and the worse one of 1740 caused famine and a sharp rise in prices which formed a recurrent pattern in the 1770s and again in 1782-3 and again the even more drastic famine of 1796. According to J.K. and B. Hammond on each of these occasions the harvests caused a crisis throughout not only the agricultural industries but in trade and factory production as well.2 These were the "recent periods of pure want" which Adam Smith referred to.3

Often in response to these years of drastic poverty there were combinations of workers to raise wages which also resulted in

---

1 WN I, p. 114.

2 Reports of rioting and violence are recorded by many histories of the period. See Hamilton throughout chapter four- of his Ec. Hist. of Scotland, op.cit., pp. 375-95. See Ashton, An Economic History, op.cit., final chapter on Labour, pp. 224-35. See John Lawrence (and Barbara) Hammond, The Skilled Labourer 1760-1832 (London, 1920), pp. 53-55, 194-5, and The Town Labourer 1760-1832 (London, 1936), pp. 95-110, 247-8.

3 As Ashton points out "In the dearths of 1756-7, 1766-7, and 1772-4 ... falling wages, and unemployment [resulted]. It was on the poorest that the burden of a failure of the harvest bore most heavily ... the classes most heavily hit far exceeded in numbers those who escaped with a relatively small curtailment of income." Ashton, An Economic History, ibid., p. 225.

in riots[1] of the labourers. In these times Smith says:

> They are desperate, and act with the folly and extravagance of desperate men, who must either starve, or frighten their masters into an immediate compliance with their demands. The masters upon these occasions are just as clamorous upon the other side, and never cease to call aloud for the assistance of the civil magistrate, and the rigorous execution of those laws which have been enacted with so much severity against the combination of servants, labourers, and journeymen. The workmen, accordingly, very seldom derive any advantage from the violence of those tumultuous combinations, which, partly from the interposition of the civil magistrate, partly from the superior steadiness of the masters, partly from the necessity which the greater part of the workmen are under of submitting for the sake of present subsistence, generally result in nothing, but the punishment of the ringleaders.[2]

Social unrest in Smith's time though mainly associated with periods of bad harvests was also connected with trades,[3] and townsmen and the new shops for these were the foremost groups to take part in the riots. But the agricultural workers who had

---

1 For a discussion of 18th century class conflicts see Edward P. Thompson, Making of the English Working Classes, op.cit., p. 60, "the distinction between the legal code and the unwritten code ... have rarely been so sharply distinguished from each other than in the second half of the 18th century. Riots and capital offences drastically increased after the accession of George III."Thompson give figures for these. They were not only petty theft but destroying looms, tearing down fences of enclosures, etc.

2 WN I, pp. 75-6.

3 Hamilton, Ec. Hist. of Scotland, op.cit., p. 343. Many newer trades where there was heavy demand for capital experienced "a deep division between employer and employed."

a tradition of bare subsistence, appalling wages, and "voluntary service" to laird, church, mill and town, also rioted.1 Indeed all crimes against property greatly increased and the death penalty became common for even petty theft because thieves were rarely caught.2

Yet though sparked by famine, the rioters attacked tolls, factories, equipment and enclosures simultaneously, indicating a broader antagonism.3 In "The Machine Breakers", Hobsbawm shows that much of the breaking of equipment took place in rural areas and that the wreckers received a sizeable majority of public sympathy.4 The action of coal miners in 1740 who set the mines on fire and smashed the pit gear, of textile workers in Nottingham

---

1 See John Lawrence (and Barbara) Hammond, The Village Labourer 1760-1832 (London, 1932), pp. 89-101. See also Ashton, An Economic History, op.cit. reached the Home Office of the pulling down of corn mills ... and the rough handling of dealers. In spite of the drastic penalties the same thing occurred in each of the later dearths of the century; in 1762, 1765-7, 1774, 1789."

2 Plumb, Four Georges, op.cit., pp. 1-25.

3 E.J. Hobshawm, Labouring Men, Essays in the History of Labour (London, 1967), pp.5-22. Hamilton, Ec. Hist. of Scotland, op.cit., p.346. See especially views on class conflicts in agricultural communities against enclosures, pp.81-85. Both Ashton and Plumb provide inaccurate explanations of the Machine breakers according to Hobsbawn, p. 5. They suggest that these acts were "pointless, frenzied, industrial Jacquerie" due to excitement and high spirits rather than resentments. See J.H. Plumb, England in the Eighteenth Century (Harmondsworth, 1950), p.150, and Ashton, The Industrial Revolution, op.cit., p.154.

4 Plumb, ibid., p.13.

who destroyed machinery, and knitting frames, and the destruction of Arkwright's mill at Birkacre in 1779; all demonstrate fear and antagonism to the labour saving devices.[1]

Plumb provides excellent examples of the ways in which such industrial riots reflected a sort of economic-political desperation in the workers as he says:

> No nation rioted more easily or more savagely from 1714 to 1830 angry mobs burning and looting, were as prevalent as disease, and as frequent in the countryside as in the great towns. Time and again the gentry were forced to assemble to put down rioting workmen by force.[2]

Plumb, Hobsbawm, Thompson, the Hammonds and Ashton all provide extensive descriptions of the numbers of rioters, their causes and degree of seriousness throughout the 18th century.[3] Plumb concludes one of his catalogues of these civil disturbances and class conflicts saying:

> Gloucester was so riotous in 1734 that the army was needed to restore order. Suffolk later in the century, suffered a miniature civil war. For a few days in June 1780 London and Southwark were at the mercy of the mob. Mobs and destruction - they were part of life, an expression of those sharp conflicts in society.[4]

---

1 See Hammond, The Skilled Labourer, op.cit., pp. 54-55.

2 Plumb, Four Georges, op.cit., p. 14.

3 Plumb, ibid., p. 15. Hobsbawm, Labouring Men, op.cit., pp. 1-12. Thompson, op.cit., p. 60. Hammonds, The Skilled Labourer, op.cit., pp. 17, 22, 35, 53-5.

4 Plumb, ibid., pp. 14-16.

But Ashton asserts that the rioters themselves did not really comprehend "those sharp conflicts in society."

> They must have realised that their action would result in unemployment, but their immediate concern was to assert their strength and inflict loss on stubborn employers. There seems to have been little or no social theory in the minds of the rioters and very little class-consciousness in the Marxist sense of the term.[1]

It is difficult to know to what extent Ashton is correct in this appraisal of 18th century workers' class-consciousness.[2] To explore Adam Smith's judgement on this we will consider his views on the effects of industry and class upon workers.

V

Much recent critical opinion has been devoted to an analysis of Smith's concept of the alienation of detail factory labourers as an important predecessor to Marx's concept of alienation.[3]

E.G. West in his article "The Political Economy of Alienation, Karl Marx and Adam Smith", provides the first comprehensive

---

1 Ashton, An Economic History, op.cit., p. 228.

2 Hammond, The Town Labourers, op.cit., pp. 95-110 and pp. 247-268. The Hammonds provide a somewhat contradictory view to Ashton. An Economic History, op.cit., pp. 96-8. See also Hammond The Skilled Labourer, op.cit., p. 55. "The extent of public sympathy with the rioters is illustrated by the tone of the petition sent up to Parliment." It speaks of "the immense profits and advantages of the Patentees and Proprietors."House of Commons Journal, April 27, 1780.

3 E.G. West "The Political Economy of Alienation: Karl Marx and Adam Smith", Oxford Economic Papers Volume 21, No. 1 (1969),

analysis of "alienation" in Smith's thought.[1] West compares three aspects of alienation described by Marx with the various comments by Smith concerning the effect on the individual of commercial industrial society. It is a valuable article and I will separate my discussion into the three aspects of alienation which West uses, namely: powerlessness, isolation and self-estrangement.

West concludes that Smith could not have thought labourers were alienated in terms of feeling powerlessness or isolation

---

pp. 1-23. Hereafter cited as "Alienation". Fritz Papeneim in his The Alienation of Modern Man (New York, 1959) says that: "Marx's concept of alienation is an outgrowth of Smith's description of commercial society." Nathan Rosenberg says Smith's works 'constitute a major source of inspiration for the socilist critique of capitalist institutions as Marx himself acknowledged'. 'Adam Smith on the division of labour: two views or one?' Economica, 30, (1963), pp. 23-32. Jacob Viner, "Guide" introduction to John Rae's The Life of Adam Smith (New York, 1965) says the "Scottish Historical School were writers on alienation in the general Marxian sense." Duncan Forbes insists "it appears to have been Adam Smith who first broached the potentially explosive topic of the [Marxian alienation] effects of the division of labour". Douglas Young and others, Edinburgh in the Age of Reason (Edinburgh, 1967), p. 47. George Elder Davie described Smith as "lucidly pointing forwards to the industrial society with its problems of "alienation and atomization." Edinburgh in the Age of Reason, ibid., p. 24. See also William F. Campbell, "Adam Smith's Theory of Justice, Prudence and Benevolence", American Economic Review 57 (1967), pp. 571-96, esp. p. 577. And see Meek, "Scottish Contribution", op.cit., pp. 84-103.

1 This article of West's developed from conclusions reached in his earlier article, "Adam Smith's Two Views on the Division of Labour", op.cit., pp. 23-32. Nathan Rosenberg then took up this discussion in his article "Adam Smith and the Division of Labour: Two Views or One", op.cit., pp. 127-139. Rosenberg provides a much deeper analysis of division of labour in Smith than West's two articles but he does not dwell on Smith's idea of alienation.

because West defines these terms in a limited and modern fashion. Furthermore, West only acknowledges Smith's beliefs that factory workers are alienated or self-estranged with the proviso that this conclusion is at variance with Smith's more general opinion that extensive division of labour cannot but improve men technically, socialy, and morally. I intend to show that Smith believed workers to be alienated in these ways, I hope to show the interrelated effects of commerce upon individuals. By keeping Smith's integrated system of moral philosophy in mind and the historic conditions of labourers in the various industries he describes I hope to provide a deeper analysis of Smith's views on "alienation" and the general effects of commerce and industry upon individuals than has been shown by existing analyses.

West has chosen Smith's views of the effects of commerce from theoretical statements about how the market ought to operate, not those passages where Smith is actually describing the commercial industrial market society he lived in. West quotes Smith's theoretical view of commerce as this "happiest and most comfortable", "cheerful and hearty state to all the different orders of society".1 But this theoretical appraisal must be contrasted with Smith's actual description of existing commercial

---

1 West, "Alienation", pp. 7-10.

"conditions so justly lamented".[1] Where except in theoretical terms are workers at work ever described by Smith as happy, cheerful, and hearty? "Misery", "and want" are occasionally used by Smith to describe the feelings of the poor in times of bad harvests but "happy, cheerful" Smith reserves only for their periods of amusement when they are not working.

Though I do not assert that Smith believed the worker suffered abject poverty, wage slavery and starvation it is important to see the clear broad picture of workers' conditions, Smith described at his time and not simply the theoretical happy, cheerful and hearty state they could be enjoying in theoretical perfect market conditions of the ideal progressive state.

Smith's comment about workers' attitudes and sentiments indeed suggest powerlessness. For example:

> The poor labourer who has the soil and the seasons to struggle with, and, who while he affords the materials for supplying the luxury of all the other members of the commonwealth, and bears, as it were, upon his shoulders the whole fabric of human society, seems himself to be pressed down below ground by the weight and to be buried out of sight in the lowest foundations of the building.[2]

---

1 See esp. WN p. 519, "Commerce, which ought naturally to be, among nations, as among individuals, a bond of union and friendship, has become the most fertile source of discord and animosity."

2 Draft of the Wealth of Nations, p. 328. And see Lectures, p. 163 and WN I, pp. 2, 54-5.

Smith describes such a worker as "the lowest and most despised member of civilised society,"[1] which contradicts West's assertion that "there is no complaint in Smith that such subordination is undignified."

West therefore appears to have inadequate justification for his statement that "If one can speak of any subordination in Smith's economic system it is not to any one social group but to the consumer." Smith distinctly describes these existing conditions as "exhibiting so much oppressive inequality."[2] And Smith draws a diagram of subordination,

> The opulent merchant, who spends a great part of his time in luxury and entertainments, enjoys a much greater portion of the profits of his traffic, than all the clerks and accountants who do the business. These last, again, enjoying a great deal of leisure, and suffering scarce any other hardship besides the confinement of attendance, enjoy a much greater share of the product than three times an equal number of artisans, who under their direction, labour much more severely and assiduously.[3]

As described earlier "the poor workman" is even more subordinate than these lowly artisans. Smith's entire diagram is well summed up by him with the statement that "those who labour most get least."[4]

---

1 Draft, p., 328, and WN II, p. 308, "contemptible".

2 Draft, p. 328. And for explicit descriptions of oppression in WN see WN I, p. 278, II, p. 483.

3 Draft, pp. 327-8, and WN I, p. 2.

4 Draft, p. 327.

As indicated earlier Smith was fully aware that workers' conditions throughout the century were fluctuating with harvests, wars and bank crises, and as he demonstrated, even where the wage stayed the same for half a century the price of provisions sometimes doubled in a month owing to floods or droughts. Therefore Smith did not assume that in this relatively progressive state of England and Scotland in the 18th century workers necessarily were happy, comfortable, cheerful and hearty. Nor did he fail to recognise the prevalence of exploitation.

> In a civilised society the poor provide both for themselves and for the enormous luxury of their superiors. The rent, which goes to support the vanity of the slothful landlord, is all earned by the industry of the peasant. The monied man indulges himself in every sort of ignoble and sordid sensuality, at the expense of the merchant and tradesman, to whom he lends out his stock at interest. All the indolent and frivolous retainers upon a court, are, in the same manner, fed, clothed and lodged by the labour of those who pay the taxes which support them.[1]

And on the following page Smith again returns to this theme of exploitation when he says:

> But with regard to the produce of the labour of a great society there is never any such thing as a fair and equal division. In a society of a hundred thousand families, there will be perhaps one hundred who don't labour at all, and who yet, either by violence or by the orderly opposition of the law, employ a greater part of the labour of the society than any other ten thousand in it. The division of what remains too after this enormous defalcation, is by no means made in pro-

---

1 Draft, p. 326.

> portion to the labour of each individual. On the contrary those who labour most get least.[1]

Though Smith did not in his Wealth of Nations take these views as far as he did his Draft of the book, there are unmistakably similar viewpoints expressed by him when he says "For every rich man there must be at least five hundred poor" and when he describes the "mean rapacity and monopolising spirit of merchants and manufacturers",[2] landlords who "love to reap where they never sowed", and the merchants "who conspire against the public at every opportunity." Merchants, manufacturers, landlords and dealers "have generally an interest to deceive and even to oppress the public, and who accordingly have, upon many occasions, both deceived and oppressed it."[3] It is abundantly clear that Smith's numerous suggestions of the exploitation of workers did not lead him to the Marxian conclusions that private property, or the distinction of ranks among classes, or even the functions of the different classes should be abolished. Yet his advocacy of economic, social and political reforms stemmed from his criticisms, and his candid observations of the social relations of his time.

Smith did not go into detail on particluar acts of exploitation by particular merchants or factory owners, nor statistics of

---

1 Draft, p. 327.

2 WN I, p.519.

3 WN I, p. 278.

amounts of labour which had been exploited in any one industry or one year. To some extent Smith was simply expressing the conventional wisdom of his group of Scottish authors who each make virtually identical comments. For example Hume said "Where riches are in few hands, those must enjoy all the power and will readily conspire to lay the whole burthen on the poor,"1

Such statements by Hume and Smith do not deny that workers were better off than savages or even kings of savages, but they do serve to put into perspective the relative exploitation, subordination and poverty which workers experienced or felt in existing commercial society.

West does not present the "abundant evidence" that "Smith believed labour commanded capital no less than vice versa". While this is true in the abstract, Smith's famous description was that:

> It is not, however, difficult to foresee which of the two parties must, upon all ordinary occasions, have the advantage in the dispute, and force the other into a compliance with their terms. The masters ...2

Smith goes on as we have described into the advantages and disadvantages respectively of managers and workers which lead capital to command labour. He concludes "In the long-run the workman may be as necessary to his master as his master is to him, but the

---

1 David Hume, Political Discourses in Essays, op.cit. (originally published in second part of Essays, 1752), p.18.

2 WN I, p. 74.

necessity is not so immediate."1 That is "... the necessity which the greater part of the workmen are under of submitting for the sake of present subsistence..."2

VI

Because of "Smith's general emphasis upon the private property in labour-skill,"3 West does not believe Smith could have considered labourers to be "powerless". West does not mention that according to Smith although workers theoretically possessed "the most sacred property" in their labour skill they were repeatedly referred to by Smith as actually "the propertyless". It was their actual condition which rendered them powerless in terms of contract disputes, famines or natural disasters or government legislation, or control of their working conditions.

In factual descriptions4 of workers Smith described them as "without property", "the propertyless", or having "none at all".5 Clearly the distinction between those who had "some" property and those who had "none at all", did not refer to those

---

1 WN I, p. 75.

2 WN I, p. 76.

3 West, "Alienation", p. 9.

4 As opposed to such abstract descriptions of "The property which every man has in his own labour as it is the original foundation of all other property, so it is the most sacred and inviolable."

5 WN II, p. 236.

who have no labour, or could not labour. This was simply the difference between the rich and the poor.1

Smith at various points describes workers being obliged to accept various conditions of employment, and the difficulties of workers refusing or disputing these conditions. While the worker is not necessarily powerless he is usually circumscribed by obligations, conditions, restrictions and legal and extra-legal forms of coercion which make him always subordinate, often exploited, and in the majority of cases, effectively powerless according to Smith in contracts, wages, hours, forms of payment and in any disputes.

Of independent workmen, Smith says

> Such cases, however, are not very frequent, and in every part of Europe, twenty workmen serve under a master for one that is independent; and the wages of labour are everywhere understood to be, what they usually are, when the labourer is one person, and the owner of the stock which employs him another.2

In wages contracts the masters "force the [workers] into a compliance with their terms."3

The worker is usually powerless in the decision as to what kind and what amount of work he will do for his wage; the number

---

1 Smith's confusion on whether he believed labour to be property will be dealt with at the end of this chapter.

2 <u>WN</u> I, p. 74.

3 <u>WN</u> I, p. 74.

of pieces in piece work and the speed or length of time of his work in hourly labour.

The worker is powerless to decide the form of payment he will be given in credit or truck, cash, or vouchers from private stores.

Labourers usually were powerless in other disputes with their employers. "The workmen, accordingly, very seldom derive any advantage from the violence of those tumultuous combinations ... nothing, but the punishment or ruin of the ringleaders."1

Each of these aspects of workers' usual powerlessness which Smith describes is fully documented in the conditions of employment described by the economic histories of Smith's times,2 and the declarations of the pinmakers3 at the end of the 18th century.

West asserts that "There is no evidence to show that Smith believed that the "detail workers" of capitalism felt isolated."

> The propensity to barter and exchange leading as it did to the division of labour under one roof worked towards, not against, the direction of social intercourse. Such communion provided men with the "impartial spectators" which they needed as a 'mirror' of their actions. The whole process was thus a coherent, positive, and

---

1 WN I, p. 76.

2 Hamilton, Ec. Hist. of Scotland, op.cit., p. 52 and see Thomas Johnston, op.cit., Chapter on "Forced Labourers", pp. 72-84.

3 Pinmakers document in Tracts Relating to Trade, op.cit., Manuscript 13, p. 816.

> constructive social process which led not into but out of a condition of isolation.[1]

West in his effort to compartmentalise the various aspects of alienation, into "powerlessness", "isolation" and "self-estrangement" has lost sight of their interconnection in what has been shown earlier to be a total system of Smith's moral theory. This system of moral sentiments dictated that men gained their social values from society and if they became self-estranged, (as West is willing to concede) then according to Smith's interconnected moral system, they become automatically isolated from others. For example, West claims that "the whole process [of detail factory labour] was thus a coherent, positive, and constructive social process", whereas Smith says that detail factory labour "renders him [a man] not only incapable of relishing or bearing a part in any rational conversation, but of conceiving any generous, noble or tender sentiments, and consequently of forming any just judgement concerning many even of the ordinary duties of private life." As labour became more subdivided into the most confined "few simple operations, frequently but one or two", Smith nowhere argues as West does[2] that "such communion provided men with the impartial spectators which they needed as a mirror of their

---

1 West, "Alienation", p. 10.

2 And West is joined in this misunderstanding by Milton M. Meyers, "Division of Labour as a Principle of Social Cohesion", Canadian Journal of Economics and Political Science XXXIII No. 3, Aug., 1967, p. 432.

actions." On the contrary such activities completely destroyed their ability to sympathise or hearken to their internal impartial spectator. Men became isolated by the very fact of their self-estrangement. For in Smith's theory, one is only social to the extent that one is capable of sympathy. Destroy his faculties for sympathy and the detail worker is by Smith's own definition, isolated. Smith directly agreed with Ferguson and Millar in this argument.1

VII

Smith viewed the effect of commercial life on the labouring individuals from several different vantage points.2 The most damaging effects of commerce were expressed in what West calls Smith's "alienation passage".3 It is significant in putting this passage in perspective that Smith introduces it by the assumption that the effects he describes could cause "the almost entire corruption and degeneracy of the great body of the people."4 Despite its length, this passage is so important that I fell it must be quoted in full.

---

1 Ferguson, History, p. 118; Millar, p. 380-382.

2 From the standpoint of production, distribution, history and conjecture. Although Ricardo argued that Smith had neglected distribution analysis there are many historical and moral comments upon class distribution of income in WN.

3 WN II, pp. 302-3.

4 WN II, pp. 302.

> In the progress of the division of labour, the employment of the far greater part of those who live by labour, that is, of the great body of the people, comes to be confined to a few very simple operations; frequently to one or two. But the understandings of the greater part of men are necessarily formed by their ordinary employments. The man whose whole life is spent in performing a few simple operations, of which the effects too are, perhaps, always the same, or very nearly the same, has no occasion to exert his understanding, or to exercise his invention in finding out expedients for removing difficulties which never occur. He naturally loses, therefore, the habit of such exertion, and generally becomes as stupid and ignorant as it is possible for a human creature to become. The torpor of his mind renders him, not only incapable of relishing or bearing a part in any rational conversation, but of conceiving any generous, noble, or tender sentiment, and consequently of forming any just judgment concerning many even of the ordinary duties of private life. Of the great and extensive interests of his country he is altogether incapable of judging; and unless very particular pains have been taken to render him otherwise, he is equally incapable of defending his country in war. The uniformity of his stationary life naturally corrupts the courage of his mind, and makes him regard with abhorrence the irregular, uncertain, and adventurous life of a soldier. It corrupts even the activity of his body, and renders him incapable of exerting his strength with vigour and perseverance, in any other employment than that to which he has been bred. His dexterity at his own particular trade seems, in this manner, to be acquired at the expense of his intellectual, social, and martial virtues. But in every improved and civilised society this is the state into which the labouring poor, that is the great body of the people, must necessarily fall, unless government takes some pains to prevent it.[1]

1 WN II, pp. 302-3.

Later Smith says in all earlier societies, "Invention is kept alive, and the mind is not suffered to fall into that drowsy stupidity, which, in a civilised society, seems to benumb the understanding of almost all the inferior ranks of people."1

Smith returns to this theme when he says of "common people":

> They have little time to spare for education. Their parents can scarce afford to maintain them even in infancy. As soon as they are able to work, they must apply to some trade by which they can earn their subsistence. That trade too is generally so simple and uniform as to give little exercise to the understanding; while, at the same time, their labour is both so constant and so severe, that it leaves them little leisure and less inclination to apply to, or even to think of anything else.2

What did Smith think of the condition of the great body of the common people he had so woefully described: namely of their,

> gross ignorance and stupidity which, in a civilised society, seem so frequently to benumb the understandings of all the inferior ranks of people. A man without the proper use of the intellectual faculties of a man, is, if possible, more contemptible than even a coward, and seems to be mutilated and deformed in a still more essential part of the character of human nature.3

I have included a sample of other passages from Smith to indicate that his "alienation passage" is by no means unique or unconnected with the rest of his thought concerning the effect of commercial/industrial society on most men. Smith refers to these

---

1 WN II, p. 303.

2 WN II, p. 305.

3 Lectures, pp. 255-258.

alienating effects of detail division of labour in his Glasgow Lectures[1] as early as 1763. There was no single "alienation passage" but many descriptions of different aspects of workers' alienation.

In his article West concedes that this self-estrangement of the detail factory labourer is the one form of "alienation" Smith may have intended. And West is willing to admit that this form of alienation Smith believed resulted from overly extensive division of labour in factory production. But he then details contradictory evidence from the Wealth of Nations to the effect that the division of labour is necessary to socialise men.

> Thus in Book I he argues that workers become "slothful" and "lazy" without the division of labour; compare this with his claim in the alienation passage that they become "stupid and ignorant" with it.[2]

Although West notes these direct contradictions, he does not explain them. The explanation would appear to be that Smith's statements about the socialising effects of the division of labour are based on his abstract conjectural model of society built up from individual propensities originating in man's innate tendency to truck, barter and exchange. Whereas his critique of the division of labour's effect on detail factory workers sems based more upon the real social effect of institutions upon individuals.

---

1 West, "Alienation", p. 11.

2 Ibid., p. 11.

Furthermore, the explanation of Smith's divergent conclusions about the division of labour seems based on the difference between the positive effects of the general and primitive division of labour in the petty mode of production and the detrimental effects of extreme division of labour in the factory situation[1] E.G. West denies this,[2] but it directly corresponds to Ferguson's and Millar's explanation of the contrary effects of the division of labour. On this explanation Smith and others of the Scottish School would probably have been in agreement since their descriptions of the harmful effects of detailed division of labour, and positive effects of broad general divisions of labour are so similar to one another.[3] Ferguson frequently contrasts these two effects which Smith only contrasted by implication.

> The separation of professions, while it seems to promise improvement of skill, and is actually the cause why the productions of every art become more perfect as commercial society advances; yet in its termination, and ultimate effects, serves, in some measure, to break the bands of society, to substitute more forms and rules of art in place of ingenuity, and the withdraw individuals from the common sense of occupation, on which the sentiments of the heart, and the mind, are most happily employed.[4]

---

1 Nathan Rosenberg, op.cit., p. 128 contends there is no contradiction; but on p. 139 admits there is some.

2 West, "Alienation", pp. 11-15.

3 Compare Smith, WN II, pp. 302-3 to Ferguson, History, p. 218 and Millar, p. 381 and p. 382.

4 Ferguson, History, p. 181 and see generally pt.iv, sect. 1 and part v, sect. 3, 4.

Also in a similar fashion to Smith, Ferguson warns that extreme division of labour destroys or dismembers the human character,[1] while directly contrasting this with the great productivity which such division makes possible:

> By having separated the arts of the clothier and the tanner, we are then better supplied with shoes and with cloth. But to separate the arts which form the citizen and the stateman, the arts of policy and war, is an attempt to dismember the human character, and to destroy these very arts we mean to improve. By this separation, we in effect deprive a free people of what is necessary to their safety:...[2]

As Duncan Forbes says,[3] this alienation or self-estrangement theme is found earlier than Ferguson's Essay or Smith's Lectures in Jean Jacques Rousseau's Discourse on the Origin of Inequality.[4] Several authors have all in passing mentioned the similarity between Rousseau and Smith in recognising this

---

1 History, p.250. "If that respite from public dangers and troubles which gives a leisure for the practice of commercial arts, be continued, or increased, into a disuse of national efforts; if the individual, not called to unite with his country, be left to pursue his private advantage; we may find him become effeminate, mercenary, and sensual; not because pleasures and profits are become more alluring, but because he has fewer calls to attend to other objects; and because he has more encouragement to study his personal advantages, and pursue his separate interests."

2 History, p. 353.

3 Duncan Forbes Introduction to Ferguson's History, p. xxxi. See Forbe's detailed examination xxxi-xxxiii of alienation.

4 See Smith's comments on Rousseau's Origin of Inequality in his letter to the Edinburgh Review, 1755-6.

corruption of the individual by commercial society. However, the key difference between Rousseau and the Scottish School was that Smith, Ferguson, and Millar directly attributed this alienation or self-estrangement to the process of the division of labour which Rousseau's Discourses did not mention. Ferguson expanded on Smith's view of the kind of psychological self-estrangement modern commercial/industrial society caused, by showing that

> The lower orders are not only ignorant, but meanminded, envious and servile.[1]

John Millar repeats Ferguson's view that competition lessens the bonds of society; and dwelt at greater length than Smith on these psychological effects of the division of labour. Millar concluded, "There are limits beyond which it is impossible to push the real improvements arising from wealth and opulence."[2] In Millar's lectures according to John Craig's Life, he examined "at some length the question of whether the progress of civilisation can be continued without end or whether it is subjected to certain limitations, from the nature of Human affairs."[3] Millar says for example:

> But in a country where nobody is idle, and

---

1 Cited by Duncan Forbes Introduction to History, op.cit., p.xxxiii. Ferguson contrasts this with "The savage who knows no superior and cannot be servile, also knows no distinction of wealth and cannot be envious."

2 Duncan Forbes, "Scientific Whiggism. Adam Smith and John Millar", op.cit., p. 650.

3 John Craig, Life of John Millar appended to Origin of the Distinction of Ranks (Glasgow, 1806), 3rd ed. p.xivii-ix.

> where every person is eager to augment his fortune, or to improve his circumstances, there occur innumerable competitions and rivalships which contract the heart, and set mankind at variance. In proportion as every man is attentive to his own advancement, he is vexed and tormented by every obstacle to his prosperity, and prompted to regard his competitors with envy, resentment, and other malignant passions.[1]

Also, Millar insists that the minds and bodies of the labourers suffer from the division of labour, and in a direct echo of Smith's famous alienation passage, Millar states that this suffering appears preventable only through the exertions of education.[2] Thus we find that the Scottish School shared Smith's concern in asserting that the effects of the division of labour and commercial society were beneficial when these increase social intercourse and the development of men's sentiments, and are harmful[3] when they become so advanced, detailed or narrowing that the individual becomes incapable of sympathies.

Smith therefore from the foregoing analysis would appear to have shown that labourers have experienced powerlessness in contracts and disputes, and isolation by their loss of the social faculty of sympathy to enter into or comprehend the situation of

---

1 Millar, p. 387.

2 Millar pt. IV sect. 6 and especially p.381.

3 James McCulloch in his edition of the Wealth of Nations (London, 1843) sharply criticised Smith for coming to these "untrue conclusions that the division of labour could harm" or make morons. McCulloch argued the division of labour always improved men.

others or the larger issues of their country. They are corrupted in their bodily, mental and moral capabilities by reason of their narrow tasks and can be justly termed estranged from their ordinary human being. Therefore, it seems reasonable to conclude that Smith anticipates all three types of alienation identified by Marx. Namely, Smith suggests various ways in which labourers are powerless, isolated, and self-estranged by the working and class conditions of advanced commercial/industrial society.

## VIII

Smith did not realise that the basis of men's alienation, as he describes it, had been inchoate in the very assumptions he had first made about human effort and judgment. The fundamental basis of alienation sprang from his conception of labour and sentiment. I will attempt to show how and why this was so, first in his concept of labour, then in his concept of sentiment.

The most revealing dichotomy of Smith's thought is his belief on the one hand that the origin of property is labour and hence every man has his first and fundamental property in himself and his own labour; and on the other that the labourers in commercial society are the "propertyless". Smith never really resolved this issue. Thus at the foundation of Smith's property theory was always this contradiction. The basic issue was whether labour was property or not. The deeper seated explanation goes beyond Smith's indecision as to whether property was an normative right or a positive fact, but that is the area in which a solution to this dichotomy will be found.

Labour was a "fundamental property", a birthright but labour was also "a commodity" bought and sold in the market. Labour was, however, distinct from other commodities in that according to Smith it did not rise and fall in its real intrinsic value.[1] Labour's value and price were somehow not the same as with other commodities. Though labour's price or wage might rise or fall Smith concluded that it was not the intrinsic value of labour which had changed but the price of the goods that labour created or purchased, which had altered in value. Therefore although labour was in some ways equivalent to other property commodities, in other ways it was not equivalent at all. Smith showed by this self contradiction that one cannot base a theory of value as a measure on something which cannot itself be measured. Although the labour theory as a statement of the importance of labour in all property values is not self contradictory; the labour theory of value as a measure of values is self contradictory. Depending on which argument he was using, the question "how then did Smith describe labour?" can be answered in several ways.

But Smith viewed the labour of workers he saw about him in one way only. Ordinary labour was always conceived by Smith as a

---

1 WN I, p. 37.

sacrifice, a giving up of a man's ease, effort, pleasure and time; it was always "a toil and trouble"[1] and an expense, a giving up of his real desired interests. "He must always lay down the same portion of his ease, his liberty and his happiness."[2] In short, each hour of ordinary labour was a sacrifice of the labourer's "ease, his liberty and his happiness". Here was the root of alienation, in labour itself. The basis of property alienation in exchange of labour, was also the basis of human alienation in Smith's conception of labour as a sacrifice. Labour although it was man's fundamental property or possession only had a value for men when it was being "alienated" (sold), sacrificed for cash or actual property goods.

The second fundamental source of alienation is found in Smith's description of men's moral relations with others. One principle of Smith's Theory of Moral Sentiments is that individuals all confront each other as spectators. Although individuals have the ability to sympathise or imagine the feelings of one another they only feel with or sympathise with others on the basis of viewing external behaviour of others. There is no direct relation between men's internal selves.

Smith believed that men adopt the role of "impartial spectator" to judge the conduct of other men. Eventually, they form just judgements of themselves and their own behaviour through gradually applying this same impartial spectator's judgments they

---

1 WN I, p. 34.

2 WN I, p. 37.

have used on others, finally on themselves. Only from this alien's position do we come to know and feel with others, or to judge or feel happy with ourselves.

Certain aspects of this conception of Smith's relate to Locke's description of psychology and learning processes, in his An Essay Concerning Human Understanding.1 Sheldon Wolin demonstrates in his Politics and Vision2 that Locke made conscience "an internalised expression of external rules rather than the externalised expression of internal convictions." In so doing he put forth a psychology which (though based on reason rather than sentiment) bore a certain simiarity to Smith's later view. Locke in Wolin's words,

> ushered in a new social world where men, no longer able to communicate on the basis of a common interior life, were reduced to knowing each other solely from the outside, ... man had become estranged from man, which corresponds exactly to Locke's terse description of the human condition where individual consciences are strangers to each other: "no particular man can know the existence of any other being, but only when, by actually operating upon him, it makes itself perceived by him." Man becomes conscious of his fellows only when he and they collide; conflict and friction are thus the sources of man's awareness of man.3

Although Smith believed men can "imagine" each other's "interior

---

1 John Locke, An Essay Concerning Human Understanding 2 Vols. ed. A.C. Fraser (New York, 1959) (First ed. 1690).

2 Sheldon Wolin, Politics and Vision (Boston, 1960), pp. 138-40.

3 Ibid., pp. 138-40.

life", his descriptions of individuals developing moral judgements by random observations of external behaviour and his description of individuals randomly competing in the market extended this Lockean sketch of human psychology. Instead of using this conception of external observation only as a description of the way men learn knowledge or facts and perform rational activity, Smith broadened this conception and used it to investigate our moral, sentimental, passionate, and irrational drives in a universal social market. But what is significant in Smith is that though all men possessed the capability of sympathy nevertheless men were reduced to knowing each other primarily from the outside, and in modern commercial society "man had become estranged from man."[1]

On the very first page of the Theory of Moral Sentiments Smith lays down the primary assumption that, "we have no immediate experience of what other men feel."

> Though our brother is upon the rack, as long as we ourselves are at our ease, our senses will never inform us of what he suffers. They never did, and never can, carry us beyond our own person, and it is by the imagination only that we can form any conception of what are his sensations. Neither can that faculty help us to know this any other way, than by representing to us what would be our own, if we were in his case.

---

1 Wolin, ibid., pp. 139-40.

> It is the impressions of our own senses only, not those of his, which our imaginations copy.[1]

Although Smith's belief in men's capacity to imagine or to enter into the feelings of other men was a most profound advance upon Locke's rational theory, Smith had shown numerous ways in which men's sympathies were often directed to wealth and greatness and how men were far less inclined to enter into the feelings of the poor, the sick or the ordinary man. Moreover, Smith stated that the vast majority of the public were, because of the detrimental effects of advanced division of labour, steadily losing their capacity to enter into even the ordinary sentiments of their fellows.[2] If men's ability to sympathise with others was impaired they would be reduced to only their sensual experience which Smith stated in the passage above, to be incapable of giving us the feelings of other men. Thus, it was because men's ability to sympathise was often misdirected and, for many, was becoming steadily impaired, that Smith like Locke implied that men were becoming estranged from one another.

This chapter has attempted to show that Smith never reconciled his explanations of the two diametrically opposed effects of commerce. He showed that commerce established useful routines for working behaviour, institutions and for market standards of exchange. But also he showed that commercial society

---

1 TMS, pp. 3-4.

2 WN II, pp. 302-3.

intensified the harmful effects of class conflict, and of the division of labour. Smith's two views of the effects of commerce (actual effects versus theoretical effects) led him to the awkward position of theorising a harmony of interests between those groups engaged in production, and yet at other times led him to describe class exploitation and conflicts of interest. Commerce and the division of labour greatly increased efficiency of production and brought cheapness and plenty for the entire society. But another result of commerce and of extreme division of labour was that workers experienced alienation in terms of isolation, powerlessness and self-estrangement. Two fundamental bases of alienation I suggested might be found in the prevailing task divisions of factory labour and the consequent erosion of moral sentiments as described by Smith. Smith believed that men's ability to sympathise was often misdirected, and was becoming increasingly impaired by tasks with advanced division of labour. Smith implies that this was causing labourers to become estranged from one another so that they were no longer capable of ordinary sentiments or conversations.

# CHAPTER VIII

## EXISTING GOVERNMENT: THEORY AND PRACTICE

This chapter will deal with Smith's actual political times and activities and attempt to relate his political theory to his experience. It will be argued that Smith's political experience was of an extremely corrupt landed aristocracy and monopolising merchant class who controlled both Parliament and subsidiary political bodies. Smith's political theory was founded upon a description and criticisms of just such a government. His class argument was connected with his policies concerning internal and external monopoly trade; and connected also with his implicit social contract theory. This implicit social contract theory in his attitude to sovereignty and universal political rights is found in his discussions of: the rights to revolution; rights of colonists; rights (often denied to the vast majority of the population) to vote, or be representatives, sit on juries, or sometimes to receive due process of law. Class control of government denied individual's rights, especially property rights, and this was the essence of Smith's political critique.

### I

In essence the background to the political history of Smith's times (1723-1790) was as follows.[1] The Protestant House of

---

1 The political structure and political history of Smith's early life are best conveyed by J.H. Plumb in his books: The

Hanover from Germany in 1715 replaced the Catholic House of Stewart from Scotland. As a result the period from 1715-1745 was characterised by pressure from Scottish political groups and "Jacobites" to return the Stewarts to the throne.[1] Smith reflects upon this sentiment when he says:

> During the reign of the late king, and that of his royal father, we used to complain, that our connection with Hanover deprived us of the advantages of our insular situation, and involved us in the quarrels of other nations, with which we should, otherwise, have had nothing to do ...in those days it was the general wish of the people that Hanover might some time or other be separated from the Crown of Great Britain...[2]

---

Growth of Political Stability in England 1675-1725 (London, 1967); The First Four Georges, op.cit.; and Sir Robert Walpole, 2 vols. (London, 1956, 60). See also Keith Grahame Feiling, The Second Tory Party 1714-1832 (London, 1938) for a contrasting (but sometimes less reliable) account of the politics in Smith's early life until he left Glasgow in 1763. The political structure of Britain in the later period of Smith's life is best conveyed by Lewis Namier's two major works: The Structure of Politics at the Accession of George III, 2 vols. (London, 1929). (I have used the London, 1963 ed. hereafter cited as Structure); Lewis Namier, England in the Age of the American Revolution, op.cit. The political history of this later period is the subject of numerous books on William Pitt, and George III. The works I have found most useful are A.F. Basil Williams, The Life of William Pitt, Earl of Chatham, 2 vols. (London, 1966); Brian Tunstall, William Pitt, Earl of Chatham (London, 1938); and J.H. Plumb, Chatham (London, 1953).

1 Plumb, Four Georges, op.cit., p. 26. And see also Plumb, Chatham, ibid., p. 65. Pitt attempted by creating the highland regiments "to lessen the danger of Scottish dissent and Jacobite Rebellion." See also Trevelyan, History of England, op.cit., pp. 529-31.

2 Adam Smith, "Smith's Thoughts on the State of the Contest with America February 1778" in G. H. Guttridge, "Adam Smith on the

Scottish political groups were the most active of those who attempted to separate the Hanoverian Kings from the Crown. They spawned frequent intrigues and in 1715 and 1745 caused the famous "rebellions" which failed to overthrow the throne primarily because they lacked English support.1 Smith in the above passage written in 1775 appears to acknowledge his sympathy with "the general wish of the people [of Scotland in 1745] that Hanover might some tme or other be separated from the Crown of Great Britain." However, in his earlier Lectures in 1763 Smith had appeared somewhat scornful of the various participants in the so-called "rebellion".

> In the year 1745 four or five thousand naked unarmed Highlanders took possession of the improved parts of this country [Scotland] without any opposition from the unwarlike inhabitants. They penetrated into England, and alarmed the whole nation, and had they not been opposed by a standing army, they would have seized the throne with little difficulty. Two hundred years ago such an attempt would have roused the spirit of the nation.2

---

American Revolution. An Unpublished Memorial." American Historical Review, xxxviii (1932-3), pp. 714-20. The passage cited above is taken from a comparison of the separation of Great Britain from the House of Hanover, to the separation of Great Britain from her American colonies, p. 717-718. (Smith's writing in this will be cited hereafter as AR. The introduction by Guttridge is cited separately).

1 Plumb, Political Stability, op.cit., p. xviii. Trevelyan, op.cit., pp. 529-31. Plumb, Chatham, op.cit., p. 65.

2 Lectures, p. 258.

From such observations and other information about Smith's political views, clubs, and activities, it appears clear that Smith was not a Jacobite, nor was he overly exercised over the Hanoverian succession.

In practical terms of British politics the threat of Stewart Jacobinism and revolution kept the Whigs united in Parliament and the other opposition groups in disarray. With the Whigs firmly in power there occurred the period of relative Parliamentary calm and stability under Robert Walpole from 1721 to 1742 that brought respite from the torments of the previous century.

Walpole's years of relative calm were, however, bought by means of his accommodation with the corrupt forces controlling Parliament and the squirearchy, and it was this wholesale corruption throughout government which formed a second continuing characteristic of politics in Smith's formative years. In the tense and unsettled fifteen years after Walpole and before the improvements of William Pitt (the Elder), corruption reached its peak with blatant buying and selling of "rotten" and "pocket" parliamentary seats, government contracts, and the "Secret Service" accounts of the Duke of Newcastle. When Pitt (later Lord Chatham) attempted to remove some of this corruption, he was ultimately forced to make a deal with Newcastle in order to obtain funds to continue the Seven Years War. Corruption was, therefore, thoughout Smith's life a key feature of British politics.

Lewis Namier in his The Structure of Politics at the Accession of George III has three relevant chapters on this extraordinarily widespread corruption.[1] The numerous forms which it took were constantly interrelated. These forms of corruption included most notably the selling of government contracts, positions and Parlimentary seats, Namier deals with all the variety of deals and political relations and shows how they were founded upon the basic limitation of the franchise.

> The obsolete distribution of seats naturally produced electoral absurdities and corruption.[2]

Not only did London have but 10 of the 558 seats, but all of the major cities were similarly under-represented. The Parliamentary seats from the over-represented southern countries with their rotten boroughs, were used "for professional politicians, civil servants and big merchants."[3]

---

1 Namier's first chapter entitled "Why Men Went Into Parliament" contains not only a general account of each group of members, such as Lord's sons, country gentlemen, merchants and military gentlemen, but a section on "Private and Pecuniary: The Placemen and the purveyors of favours" and another on "Contracts, Remittances, and Loans: The Merchants and Bankers". Namier's second chapter contains the most exhaustive description of "the distribution of seats" and "Patronage". He concludes that seventy-three percent of the House was from below Bristol and the Thames.

2 Structure, p. 63.

3 Structure, p. 63.

Yet perhaps the most interesting section of Namier's analysis is Chapter IV "Secret Service Money Under the Duke of Newcastle"[1] and his appendix[2] which lists Newcastle's actual accounts from 1754-60. However, it is important to emphasise that though the Secret Service Money was the most notorious form of political corruption, the number of injustices and arrangements and payments for service were actually far more widespread and universally felt than the famous Secret Service Lists might suggest. The reason for this was partly that:

> There were no party funds from which to cover election expenses, and secret service money did not go far in this matter. Offices and sinecures (or contracts in the case of merchants) were therefore used to compensate faithful adherents of government for their electoral expenses and to reward their services.[3]

There were two other key aspects to existing corruption which must be kept in mind when considering Smith's comments on the existing condition of politics. Firstly, as shown by Edward and Annie Porritt in The Unreformed House of Commons, Parliamentary Representation Before 1832 the franchise since 1430 and the

---

1 Structure, pp. 173-235.

2 Structure, pp. 427-483.

3 Structure, p. 20.

4 Edward and Annie Porritt, The Unreformed House of Commons, Parliamentary Representation Before 1832, 2 vols(Cambridge,1909).

reign of Henry VI had remained almost the same. The electorate still consisted, to a considerable extent, of forty shilling freeholders. Although by 1760 there had been a lowering of the value of money, and some leaseholders for life, and proprietors with heavy mortgages, and even "a few petty offices" or non-land-owning townsmen now had the vote,1 the total electorate did not exceed 160,000.2 Moreover, Smith reminds us that in Scotland no leaseholders were permitted parliamentary franchise as some groups were in England.3 Second and even more important, Namier warns us against thinking even this number of voters were actually permitted to exercise political choice.

> This might seem a numerous electorate. But as the voting was open and recorded in poll-books, people in dependent positions could seldom exercise a free choice; and as the agricultural interest was dominant in the countries, the result of the county elections was determined as a rule by the big landowners - the territorial magnates and the country gentlemen. Most countries, in fact, represented this one class only, and the candidates were often fixed upon at the Assizes or local races.
>
> In a few countries only was there any serious influence of a different character.4

---

1 Namier, Structure, p. 75, describes the five types of franchise in English boroughs. These ranged from a few boroughs where suffrage was almost universal to others where the forty shilling freehold rule was strictly enforced.

2 Porritt, *op.cit.*, I, pp. 22-23.

3 *WN* I, p. 416.

4 *Structure*, p. 65. Namier describes the five types of franchise in English Boroughs. *Structure*, p. 75, thus indicating the great variety of political rights and forms of representation.

II

In Smith's Scotland the political sentiment and resentment against all these forms of corruption was much stronger than in England of this same time. The Union of Parliaments of 1707 had abolished the Scottish Parliament and her political sovereignty. In 1715 the accession of George I ended the Scottish Stewart basis for cooperation with England and raised the flag of political unrest which Smith was to find familiar throughout his life. The Scots as a residual effect of the wars of the previous century and of these recent shifts of allegiance, were much less obedient to law, especially English Law throughout this period, than the English.1 They did not dread civil war the way the English did, and Scottish Jacobites would take up arms with little provocation.2

Smith, Hume and Ferguson and many others of the broad "Scottish School" were intimately aware of these developments and

---

1 Plumb, The Growth of Political Stability, op.cit., p. xviii and pp. 179-83. Scotland was a "dangerous" territory "liable to revolt on behalf of the Stewarts." Bell, "Adam Smith Clubman", op.cit., p. 113. Life, pp. 136-7.

2 Plumb, ibid., p. 169 "... between 1714 and 1724 the Jacobites raised a full scale rebellion in Scotland and invaded England", and on p. xviii Plumb describes Scottish instability, p. 18 "the Scottish" problem, and on p. 23 "It seemed unlikely that Scotland or Ireland could be brought to heel without Strong monarchy backed by force. And if they were not brought to heel what government in England could ever feel secure."

politically in sympathy with certain of the dissidents' desires: for political rights to bear arms, assemble, petition and speak against discriminatory acts against Scotland. As Rae, J.F. Bell, Dunn, and others have made clear, Smith was one of the founders, or at least one of the original memebers, of the Edinburgh Poker Club in 1762. The Poker Club was really a committee for political agitation, to stir public opinion especially among important political leaders to create a Scottish National Militia.1 There was wide popular support for this and many of the most important Scotsmen were members of this Club. It was intended that after the establishment of the national Militia other questions would be taken up concerning Parliamentary reform to do away with certain corruptions, but the militia question was not solved in that generation.2 The English were not ready to grant arms to the Scots so soon after their sponsorship of the "rebellion" of 1745.3

---

1 Bell, op.cit., pp. 113-115. For English Goverment views of a Scottish Militia and the political patronage and intricate maneuvering of ministers to strip Scottish Jacobites of power, see Patrick William J. Riley, The English Ministers and Scotland 1707-1727 (London, 1964).

2 Life, p. 135. "George Dempster of Dunnichen for example, an old and respected parliamentary hand of that time, wrote Dr. Carlyle in 1762 that when they get their militia they ought to agitate for parliamentary reform, 'so as to let the industrious farmer and manufacturer share at last in the privilege now engrossed by the great lord, the drunken laird, and the drunkener baillie.'"

3 Bell, op.cit., p. 113. Arms had been forbidden to the Scots since "the Rebellion of 1745". The Militia would restore arms and dignity to Scotsmen. "The English took a dim view of this and were unable to see peaceful aims in their motives."

Smith may have been more interested in these other questions of reform of Parliament, or he may have simply changed his mind about the value of a Scottish national Militia. For, though Smith remained a member of the Club until 1774, in 1776 when the Wealth of Nations appeared, Smith advocated a standing army as the more efficient form of defence than a militia. Though Smith praised the highland militia, he said that divison of labour had now imposed itself on the art of war to the extent that professional soldiers were better than part-time farmers. Ferguson, the fervent leader of the militia proponents, and organiser of the Poker Club, sharply criticised Smith on this apparent change of view.1

In addition to this general internal unrest and corruption in British politics, there was the even more explosive character of continental and colonial relations during Smith's life. The comparative success of British Colonies in America, the West Indies and partially in India during the 1740s under Walpole's period of calm (in contrast to the 1770s) had been achieved because of Walpole's cautious avoidance of wars. (And it was this which formed the basis for Smith's praise of Walpole's financial administration.2 Yet finally Walpole was forced to go to war

---

1 Life, pp. 134-8. And see Adam Ferguson, Reflections Previous to the Establishment of a Militia (London, 1756). In Lectures, p. 263 as early as 1763 Smith advocated standing armies.

2 See W.R. Scott. "Adam Smith at Downing Street", op.cit., p. 80. Smith compiled and partially wrote a history of the sinking fund for Townshend in 1766 in which Walpole's administration was praised as "the first symptom of regular Finance."

and in the turbulent fifteen years following him there occurred several confrontations arising from colonial disputes with other European powers, bad colonial relations, and enormous national debts. By 1756 at the beginning of the Seven Years War the mistakes of British colonial policy (except for India where Clive was successful) had led to a certain ascendancy of French foreign interest. The Whig party proved unable to govern and corruption in it was so rife that it could hardly perform the day to day functions of normal administration.1 The old Tory party was equally unwieldy and thus a period of political uncertainty amid changing governments ensued until Pitt took over.2

Adam Smith's connection with politics, aside from being a loyal Scot and a member of Ferguson's notorius "Poker Club", began during Pitt's administration. Smith's formal political activity began under Charles Townshend, that brilliant but capricious minister of various governments from 1749-1767. Townshend is best known for his famous taxation acts upon the American Colonies in 1765-7 when he was Chancellor of the Exchequer, which led to the American Revolutionary War.3 Smith was an adviser to Charles Townshend at Downing Street during this last most crucial period 1766-7 and probably resigned because he was unable to dissuade

---

1 Feiling, The Second Tory Party 1714-1832, op.cit., p. 73. "In 7 years there were 5 ministries."

2 Feiling, The Second Tory Party 1714-1832, ibid., p. 76. "In all this the Tories were ... divided."

3 Life, p. 1346.

Townshend from his disastrous policy.[1] Namier's Charles Townshend, His Character and Career provides the clearest analysis of the man and his consistent dedication to the policy of colonial taxation from 1749-1767 while illuminating the peculiarly confused personal and political sitiuation Smith must have found himself in as an adviser on colonial policy. Although little information is available on Smith's actual political activities as adviser, W.R. Scott in his article, "Adam Smith at Downing Street 1766-7",[2] has pieced together what facts are known with Smith's famous views on colonial policy and administration expressed in their most fulsome form in the Wealth of Nations, Bk. IV and V. W.R. Scott stresses the awkward position Smith must have felt himself in and the inevitable clash of his views with Townshends'. It was between this period and 1776 that Smith worked out in detail the sections of the Wealth of Nations on colonial policy. However he had in an early speech, his Lectures and Draft set out the initial statement of policy which did not change.[3]

According to Smith, colonies were the most drastic form of monopoly. Colonies were set up for the benefit of the mother

---

1 Lewis Namier, Charles Townshend, His Character and Career (Cambridge, 1959).

2 Scott, "Downing Street", op.cit.

3 WN IV and V. However, Smith first enunciated this policy in broad outline in a speech delivered in 1749 which he later publicly claimed to be the first advocacy of his laissez-faire policy and where in fact that exact term is used. See Rae, Life, p. 36.

country and specifically for the benefit of certain classes of merchants and landlords, and exploited for many generations by being denied freedom of trade or representation in the British Parliament.1 In addition to this fundamental view Smith believed colonies inevitably were at best a mixed blessing and often proved more of a burden than an advantage since colonists rightfully resented their subservient position to the mother country economically, politically and legally. Colonies required inordinate defence expenditure to secure them from other great powers which might offer the colonists greater self-determination.

After 1740, which had been a high point for British Colonies in America, the West Indies, and India, there had developed by 1776 a confused pattern of colonial mismanagement. In America, with no French threat, after "the French and Indian" and "Seven Years" wars, the colonists no longer depended so much on British protection. Yet, because of the vast expense of these wars, the British felt the need for the colonists partially to reimburse them for their previous defence. Smith was extremely well versed in these colonial relations and he was convinced that for various economic and political reasons Britain eventually, would be forced

---

1 WN II, p. 146. Colonies are monopolies. Smith's Colonial policy criticisms are most comprehensively expressed in Bk. IV and V of the Wealth of Nations but more particular criticisms are contained in "Smith's Thoughts on the State of the Contest with with American February 1778", op.cit. and Smith's "Memorandum on Irish Free Trade" written at the request of Lord North's ministers during the turbulence of 1779. See Life, pp. 346-56.

to give them up.[1] But Smith in the meantime urged that revolutionary war should be averted, and the colonists offered concessions from the British Parliament to keep them quiet so that constructive economic relations could continue. Smith was convinced also, that if separation did occur, America would provide a most useful trading partner for Britain. But, in the immediate period he wished to avoid bloodshed and so suggested diminishing the political unrest by incorporating 60 colonists into the British Parliament.[2]

Smith while working for Townshend on colonial administration exchanged various memoranda and letters with him. Scott reproduces one letter, probably from Townshend to Smith dealing with colonies and especially the sinking fund, and concludes from it:

> Considering the momentous consequences which were involved, it is an altogether new light on Adam Smith's life to find him involved in these great transactions. It is unfortunate that there is no trace of the end of the association of Townshend and Adam Smith. The latter was most outspoken. If his views on taxation and representation were the same as he expressed in 1776 and 1778, and from his whole type of thought there is no reason to doubt it, he may have expressed his disagreement forcibly and returned to Scotland.[3]

---

1 <u>Life</u>, pp. 353-5.

2 <u>WN</u> II, p. 139.

3 Scott, "Downing Street", <u>op.cit</u>., pp. 88-9.

Yet, outspoken as his political views often were, he was always in his letters and relations with Townshend extremely cordial and it had not been without considerable effort that Smith had secured the original position of tutor to Townshend's nephew[1] and he probably endeavoured to maintain the high opinion Townshend had of him which is evident in a letter Scott reproduces. In this letter Townshend describes his great respect for Smith's political knowledge:

> Mr. Smith, among other advantages, possesses that of being deeply read in the constitution and laws of your own country. [Scotland] He is ingenious without being confined. He is general without being superficial and too systematical, he is learned without being singular in his notions of our Government, and from him you will grow to be a grounded politician.[2]

After returning to Scotland from advising Townshend, Smith spent the next nine years in semi-seclusion finishing the Wealth of Nations. He then spent another year in London (1776-7) "among the great" enjoying the acclaim his book received especially among those in government. He may well have advised the government informally during this period, for in November 1777 Lord North appointed him Commissioner of Customs for Scotland. Not only had Lord North himself been favourably impressed by Smith's <u>Wealth of</u>

---

1 Scott, <u>Adam Smith as Student and Professor</u> introduction to Smith's <u>Draft of the Wealth of Nations</u>, pp. 317-21.

2 Scott, "Downing Street", <u>op.cit</u>., p. 83. Letter dated Sept. 10, 1764.

Nations but so had several of his key ministers and in 1778 before Smith took up his post in Scotland he was urgently consulted for his opinion on the colonial war with America following the British defeat at Saratoga. Smith's extensive views were sent to Lord North's government in a document now titled "Smith's Thoughts on the State of the Contest with America February 1776". G.H. Guttridge in his article "Adam Smith on the American Revolution an unpublished Memorial"1 has examined this document in detail to prove Smith's authorship and to compare its views with those expressed by Smith in other works.

The "Memorial" contains several passages which are important for a complete understanding of Smith's political theory. The document was ostensibly an examination of four possible outcomes of the Revolutionary War and the opening sentence sets this out:

> There seems to be four, and but four, possible ways in which the present unhappy war with our colonies may be conceived to end.2

These were (1) complete "submission", (2) "complete emancipation of America", (3) restoration of old colonial system yet with America "contributing little or nothing" to defence, (4) "the submission of a part, but of a part only, of America; Great Britain, after a long, expensive and ruinous war, being obliged to acknowledge the independency of the rest". Smith then goes on to

---

1 G.H. Guttridge, "Adam Smith on the American Revolution an unpublished Memorial", op.cit., pp.714-20.

2 AR, p. 715.

examine in detail some "advantages and disadvantages which might be expected from each."1

Couched in these practical terms of four outcomes Smith proceeds to outline several of his conjectural political theories. Conquest would require continuing military occupation and the Americans would forever resist it. "They will, for more than a century to come, be at all times ready to take arms in order to overturn it." Only by treaty could peaceful submission of America to Britain be achieved and this Smith says is the least likely of the four possible outcomes because Americans and British in their present conditions oppose it. "The plan (of a constitutional union with the colonies) which, if it could be executed would certainly tend most to the prosperity, to the splendour, and to the duration of the empire, if you except here and there a solitary philosopher like myself, seems scarce to have a single advocate." Nevertheless, Smith persists in advocating such a union of Britain with the Colonies by treaty because:

> The Americans, I imagine, would be less unwilling to consent to such a union with Great Britain as Scotland made with England in 1707; than to the restoration, or to anything like the restoration of the old system. The leading men of America, we may believe, wish to continue to be the principal people in their own country. After a union with Great Britain, they might expect to continue to be so; in the same manner as the leading men of Scotland continued to be the principal

---

1 AR, p. 716.

> people of their own country after the Union with England.1

By contrast Smith argues that after conquest, or restoration of the former system, these native American leaders would be replaced. This appeal to the self preservative instinct of the "leading men" of America was a repetition of the argument in the Wealth of Nations urging 60 American representatives for Parliament.2 It can be taken to be once again a reflection of Smith's key principle of class dominated politics. This principle was found in his conjectural origin of government from the preservation of property by the rich; and in his reflections upon monopolies legislation. It was also the basis of his attacks on the interests and character of the members of Parliment.

But Smith's political theory was far subtler than simply a recognition of the prevailing class rule.3 Basing his political theory upon the need to satisfy the "leading men of Britain and America" he urged a high level form of deceit, a fake

---

1 AR, p. 718-9. Compare this to WN II, pp. 136-9.

2 WN II, p. 137.

3 Evidence that class rule and localised elites were the hallmarks of 18th century British and especially Scottish Politics is provided by Namier, Structure, ibid., p. 64. Plumb, Political Stability, op.cit., p. xviii. The prime causes of political stability which Plumb considers were "In England as I hope to show, there were three major factors: single party government the legislative firmly under executive control and a sense of common identity in those who wielded economic, social and political power." Plumb, Four Georges, op.cit., p. 7 states that the House of Commons was "A body however which was representative of only the wealthiest classes."

restoration:

> An apparent restoration of the old system, so contrived as to lead necessarily, but insensibly to the real dismemberment of America, might, perhaps, satisfy both the people of Great Britain and the leading men of America; the former mistaking, and the latter understanding the meaning of the scheme.1

Though Smith later admits that "the secrecy, the prudence necessary for conducting a scheme of this kind, "are virtually impossible, it is of utmost importance that this deceit was the one outcome: "perhaps, of all those which are likely to happen the most advantageous to the state." When we reflect upon the magnitude of this political deceit Smith was advocating with regard to the colonies we find there may be another conclusion than simply Smith's desire for the end of Britain's colonial establishment. This other conclusion is that the political objectives he found "the most advantageous to the state" might on other occasions be achieved by deceit of the general public. This does not mean Smith's political theory must be equated to Plato's theory of the "noble lie" but it does lay the foundation for an understanding of certain state activities he advocated. Smith recommends the State act on the half of those individuals and classes who do not know what is in their own best interest. The state must at times direct and even make sane decisions for the labouring classes and must "contrive": laws to make it "seem in men's best interest to be just". Although this will be dealt

---

1 AR, p. 719.

with more fully later, for the present, it may be mentioned that Smith in moral Sentiments said men's drive for wealth and frivolous utilities was another colossal delusion, for he believed all men are equally capable of happiness, and the beggar lying by the side of the road has the happiness and peace which kings are fighting for.

Smith in this same memorial on The Revolutionary War reflects in a similar vein that if the colonies become independent another contrivance - an international deceit would keep the colonies allied to Britain.

> If, with the complete emancipation of America, we should restore Canada to France and the two Floridas to Spain we should render our own colonies the natural enemies of those two monarchies and consequently the natural allies of Great Britain. Those splendid, but unprofitable acquisitions of the late war, left our colonies no other enemies to quarrel with but their mother country. By restoring these acquisitions to their ancient masters, we should certainly revive old enmities, and probably old friendships.[1]

I have dwelt on these supposedly practical proposals of Smith's to Lord North's government in order to indicate how his political theory, like his economic theory, although drawn from factual issues and policies of his time, tended to seek a contrived harmony of interests. The contrivance of the equal proprietors in the free market exchanging labour for wages, in ths way paralleled the contrivance of equal parliamentary representation. The

---

1 AR, p. 718.

inferior colonists like the poor labourers would lose their discontents in the larger political whole. Likewise the achievement of international harmony was to be achieved by a contrivance of enmities and friendships, as in the above case of America.[1]

Smith concluded his Document on America with the assumption that the submission or conquest of part of America was both the most likely and most disastrous outcome of the revolutionary war. This Smith said would result in eternal animosities and defense expenditure.

Smith when he had taken up his quite demanding post of Controller of Customs for Scotland and Collector of the Salt Tax was thought by several of his friends to be wasting his time instead of doing new writing. Although Rae makes this argument quite forcibly, according to Sir John Sinclair's Correspondence[2] Smith on the contrary in his customs post was learning "how essential practical knowledge was to the thorough understanding of political subjects." H.B. Vanderblue in his article "An Incident in the Life of Adam Smith Commissioner of His Majesty's

---

1 Smith's conception of politics as a contrivance did not go as far as Hobbes' in imagining a Mechanistic political contrivance for absolute obedience, but Smith did believe in contrived harmony.

2 Sir John Sinclair, Correspondence, 2 Vols. Vol. I., p. 389 and quoted by Rae, Life, p. 332.

Customs"[1] argues that Smith's friends and Rae have misunderstood the importance of this period of practical work for the development of Smith's political thought. As Vanderblue says "During this same period he wrote certain of the significant passages in the text of the Wealth of Nations as it has come down to us."[2] Mainly these new passages had to do with Treasury matters; and additions to the chapters on "Drawbacks" and "Bounties", and an entirely new chapter on the "Conclusion of Mercantile System". But the most significant additions were to the chapter upon the "Expenses of the Sovereign", Smith's foremost political chapter of the entire book. However Vanderblue does not provide details on what these additions were, and from Gannan's annotations it would appear that the new political material was on administration, not political theory.

Nevertheless, it is known that while in this important Customs post Smith was consulted upon various political matters by the British government. For example, Smith was sent an urgent solicitation for advice by two members of the Board of Trade concerning the Irish unrest in 1779. Commercial restrictions upon Irish trade had been so severe that Irish merchants were not allowed to trade with British "colonies because they were aliens and they were not allowed to trade as they would with foreign

---

1 H.B. Vanderblue "An Incident in the Life of Adam Smith Commissioner of His Majesty's Customs". American Historical Review XXVII (1937) pp. 305-8.

2 Vanderblue, ibid., p. 305.

countries, because they were British Subjects."[1]

The result of this systematic oppression was enormous scarcity and unemployment. Smith was called in to advise on free trade for Ireland, however, only when its proposal by the British government had met with widespread attack by English merchants. Smith's advice was his familiar free trade argument, that under whatever variety of conceivable Irish demands and conceivable circumstances "Britain would not be hurt by it." Again in this document he returns to the issue of class control of government and monopoly legislation in a conception that was to form the foundation for most of his political theory.

> Nothing, in my opinion, would be more highly advantageous to both countries than this mutual freedom of trade. It would help to break down that absurd monopoly which we have most absurdly established against ourselves in favour of almost all the different classes of our own manufacturers.[2]

Monopolies are always "in favour of almost all the different classes of our own manufacturers." He also stresses that they are always "Against ourselves", meaning the vast majority of the public.

---

1 Life, p. 346.

2 Life, p. 355.

## III

We turn now from Smith's political experience to his political theory.[1] Smith's Lectures stated that there are two principles of government, "the principles of authority and utility".[2]

> In all governments both these principles take place in some degree, but in a monarchy the principle of authority prevails, and in a democracy that of utility.[3]

Although Smith says there are three forms of government into which all other varieties can be reduced; namely into "monarchical, aristocratical and demoncratical",[4] he then immediately afterwards reduces the division to two forms saying: "these two

---

1 Smith's political theory is scattered throughout his works but is most extensively propounded in his Lectures "on Justice" and in the Wealth of Nations especially Bk. V chapter I "Of the Expenses of the Sovereign or Commonwealth." II pp. 233-341. Smith's political theory and especially the functions of government is considered by James Bonar, Political Economy, op.cit., pp. 175-80, and by Viner, "ASLF", p. 203, p. 219-20, and Bitterman, op.cit., pp. 518-20; and by Morrow, Theories, ch.3, Solomon, op.cit., p. 26. O.H. Taylor, op.cit., pp. 70-1 and Cropsey, op.cit., pp. 19-30 and 64-80. The specific issue of government policy is dealt with by Lionel Robbins, The Theory of Economic Policy in the English Classical Political Economy, op.cit., ch.2 and ch.6. This has also been dealt with by Samuels, The Classical Theory of Economic Policy, op.cit., ch.III and IV on "The Economic Role of the State", pp. 98-161.

2 Lectures, p. 9.

3 Lectures, p. 11.

4 Lectures, p. 14.

last forms may be called republican, and then the division of government is into monarchical and republican."[1]

To understand government Smith says we must consider "the first form of it, and observe how the other forms arose out of it."[2] However, what Smith considered the first form of government is not certain from Smith's texts. On page 14 of his Lectures Smith says "in a nation of hunters there is properly no government at all." Yet on page 20 of these same Lectures Smith says of "a nation of hunters and fishers", "The principle of authority operates very strongly and they have the liveliest sense of utility in the maintenance of law and government." And this is further confused because Smith originally stated that one of the prime reasons that nations of hunters have no proper government was that no one person had natural authority over others. The explanation for these discrepancies seems to be that "proper government" for Smith required extensive permanent property which the rich needed to protect from other groups. As previously quoted in a different context:

> Till there be property there can be no government, the very end of which is to secure wealth and to defend the rich from the poor.[3]

Thus Smith meant that "proper government" was preceded by tribal

---

1 Lectures, p. 14.

2 Lectures, p. 14.

3 Lectures, p. 15.

meetings that were primarily concerned with personal injuries and group safety, not with the unequal distribution of wealth and the protection of property rights.

It is only in herding tribes where there is some permanent property that government develops from the attempts of the rich cattle owners to preserve the inequality of fortune.1 It is in this age that the authority conferred by the possession of wealth supersedes the authority of strength, age, wisdom and birth as the key principle of social control; (birth is thereafter usually allied to wealth.) Unlike hunting tribes where there is a primitive democracy because no one presumptive leader "can do anything without the consent of the whole",2 in herding societies the leaders' power is the most absolute and monarchical. It is thus unlikely that the utility of government is appreciated by the subjects in these absolute monarchies of herdsmen who were constantly at war with one another. Rather it is the principle of the most absolute authority which is observed.

It is therefore not until the development of certain agricultural societies3 that a "proper" republican government is first established; meaning one where the general public have at least a

---

1 Lectures, p. 15.

2 Lectures, p. 15.

3 It was shown in ch. VI sec. III and ch. VII sect. I that Smith described two forms of agricultural society; republican and monarchical.

partial appreciation of the usefulness of laws and of the protection of private property. However, many other agricultural societies were monarchical, and in some an absolute despotism had prevailed.

With the agricultural stage of society there was the possibility for a greater variety of state structures than in the previous hunting and herding societies. That is, within each of the two types of farming societies, republican and monarchical, there occured many shifts in the form of government as agricultural property ownership changed. In his Lectures on Public Jurisprudence Smith traces the development of government in England from the earliest "Military Monarchies".[1] He shows that each shift in the form of government directly reflected the conditions of property's distribution among leading "ranks" of society. Military Monarchy was dissolved[2] at the end of the Roman Empire when gradually the various tribes of barbarians settled into established communities and "allodial government" was formed.[3] Allodial government originated from allodial property holdings which were owned absolutely by the local ruler.[4] This form of government therefore persisted as long as various local

---

1 Lectures, pp. 30-33.

2 Lectures, pp. 32-33.

3 Lectures, pp. 34-35.

4 Lectures, pp. 34-35.

rulers could defend their absolute possessions and so long as their respective domains remained comparatively equal.[1] Gradually the leading lords granted protection to inferior lords and thus was established the feudal form of property and government based upon a chain of dependence, protection and allegiance.[2] Unlike the absolute property holdings of Allodial society the later Feudal property rights descended from God, to the King, to the Dukes and then to the local lords or lairds.[3] Smith examines the feudal mode of property in some detail to show its relation to feudal government, and to examine certain feudal laws of property whose vestiges still persisted in his own time.[4]

It is the gradual changes in property relations between the king and his lords and also the development of non-landed wealth in the towns and cities that forces feudal government to change and enables Parliament to begin to exert considerable influence over the affairs of state.[5] A Magna Carta for the protection of the rights of lords and charters for the towns and their commercial tradesmen each reflect the independent strength of other groups besides the king. Smith traces the development of

---

1 _Lectures_, pp. 35-37.

2 _Lectures_, pp. 36-40.

3 _Lectures_, pp. 36-40.

4 _Lectures_, pp. 107-132.

5 _Lectures_, p. 40.

these other economic powers of landed aristocracy and the townsmen in their struggle with the king, for rights, privileges and political influence. Smith describes the tides of fortune experienced by Parliaments as Queen Elizabeth and later kings gained their partial financial independence from public taxes and so did not need to call or to obey the lords or public representatives.1 Smith then shows that because of financial mismanagement, later kings became again dependent upon Parliament for funds.2 With each grant of money the kings were forced to lose successive portions of their former powers of absolute government, and the strength and liberty of Parliment was increased.3

Throughout this description of the development of English government, changes of property relations between the leading social ranks were shown to cause political transformations. In Smith's extensive discussion of the development of the "English Courts of Justice" he describes a similar pattern of struggles among the leading ranks of society for justice in their respective private cases.4 English justice in the beginning was dependent upon the will of the local ruler and disputes were settled by

---

1 Lectures, p. 42.

2 Lectures, p. 43.

3 Lectures, p. 43-46.

4 Lectures, pp. 46-53.

trials of strength or torture.1 With feudal government there developed a hierarchy of judicial courts, that corresponded to the hierarchy of feudal society. With development of towns and of property disputes between new social ranks and old the courts of justice were forced to codify their laws and regularise their procedure.2 Eventually the independence of the courts from the interests of the king, Parliment or single lords was made possible because there were conflicting pressures from so many conflicting important groups.

Smith studied the "mixed" government in Britain to discover which propertied interests had predominated at different periods and specifically to discover which periods of her history were predominantly monarchical and which were predominantly republican and the causes and effects of these predominancies. He concluded that only in the present time were the divisions of powers between King, Parliament, and Courts beginning to become a true safeguard of individual's rights and liberties.3 Even in his time Smith argued that although the powers of the king and Parliament were finally in check,4 he asserted that the absolute powers of the aristocracy and landlords and monopolists over the unreformed

---

1 Lectures, pp. 46-50.

2 Lectures, pp. 50-52.

3 Lectures, pp. 45-46.

4 Lectures, pp. 45-46.

Parliament were hindering the development of the economy,[1] and denying the full rights of citizens[2] and subjects.[3]

The aspects of politics to which Smith devoted most of his efforts was the determination of the character, and activities and proper role of government in his own society.

Smith's political theory of the role of government in commerical society I will argue to consist of three parts. First, he examined propertied classes' control of government authority for the protection of wealth from the propertyless majority. Second, Smith advocated the utility of general policy and administrative changes in government for the proper or best future state. And third, he held an implicit social contract theory of rights and sovereignty. Smith's views on the utility of certain policies and types of administration will be left to a later chapter on the "Objectives of Government". In the following pages I will concentrate on Smith's theory on class control of government, his criticisms of policy, and the effect of class and corruption on the political rights of individuals.

Most interpreters have analysed Smith's political discussions as simply arguments for free enterprise. Yet such a view fails to recognise that he simultaneously was advocating the curbing of the class power of landlords and merchants who corrupted and

---

1 WN II, pp. 146, 165, 278.

2 Lectures, pp. 62-65.

3 Lectures, pp. 66-67.

controlled Parliament and its monopolies legislation. In a later chapter on "The Objectives of Government" it will be shown that Smith was advocating a far more active government than is usually thought, but to the extent that he did advocate laissez-faire he was in effect attacking the particular government and policies of his time. He was demanding that the propertied class control of both parties in Parliament,1 and specifically this control of military, colonial, monopoly, land and apprenticeship legislation, cease or be severely reduced. That is, the other side of the coin of his advocating laissez-faire was the curbing of that class which was controlling government and its corruption.2

In Smith's Theory of Moral Sentiments where he sketches the more abstract or conjectural aspects of politics he stresses a theme which recurs in both the later works3 that government not only begins with property but increases in size and authority in proportion to the property of that society. He explains this in various ways. From the standpoint of individuals' passions he

---

1 See Plumb, Four Georges, op.cit., p. 7. Viner, "ASLF" op.cit., pp. 230-32.

2 Both Namier and Plumb criticised Keith Gramm Feiling, The Second Tory Party, 1714-1832, op.cit. See Plumb, Political Stability, p. xiv. They argued that Feiling was wrong about George III's reign where he calls it "A watershead in party development." Feiling devotes four chapters to proving this "watershead" in party development occurred in the beginning of George III's reign. Namier devoted his two major works, in part, to disproving this view. Namier showed that the political parties operated on the same principles of graft, nepotism, and political deals as before.

3 Lectures, p. 9. WN II, pp. 231-2.

explains that the drives to invade property are

> passions much more steady in their operation and much more universal in their influence.[1]

than passions to kill or hurt other men. Therefore, with the increase of property there was an increase of injustice as men steadily sought to invade the property of others. And simultaneously with the increase of wealth, the rich assumed far more permanent and substantial authority than in previous societies where age, wisdom, strength and birth are the sources of authority and superiority. The rich take over the functions of government previously performed by the old, the wise, the strong and the nobly born.[2] Although Smith says that the other principle of government is utility, he is somewhat ambiguous on the questions of who appreciates government's utility, when, and for what reasons they do so. On page 10 of his Lectures he states that:

> Everyone is sensible of the necessity of this principle to preserve justice and peace in the society.[3]

At other points he says that among the general population the recognition of government's utility comes only after centuries of state protection of the property and authority of the rich, and

---

1 WN II, p. 232.

2 Lectures, pp. 9, 17-20, esp. 15. WN II, p. 236.

3 Lectures, p. 10.

the enforcement of peace on the other classes.[1] The explanation for this contradiction appears to be that the utility of maintaining peace is universally recognised but the utility of maintaining unequal wealth takes longers for the general public to understand.

Smith provides a conjectural and a factual appraisal of governments in commercial society. These appraisals do not entirely correspond. Conjecturally, the government of commercial society is centralised, and it performs more completely and exactly the functions of previous types of government. It enacts and enforces laws of "justice, police revenue and arms", and in his Lectures these activities are examined in detail. Government in commercial society is more completely divided into three branches - Executive, Legislative and Judicial - than in any previous society.[2]

At other times Smith provides a less formal and more realistic view of government in commerical Britain of the eighteenth century. The separation of powers between executive, legislature and judiciary was more one of form than of substance,[3] since he shows the same kinds of men and same

---

1 TMS, pp. 132-7. Lectures, p. 9. Men develop approval of their obedience to government. Eventually this meant their approval of the unequal distribution of wealth which government protected.

2 Lectures, pp. 17-18. WN II, pp. 243-4.

3 Lectures, p. 69.

propertied classes filled all the government services. And with the prevalence of so much injustice and corruption, office holders were often interchangeable. A persistent theme of ruling class oppression through their control of government runs through Smith's works. In the Draft of the Wealth of Nations Smith speaks of those few:

> who don't labour at all, and who yet either by violence, or by the more orderly opposition of the law, employ a greater part of the labour of the society,[1]

In the Moral Sentiments Smith derides:

> Sometimes what is called the constitution of the state is the interest of the government; sometimes the interest of particular orders of men who tyrannise the government, warp the positive laws of the country ...[2]

And finally in the Wealth of Nations he traces the effectiveness with which different groups attempt to influence the government for this or that monopoly or protectionist act.[3] In his

---

1 Draft, p. 327.

2 TMS, p. 502.

3 See esp. WN I, pp. 493-5. Plumb, Chatham, op.cit., p. 10. Plumb makes it clear that each general policy of those wishing to influence government was apparent from their source of income. "The ownership of land and the control of seats in Parliament were the ways rich merchants bought themselves a place in society and government in the eighteenth century." Namier makes the identical point, England in the Age of the American Revolution, op.cit., p. 10. But both Namier and Plumb also make the interesting reflection that because of the extensive landowners' influence on Parliament, the rotten boroughs bought by various merchant groups provided a democratising influence on Parliament. Namier, ibid., p. 4, insists "Without these [rotten] boroughs the House of Commons in 1769 would practically have represented one class only".

extensive examples of specific government laws and policies which the ruling propertied classes had erected and maintained Smith included export bounties,[1] import duties[2] and apprenticeship restrictions.[3] Smith's general attack on Monopolies is well known.[4] Smith insists that monopolies are supported by unjust and cruel laws specifically enacted because of propertied class political pressure:

> But the cruellest of our revenue laws, I will venture to affirm, are mild and gentle, in comparison with some of those which the clamour of our merchants and manufacturers has extorted from the legislature, for the support of their own absurd and oppressive monopolies. Like the laws of Draco, these laws may be said to be all written in blood.[5]

Smith condemns both foreign and domestic monopolies especially for their effect on government and individuals. By destroying

---

1 See Smith, WN, entire chapter on "Bounties", Bk. IV, ch. v. esp. WN II, pp. 10-20 and pp. 410-11.

2 See WN I, pp. 472-5 and II, p. 159, where it is shown that duties are but another way to secure a monopoly of the home market to domestic industry.

3 WN I, pp. 114-115, and 133-5. (Here the bond of servitude is explained and the actual statute of apprenticeships in England is contrasted with those of France and Scotland; then in pages 136-8 and 150 and 493 Smith describes Apprenticeships' obstruction of the free movement of labour again as an attempt by "masters" to preserve their monopoly in the labour market.)

4 On Smith see Jacob Viner in The International Encyclopedia of the Social Sciences (London, 1968), Vol. 12, p. 326. Monopolies are attacked by Smith in WN I, p. 69, II, pp. 165, 123, 143, 146-7, 424.

5 WN II, p. 165.

individual rights, and the ordinary citizen's respect for just government, monopolies had undermined internal political obedience. Yet, even more damaging he thought was monopolies' effect on foreign policy where "The sneaking arts of the underling tradesman are thus erected into political maxims for the conduct of a great empire."

Laws for monopolies were by no means a strange outgrowth from the existing Parliamentary legislation. They were not the aberration of an otherwise disinterested House of Commons. Namier is quite emphatic that:

> A majority of seats in the House had a quasi-proprietary character - they were a valuable inheritance or a costly acquisition from which proper returns were expected.1

Nor were monopolies by any means the only form of the government's financial aid to individual merchants, landlords, or investors.

> By means of taxation and government loans, agglomerations of capital were effected such as could not easily have arisen in private trade.2

The great contracts and fortunes of merchants and landlords acquired through political office or contracts were for feeding, clothing, or equipping the military services. Financial opportunities only offered by political office with the military, such as paymaster, ordinance, receivership etc., included the

---

1 Structure, p. 17.

2 Structure, p. 45.

receipt of vast public monies and of inordinate interest rates for loans in a time before the joint stock companies were common.1 All merchants from great grain dealers to ironmongers eagerly sought government military contracts and of course the most important merchants sought direct political office to make the acquisition of these contracts easier. Even for minor contracts political recommendations were essential. Merchants as Members of Parliament had by far the better chance of contracts and so sought seats rather than sinecures.

Smith condemned the:

> mean rapacity, the monopolising spirit of merchants and manufacturers, who neither are, nor ought to be, the rulers of mankind,...2

For, "their interest" is almost always in political terms

---

1 Plumb, Chatham, op.cit.,p. 34. "Paymasters could be certain of many thousands of pounds with which to speculate." And p. 35, "Another profitable sideline of the paymasters was the gifts which he received every time a subsidy was made to a foreign prince or when mercenary troops were hired." "In fact all paymasters had made immense fortunes." (William Pitt was the only one to not keep these various forms of graft.) Also Namier in Structure, pp. 45-6, describes the importance of these financial deals of political appointments to collect, hold or convey money for the armed services, colonies or land taxes within Britain, provided the largest and safest deposits of public money. As Namier points out, "private deposits and savings were as yet insignificant. On the other hand, the underwriting of Government loans was the chief financial transaction in an age when joint-stock companies were few and Government stock was the main regular object of Speculation in the Alley." Thus paymasters and receivers of public money could use it to privately reinvest in underwriting Government loans.

2 WN I, p. 519.

"directly opposite to that of the great body of the people." Smith detailed the exact kinds of pressure that manufacturers, merchants and landlords exerted on Parliment, in a passage that demonstrates his full appreciation of the political climate of his time. Of the monopolising merchants, manufacturers, and landlords' political influence on Members of Parliament and officials of the administration Smith says:

> They have become formidable to the government, and upon many occasions intimidate the legislature. The member of parliament who supports every proposal for strengthening this monopoly, is sure to acquire not only the reputation of understanding trade, but great popularity and influence with an order of men whose numbers and wealth render them of great importance. If he opposes them, on the contrary, and still more if he has authority enough to be able to thwart them, neither the most acknowledged probity, nor the highest rank, nor the greatest public services, can protect him from the most infamous abuse and detraction, from personal insults, nor sometimes from real danger, arising from the insolent outrage of furious and disappointed monopolists.[1]

Thus Smith's Draft, Lectures, Moral Sentiments and Wealth of Nations show his keen awareness of the discrepancy between the myth of universal political and property rights and the powerless, often voteless, and frequently propertyless majority. Property and politics were but different strands of a single social fabric.[2]

---

1 WN I, p. 494.

2 Not only did political rights tend to extend only so far as the ownership of property, but many property rights extended only

This fabric was based simultaneously upon exchange and a preservation of the social orders. The state in commercial society continued in existence to preserve and defend the propertied classes from the propertyless; the cause which had brought government into existence.

In 1760 the general population of Britain was put at over six and one half million[1] yet the voting electorate we have already said was scarcely 160,000.[2] Clearly, Smith was totally accurate when he said, "the number of the voters is nothing to that of the people."[3] Throughout his works Smith demonstrates that his society hardly recognised the poor as fully political beings. However, he stresses that this situation was not new. The electorate had always (after the democracy of primitive hunting tribes)[4] been narrow, where it existed at all. No republic he

---

to citizens. See Lectures, p. 64 "In Britain an alien cannot purchase or inherit land property, nor maintain a real action. He cannot make a will because it is the greatest extension of property and is founded on piety and affection to the dead, which an alien can have but few opportunities of deserving. By a particular statute an alien merchant, but not a tradesman may have a lease of a house. This arises from a whimsical principle that it would discourage our own tradesmen to allow foreigners to settle among them. This is the state of aliens in most countries."

1 Ashton, Industrial Revolution, p. 3.

2 E. Porritt, The Unreformed House of Commons, op.cit., I, p.22.

3 Lectures, p. 69.,

4 Lectures, pp. 15, 53. The primitive tribe as a whole judges crimes and chooses the chief and makes rules.

describes possessed universal suffrage, and no mixed monarchy such as Britain came anywhere near "a just political representation".1

Because of the enclosures and industrial movements and the consequent shift of population from the land there was a decreasing opportunity for the poorer classes to obtain a "forty shilling freehold", or permanent leasehold because of the necessity for larger holdings. Hence, this three hundred year old requirement for electoral franchise was becoming increasingly hard for the poor to obtain. Moreover, those with land, (either small freehold or leasehold) and a vote were not free in their choice of candidates or policy, as shown by Plumb, Feiling, Walcott and Namier.2 Nor once the poor of the villages and

---

1 WN II, p. 98.

2 Structure, pp. 62-5. A debate has persisted among political historians since Namier's two works appeared in 1929 and 1930, as to whether the political representation of the general public was increasing or remained static throughout the 18th century. Much of the controversy would have been avoided if the disputants had restricted the exact time periods they were generalising upon. R.R. Walcott, in English Politics in the Early 18th Century (London, 1956) attempted to draw Namier's conclusions about politics in 1760 and 1776 back into an earlier period. He argued politics in the early 18th century was similar to 1760. Plumb, Political Stability, op.cit., calls Walcott's book "very sound" and argues that p. xiv, "Politics in the 17th and early 18th century witnessed the growth of a large political nation with voting rights. More general elections were held between 1689-1714 than ever since." However, Plumb's argument does not make clear as Namier's does how little popular representation there was during this period of frequent elections, nor whether the infrequency of elections in the rest of the 18th century and the long periods of one party rule did not demonstrate a lack of popular representation after 1715.

towns did have the vote, was there much they as propertyless electors could do to ensure that "representatives" did represent the true interests of the general population in Parliament. In terms of political theory and practice this meant that political rights, political power, and possession of property were largely coincidental. Without property few men had during Smith's time, the same legal recourse to the courts for wage delays or defaults that an employer had to recover delayed or defaulted debts. Without property Smith makes clear the lesser amounts of justice in civil, commercial, or criminal disputes an individual could expect. The poor, he notes, had little recourse to any charge of vagrancy, public burden, public nuisance, public danger or public menace.[1] In short the labouring classes in general were definitely under the law (its influence and in some cases its subjection) whereas the rich were frequently "above the law" and able to either control its statutes or avoid its punishments.

Smith's implicit social contract theory was based on a society composed of equal units: citizens possessing equal political rights. Yet such "rights" were actually possessed by only those with a certain amount of property.[2] "It would be ludicrous to talk of any kind of 'democracy' in 39 out of 40

---

1 Smith's discussion of the Poor Law Administration, WN I, pp. 151-2 makes this clear.

2 Structure, p. 69.

countries",[1] says Namier. A man's political position "was measured by his rental".[2] However, Smith's declarations of "The equal rights of men" was not contradictory to his defence of a very limited property owning ruling class.[3] Smith believed in equality, and in upholding "the social orders" and ruling class of property owners. Smith argued for:

> a more equal land tax, a more equal tax upon the rent of houses [to begin] distributing the weight of it more equally upon the whole ...[4]

But he also asserted that the Aristocracy of Scotland was founded "in the natural and respectable distinctions of birth and fortune."[5]

Smith genuinely believed that democracy must come slowly through the gradual enlargement of the propertied classes and their concomitant achievement of the franchise.[6] Also Smith believed "the vast majority of mankind" are too exhausted, stupid and their range of political awareness too narrow to have much political understanding and they certainly should not be urged

---

1 Structure, p. 73.

2 Structure, p. 69.

3 Namier, England in the Age of the American Revolution, op.cit., p. 24. Also see Structure, pp. 69-73, esp. p. 69. "But it was at all times the first article of constitutional cant."

4 WN II, p. 470.

5 WN II, pp. 483-4.

6 WN II, pp. 483-4. Lectures, pp. 68-72.

to believe they had the political right to destroy the social peace by revolution.[1] Only those with property (or who are being deprived of it) have the knowledge, energy, time, wealth, interest, arms and a truly "just grievance" that entitles them to revolt. But though Smith believed the propertyless had less right than others to destroy the social fabric they must be granted political rights to protest and organise.[2] They must be given the vote, and be politically represented and have equal judicial procedure, in the same way as all other groups in the population.

Smith in his Lectures paraphrases Locke's entire description of the social contract theory of government in which the universal public joined to form government and yet retained certain rights to revolution. For example, Smith says

> Suppose that government is founded on contract, and that these powers are entrusted to persons who grossly abuse them, it is evident that resistance is lawful, because the original contract is now broken.[3]

And later again Smith enlarges this from a principle only of strict contractual governments to all governments.

---

1 WN I, p. 75. Such acts Smith describes as "desperate", "the folly and extravagance of desperate men."

2 Plumb, Four Georges, op.cit., p. 14. "No nation rioted more easily or more savagely from 1714-1830. Angry mobs, burning and looting, were as prevalent as disease, and as frequent in the countryside as in the great towns. Time and again the gentry were forced to assemble to put down rioting workmen by force."

3 Lectures, p. 68.

> Whatever be the principle of allegiance, a right of resistance must undoubtedly be lawful because no authority is altogether unlimited.1

And Smith, like Locke, makes the point that he means by this, not merely the unlimited single sovereign but any assembly such as Parliament that takes upon itself absolute, unjust, or even excessive power.

> The same degree of ill usage will justify resistance to a senate or body of men. It must be allowed that resistance is in some cases lawful, but its excessively difficult to say what an absolute sovereign may do or may not do, and there are different opinions concerning it. Mr. Locke says that when a sovereign raises taxes against the will of the people resistance is lawful, but there is no country besides England where the people have any vote in the matter. In France the King's edict is all that is necessary and even in Britain it is but a very figurative consent that we have, for the number of voters is nothing to that of the people. Exorbitant taxes no doubt justify resistance, for no people will allow the half of their property to be taken from them; ...1

Protection of property is again Smith's focal point for deciding a sovereign's legitimacy. This follows directly from his first presupposition that protection of property was the reason men created government initially.2 In addition to taxes which

---

1 Lectures, p. 69.

2 Lectures, pp. 1-9. WN II, pp. 232, 237. Ferguson, History, pp. 204-6, describes the unconsciousness of political consequences in social behaviour which is typical of the Scottish School's attitude to the conjectural origins of the state. "He who first said 'I will appropriate this field; I will leave it to my heirs', did not perceive that he was laying the foundation of civil laws and political establishments." p. 304.

alienate property from the citizen, Smith considers two other forms of property alienation by the State which many have thought to warrant revolution or the expulsion of the sovereign. These are, first, the confiscation of land or private holdings, or what amounts to the same thing the revaluing of the currency by "making all the sixpences, shillings" to pay off its debts. The justification given by the government for such acts Smith says is usually national emergency. During wars, lands belonging to rebels or emigres have been appropriated by the government. In times of severe national debt when, (as he shows in great detail), there is scant possiblity of legitimately paying off the nations creditors, the currency has been inflated in value. Although Smith criticises both practices, in time of national emergency they are legitimate confications of property and even in time of peace their enactment appears not to warrant or to cause revolution.1

The second form of the sovereign's alienation of the public's property which Smith appraises for its legitimacy or justification of revolution is the state's alienation or sale of its powers, offices, lands or holdings which the public have supposedly given him to administer for them, and in their benefit. Smith concludes:

---

1 Smith considers it fully reasonable that the state appropriate newly created lands such as occur from silting at the mouths of rivers, and appropriate all discovered treasure.

> Some writers allege that the king cannot alienate any part of his dominions.[1] This notion is founded on the principle of the original contract, by which indeed, though a people were willing to submit to one government, they will not have one of another's choosing. This doctrine is, however, groundless. In France and Spain great parts of the dominions have been given to the king's children as a portion without any complaint; when Florida was put into our hands, they never made any opposition. The King of Spain and the Czar of Moscovy can even alter the succession as they please. This was in general the case in all feudal jurisdictions, they were divisible at the pleasure of the lord.[2]

Yet for Smith there are ultimate limits to the sovereign's permissible permanent alienation of properties, rights or responsibilities from the citizens of the state. And once again Smith, like Locke, ultimately decided that a majority of the universal public must control government without quite specifying how or when a reform of the suffrage must, or would, take place.[3] In the case of James II, Smith, like Locke before him,

---

1 See Puffendorf, De Juri Natural and Contium, op.cit., and Grotius, De Juri Natural, op.cit., the two writers Smith cites and whom Locke cites on this same point. And Smith includes Hutcheson in these "writers" in his System of Moral Philosophy, Vol. II, pp. 297-299.

2 Lectures, pp. 69-70.

3 Smith was aware that the laws of franchise differed drastically between Scotland and England. He mentions leaseholders' disenfranchisement in Scotland in contrast to parts of England. E. and A. Porritt, Unreformed House, op.cit., Vol. I, pp. 22-23, and Namier, Structure, p. 75, make suffrage, in 80 a franchise restricted to freemen but 110 boroughs split their qualifications for franchise between those in the town "corporation", or who paid "Scot and lot", or to those who held certain houses or plots called "Burgages".

actually abandoned equivocation in deciding when deposition of a sovereign is justified, and concluded his removal was just. Smith says of James II, for instance:

> He, in return told them [the parliament] that he would never any more bring down his sentiments to theirs, nor consult them on any occasion. It was no wonder that by such practices the Revolution was brought about ...
>
> Thus King James, on account of his encroachments on the body politic, was with all justice and equity in the world opposed and rejected.[1]

That which distinguishes a just sovereign who has alienated some of his responsibilities and part of the nation's properties from an unjust or tyrannous sovereign who has usurped the properties, and rights of his subject is, Smith says, very difficult to determine. Yet Smith's "no people will allow the half of their property to be taken from them", is suggestive of the scale of massive injustice necessary to justify resistance or condemnation of a sovereign's alienation of property or rights through sale, confiscation or excessive taxes.

Smith repeatedly says the general public will submit to, and by his descriptions, are submitting to continual corruptions and injustices and alienations of their properties and rights.

> ... but though the highest propriety be not observed if they have any degree of moderation, people will not complain.[2]

Nevertheless, the degree of the sovereign's alienation of the

---

1 Lectures, pp. 71-72.

2 Lectures, p. 69.

individual's property whether life, liberty or estate remained the heart of Smith's political theory in the determination of the justice or tyranny of states. Following Locke, and more specifically Montesquieu, Smith outlined the ways in which the power and authority of the sovereign was checked by separate legislative, and judical bodies.1 Smith, though he outlined their separation and distinct functions, tended to agree with Locke that these authorities "though ... really distinct in themselves are hardly separated", and "are almost always united." The clearest example Smith provides of this same opinion is that of Parliament's consent to the king's new taxes which Smith called "a very figurative consent."2

According to Smith what then were the checks upon tyranny: whether tyranny of sovereign, Parliament, aristocratic landlords or merchants? He admitted that government in his time was riddled

---

1 Smith did believe there to be a certan inbred traditional character of legislative and executive as opposed to judicial institutions, which did give them a certain independence, more because of bureaucratic allegiance to separate traditions than from really distinct vital interests such as distinct forms of property possession or membership in different classes. For Smith the unitary class control of the three branches of government was based on their united interest in protecting their private property.

2 Lectures, p. 69. See Structure, op.cit., p. 73. "Taking England as a whole, probably not more than one in every twenty voters at every county election could freely exercise his statutory right." If we take Porritt's figure of 160,000 in the electorate among a population of 6 million which Ashton puts forward, then Namier's one freely exercised vote in twenty would mean that only 8,000 freely cast votes were declared for the entire population of 6 million.

with corruption. He also acknowledged that there was no legal or real political check upon those who ruled except sporadically. What made him consider the prevailing government just? Essentially, Smith believed fear of violence of insurrection was the only substantial check on the tyranny of these various organs of government. All other checks (such as the press) were either derivative in their force from this threat of popular revolution or violence, or they were imaginary and not substantial checks at all. The operation of this check by the popular force and the press were, Smith says, "irregular".

Thus, although Smith rejected the original social contract theory as an historic fact he did accept the social contract as an implicit principle of political rights[1] and a useful fiction, much as his teacher Hutcheson had. Smith in some respects took this implicit contract even further than either Hutcheson or Locke by devoting an entire chapter of his Lectures to "Contract Implied in Law". In this chapter he states that such implicit contracts could be either political or economic and were in some ways the most normal contracts in a commercial society. For example, he shows that workers like citizens are required by their circum-

---

1 Ernest Barker, Social Contract, op.cit., p. vi has remarked in terms that apply equally to Smith as to Hume. "Even if there had never been a contract, men actually behaved "as if" there had been such a thing; and behaving and acting in terms of quasi-contract - or what the lawyers call "contract implied in law", an idea which may be extended to cover the case of "contract implied in government" they made those terms of quasi-contract serve good and admirable purposes."

stances and for survival to accept implicit contracts (of employment or of political obedience) which are often forced upon them by those in higher social ranks. The poor are only liable to break these implicit contracts if forced by immediate necessity or long infringement by employer, sovereign or those in higher social ranks. When breaking these contracts at this ultimate stage, Smith suggests, the citizen and worker have a certain right and justice in their actions.[1]

Smith's interpretation of the implicit social contract appears drawn from commercial contracts of his day somewhat in the fashion that Locke's was drawn from the laws of equity and trust of his day.[2] Neither of such implicit contracts in commercial society is ordinarily revokable by individual citizens or workers, nor necessarily adhered to by representatives of government or employers.[3] Such implicit contracts, however, do persist in regulating most of the informal economic and political conflicts of interests.

---

1 Lectures, p. 69.

2 Barker, op.cit., p.xxvi has said that concerning Locke's social contract "Here in the conception of trust, Locke is drawing on the English law of equity." And Laslet in his introduction to Locke's Two Treatises has demonstrated that Locke drew his famous theory of property also from the law of his time: "In this paragraph Locke is typically, using the landlaw of his time and country to illustrate what was to him, a universal principle." See also Two Treatises, pp. 306-7 on Locke's discussion of "commons and enclosures".

3 The non-adherence to contracts by rulers and employers raises the difficult problem of alienable and inalienable rights and

In conclusion, Smith's political experience was with a Parliament controlled by an extremely corrupt landed aristocracy, and monopolising merchants, and this was reflected in his attacks upon government monopolies and the class control of politics. His attacks upon the vast corruption of his own existing government were not attacks upon all government. As Harold Laski has said, "the general context of his book required less emphasis upon the virtues of state-interference than upon its defects."[1]

Although a later chapter will examine in detail what Smith's objectives of government were, we can from this chapter summarise certain conclusions Smith made. He believed government was simultaneously a natural and a social creation. Although states were based on natural rights[2] their forms were the contrivances of ruling classes to control others. And thus the best government

---

properties which will be dealt with fully in the following two chapters. Suffice it for the moment to say that this alienation or "giving up" of the individual's rights to the sovereign or ruling class and of the workers' labour to the employer or class of property owners, because it is ordinarily unrevokable by the citizen or labourer, is a relatively permanent alienation. These alienated rights and alienated labours become permanent institutional possessions of central governments or ruling classes who control these institutions as their property to alienate in part or sometimes wholly to other persons, countries, other interests, corporations or to subsidiaries.

1 Laski, Political Thought in England From Locke to Bentham, op.cit., p. 302.

2 See Smith's discussion of political rights, Lectures, pp. 66-72 and Duncan Forbes, "Scientific Whiggism", op.cit., p. 653. Forbes contends that Smith believed "political rights stemmed from authority in early ages and from utility in modern times."

would attempt a contrived harmony of interests among sects, classes, individuals and in international arrangements.[1] Nevertheless, Smith was a firm believer in an enlargement of the franchise, and implies his belief in an eventual equality of political and judicial rights.[2] But because he was convinced of the need to continue some "distinction of ranks", to ensure the moral "emulation" of the qualities of excellence in the virtuous man, he muddled to some extent the question of the degree of economic and social equality to be sought through legislation. He never makes clear how strong was his political conviction for reform of Parliament on specific issues though his general approval is clear.

The following two chapters will attempt to indicate what was Smith's conception of future property and the policies he urged the state to adopt to achieve those future property relations. I will attempt to show that Smith envisaged a strong, active, reformed, and selectively interventionist state, not the inactive laissez-faire government he is often thought to have advocated. Furthermore it will be shown that this strong selectively interventionist state must persist in even the most distant future.

---

1 AR, pp. 718-19.

2 WN II, p. 98.

# CHAPTER IX

## FUTURE PROPERTY RELATIONS: PRESCRIPTIONS AND PROJECTIONS

The previous three chapters dealt with Smith's theory of how commercial property relations affected existing markets, individuals and governments. This chapter and the following one will concentrate on future property relations Smith expected and/or desired, and why, and how they would show that the end or goal of future property relations which he wished to achieve was the creation of virtuous and prudent men rather than maximisation of national or individual wealth. Virtuous and prudent individuals required material, moral, and educational standards of living (for the general populace) far in excess of those existing in Smith's time. These standards would be achieved through a relatively harmonious market with extensive freedom of trade for all forms of private property, though kept in check by an exact administration of impartial justice. According to this interpretation, the relatively harmonious market is the means, not the end of Smith's future property relations.

The actual future property relations Smith desired are contained in scattered prescriptions throughout the Wealth of Nations. Though certain aspects of Smith's policy proposals have been studied by Viner,[1] Robbins[2] and Samuels[3] in their works on Smith and the "classical theory of economic policy" their concern has not been with the actual form of future property relations Smith put forward. That is, they have dealt with future property only as an aspect of proposed government policy, and not primarily as a study of the end of goals Smith set forth for property itself. This end, therefore, will form the subject of this chapter. In order to study it, the future property relations he expected will be compared to those he desired. In the following chapter I will deal more specifically with Smith's future government policy proposals by which this end might be acheived.

I

Because Smith believed that labour generally within agriculture "does not admit of such subdivisions as manufactures"[4] this impossibility of separation prevents agriculture from improving equally with manufacturers.[5] Thus from this simple principle Smith concludes that agriculture is not to be promoted by discour-

---

1 Jacob Viner, "Adam Smith and Laissez-Faire", op. cit.

2 Lionel Robbins, Theory of Economic Policy in English Classical Political Economy, op. cit.

3 Waren J. Samuels, The Classical Theory of Economic Policy, op. cit.

4 WN, I, p. 9.

5 WN, I, p. 10.

aging manufacturers.[1] Nonetheless, he hoped in future that improvements in agriculture would accompany those in industry. He encouraged such improvements as the enclosure movement, the new forms of crop rotation, root and seed science, and the new breed of cattle, which had all improved agriculture,[2] and which he had witnessed in Scotland.[3]

Because of the natural fertility of the soil he did believe that the future of agriculture in North America[4] offered greater potential for improvement than in Great Britain. And Smith insisted that the future profits of agriculture in England and Scotland had been exaggerated by projectors and landlord Members of Parliament.[5]

Smith attacked the Corn Laws and those Members of Parliament who continued them.[6] And Smith, like Ricardo, asserted that the Corn Laws were harmful because the money price of corn regulates that of all other home-made commodities.[7] He insisted that agriculture is not really encouraged by the bounty on the expor-

---

1 WN, II, pp. 207-8.

2 WN, I, pp. 244, 384-5.

3 WN, I, p. 246.

4 WN, I, p. 247.

5 WN, I, p. 397.

6 WN, II, pp. 32-51.

7 WN, II, p. 14.

tation of corn. It is only the profit of the farmer not agriculture itself which is improved.[1] (For it neither raises the real price, nor employs a greater quantity of labourers with an equal quantity of corn.) Effectively, these Corn Laws merely lay a tax on the whole community which hurt the public more than they aid those who receive it.[2] Thus future property in land, agricultural produce, and profits depended very much on whether the Corn Laws were kept or repealed. Smith hoped and optimistically suggested they would be repealed because of their obviously harmful effects, not only on the economy generally, but because tillage was not really encouraged by them.[3] In the end, however, he merely sketched how a liberal system of free corn importation and exportation among nations would operate[4] and hoped the obvious need for them would be appreciated. If the "Corn Laws" persisted, Smith was as convinced as Ricardo that this would lead to "the stationary state." So long as the corn monopoly persisted Smith felt that control of corn prices by law was justified, most especially in time of famine, a bad harvest or general scarcity.

---

1 WN, II, p. 14.

2 WN, II, p. 15.

3 WN, II, pp. 12-14.

4 WN, II, p. 48.

Property in land and agriculture produce, Smith said, is preferable to that in manufactures[1] when they are considered on equal terms, because the wealth arising from them is more solid and durable than that which proceeds from commerce.[2] Agriculture was capable of absorbing considerably more capital than had been applied to it,[3] and would naturally benefit proportionally to that investment, though never to the extent of industry in manufactures. To encourage both good husbandry and profit, and a greater appreciation of land and agricultural produce, Smith urges that landlords ought to be encouraged to cultivate part of their own land.[4]

> It is of importance that the landlord should be encouraged to cultivate a part of his own land. His capital is generally greater than that of the tenant, and with less skill he can frequently raise a greater produce. The landlord can afford to try experiments, and is generally disposed to do so. His unsuccessful experiments occasion only a moderate loss to himself. His successful ones contribute to the improvement and better cultivation of the whole country.[5]

However, Smith thought it wise to urge landlords to cultivate only a part of their lands, not the whole of them, for:

---

1 WN, I, p. 403.

2 WN, I, p. 445.

3 WN, I, p. 397.

4 WN, II, p. 357.

5 WN, II, p. 357.

> If the landlords should, the greater part of of them, be tempted to farm the whole of their lands, the country (instead of sober and industrious tenants, who are bound by their own interest to cultivate as well as their capital and skill will allow them) would be filled with idle and profligate bailiffs, whose abusive management would soon degrade the cultivation, and reduce the annual produce of the land, to the diminution, not only of the revenue of their masters, but of the most important part of that of the whole society.[1]

The actual measures government should take to improve agriculture and the probable effect of tax incentives will be discussed in the following chapters. For the moment it is useful simply to summarise Smith's argument concerning future property in land and agricultural produce. Agriculture was less to be encouraged than industry[2] but was capable of progressive improvements with new advances of capital, scientific advances, and tax incentives. The improvements should be initiated by landlords cultivating part of their own land themselves. But long range productivity required that thrifty tenant farmers cultivate the bulk of the nation's

---

1 WN, II, p. 357.

2 O.H. Taylor's A History of Economic Thought, op. cit., asserts that Smith was quite similar in outlook to Thomas Jefferson in approving agriculture and its effect on men and disapproving of industry and its effect upon men. Taylor appears to go somewhat far in this judgement. Although Smith believed agriculture was better for workers and landowners than industry was for its owners or labourers, Smith nonetheless expected industrial growth to far outdistance agriculture and thus Britain's industry would be the source of greater cheapness and plenty than her farms. (In this belief Smith was not wholly correct yet it was his belief which inaugurated the prime maxim of several ages of economists that industry was the primary road to improvements, not agriculture.)

lands. Though he was in favour of a free market in land and produce he stipulated price control of corn and of certain lands by government in times of emergency, so long as landlords held a monopoly through corn laws and their control of Parliament.

We turn from Smith's proposals for future agriculture to his conception of future property in industrial manufactures. Manufacturing's great advantange over agriculture resulted from its capability of almost indefinite division of labour[1] for which he provides many examples.[2] Smith proposed that for this future society the most efficient and productive forms of manufacturing would be in towns, rather than in the countryside near the coal fields or remote rivers or lumber camps.[3] This was because optimal division of labour required that areas with a large work force replace geographical distribution or resources as the criterion of where factories would be situated.[4] Manufacturers will increase in towns because "the inhabitants of a town, being collected into one place, can easily combine together."[5] Division of labour will be more easily effected in these factories situated in towns, not only because of the greater numbers of

---

1 WN, I, p. 8.

2 WN, I, p. 15.

3 WN, I, p. 140, II, p. 404.

4 Smith analyses the reasons manufactures are usually situated near coal fields, WN, II, p. 404.

5 WN, I, p. 140.

people but because of the greater variety of skills the towns attract. Also the greater fortunes which have been amassed there in the past can help to maintain this high level of employment.

Among those cities and towns which would prosper most, the greatest progress would occur in those near coal fields, and then (with improved transport and its reduction in cost) in cities with harbours for foreign trade.[1] For, manufacturers are more influenced by the markets they sell to, (wherever they are) than by the resources or conditions in the place where the goods are made.[2] Therefore, England's many populous towns and cities along her extensive seacoast and harbours, Smith argued, ensured her a continuing future natural advantage for exporting her manufactures.

> England, on account of the natural fertility of the soil, of the great extent of the seacoast in proportion to that of the whole country, and of the many navigable rivers which run through it, and afford the conveniency of water carriage to some of the most inland parts of it, is perhaps as well fitted by nature as any large country in

---

1 This is because: first, manufactures are the principal source of foreign trade. (_WN_, II, p. 201.) And second, because manufactures require a more extensive market than agriculture. (_WN_, II, p. 203.) But, he says, _WN_, II, p. 404. "The price of fuel has so important an influence upon that of labour, that all over Great Britain manufactures have confined themselves principally to the coal countries; other parts of the country, on account of the high price of this necessary article, not being able to work so cheap. In some manufactures, besides, coal is a necessary instrument of trade; as in those of glass, iron, and other metals."

2 _WN_, I, pp. 94-5.

> Europe, to be the seat of foreign commerce, of manufactures for distant sale, and of all the improvements which these can occasion.1

In the new manufacturing cities there will be keener competition than at present among companies for resources and labour2 and this will force the increase in efficiency. Smith says "the efficiency of" the division of labour ... is most extensive in the countries which enjoy the highest degree of industry and improvement."3 Schumpeter concludes from Smith's remarks about the efficiency of the division of labour in industry that "Nobody either before or after A. Smith, ever thought of putting such a burden upon division of labour. With A. Smith it is practically the only factor in economic progress."4

Manufactures increased efficiency will result in a lowering of prices in efforts to remain competitive. In this progressive state of low competitive prices, manufactured articles will greatly increase5 and thus the total property produced by

---

1 WN, I, p. 442.

2 WN, I, p. 77. "When in any country the demand for those who live by wages; ... is continually increasing ... the scarcity of hands occasions a competition among masters who bid against one another, in order to get workmen, and this voluntarily breaks through the natural combination among masters not to raise wages."

3 WN, I, p. 9.

4 Schumpeter, op. cit., p. 187.

5 Smith takes for granted our knowledge of machines great productivity: WN, I, p. 13. "Everybody must be sensible how much labour is facilitated and abriged by the application of proper machinery. It is unnecessary to give any example. I shall only

future society will consist increasingly of factory goods. There will result not only a great increase in general consumer articles for the general public, but an increase in property in machines, stock, factories, warehouses, and capital supporting these increased manufactures.

Since the overall result of this increase in manufactures will be "cheapness and plenty" and will encourage all forms of consumption, this "great business"[1] of "poitical economy" will have been accomplished.

As Schumpeter has pointed out:

> Smith tries to show why, at least on the whole, the price - the real price - of agrarian products will rise in consequence of the Progress of Improvement and, in an additional digression that the real price of manufacturers will fall. In a sense, this foreshadows the nineteenth century doctrine of decreasing returns in agriculture and increasing returns in industry toward which he may be said to have cautiously felt his way and which might have been distilled from his pages.[2]

---

observe, therefore, that the invention of all those machines, by which labour is so much facilitated and abriged, seems to have been originally owing to the division of labour." And WN, I, p. 304, "In manufactures the same number of hands, assisted with the best machinery, will work up a much greater quantity of goods than with more imperfect instruments of trade." And finally Smith concludes: "It is upon this account that all such improvements in mechanics, as enable the same number of workmen to perform an equal quantity of work with cheaper and simpler machinery than had been usual before, are always regarded as advantageous to every society." WN, I, p. 304.

1 WN, II, p. 179, my emphasis.

2 Schumpeter, op. cit., p. 191.

It was Smith's faith in the division of labour and factory machine production which led him to believe future industry would produce cheapness and plenty and create optimistic conditions for the general public. While these optimistic conditions Smith desired were by no means guaranteed, according to his complex set of conceivable future circumstances, he is generally thought to have expected this progressive future state.

Smith repeatedly asserted that the progress of society and the improvement of men required the continual introduction of new machines into industry so that men would be free for other pursuits.

> The undertaker of some great manufactory who employs a thousand-a-year in the maintenance of his machinery, if he can reduce this expense to five hundred, will naturally employ the other five hundred in purchasing an additional number of workmen. The quantity of that work, therefore, which his machinery was useful only for performing, will naturally be augmented and with it all the advantage and conveniency which the society can derive from that work.[1]

Smith, unlike Ricardo and Marx, suggested that the initial effect of the introduction of machines was primarily beneficial to the labourer.[2] Yet, this point does not change the overriding

---

1 WN, I, p. 304, my emphasis.

2 WN, I, p. 304, Also see Smith's comments on the effects upon labourers from the introduction of machines into industry (BKTV). He compares these effects on the labour force with those arising from the recent disburesement of a large segment of the navy. In each case Smith suggests the unemployment problems are slight. WN, I, p. 492.

belief they all held that machine industry was essential for the progress of improvement and the betterment of man, in the long run.

II

We will now consider the condition of constituent forms of future property: including land, capital and labour.

Though future land might be created along the seacoast and mouth of rivers, Smith's principal concern was the advantages to be gained from the more productive use of existing lands: through enclosure, scientific fertilizer, root crops, and through new kinds of owners or users. This last was to Smith the most important, for, as shown earlier, until land could be freely sold, rented and mortgaged, it could not belong to those who would have the funds or interest to improve it.

Among his various theories of rent, analyzed in a previous chapter, Smith maintained a differential theory that is virtually identical to Ricardo's. Lands of greatest fertility would be used first. As a consequence of his partial statement of this theory, along with other conflicting theories of rent, it is impossible to say for certain what he believed future rents would be. Like Ricardo, Smith pondered over the vital effects of the "Corn Laws" on future corn prices, and, like Ricardo, he stressed their crucial effect on the prices in other industries. However, Smith, on the whole, seems as pessimistic as Ricardo concerning the continued increase in rents. Smith recognises that rent will increase directly or indirectly with every improvement in the circumstances of society,[1] and that it will probably continue to constitute a third part of the price of most kinds of goods.[2] Smith argues that with the repeal of the Corn Laws only one substantial danger for future prosperity will be removed. The basic tendency of rent to increase and to affect other industries will remain. But also, evidently he did not consider the repeal of the Corn Laws any more likely than Ricardo.

The increase in agricultural and manufactured produce Smith expected, was based on certain important assumptions about the continued employment of capital in these fields. Though some of this invested capital would be drawn initially from rent and wages, by far the greatest part would be from profits. It is thus important to clarify Smith's assertion that future factory production where the competition was keenest would have the lowest prices and the lowest profits, and yet the greatest creation of new capital. The reason for this was:

> In countries which are fast advancing to riches, the low rate of profit, may, in the price of many commodities, compensate the high wages of labour and enable those countries to sell as cheap as their less thriving neighbours, among whom the wages of labour may be lower.[3]

---

1 WN, I, p. 276.

2 WN, I, p. 56.

3 WN, I, p. 109.

This then is the progressive and most desired condition for future property in the form of capital. "Diminution of profit is the natural effect of its [trade's] prosperity, or of a greater stock being employed in it than before."[1] There was, for Smith, an important corollary to his belief that the progressive state of low profits produced the greatest capital, which was that he believed a high rate of profit everywhere destroys "thrift".[2] And great wealth tends universally to destroy virtuous and law abiding conduct. A further important corollary of his advocacy of low profit was that high profits tended to increase prices more than increased wages did.[3] Cheapness and plenty were the ends he set for political economy, since they produced both the greatest capital formation, and the tendency towards parsimony and morality.

The condition of labour in future society Smith considered in several different ways. Future rewards to labour, Smith insisted, should be "liberal".[4] He advanced this conclusion on both economic and moral grounds. Economically the low profits and prices of the competitive industries would tend to increase wages in the new manufacturing towns. Smith considered the circum-

---

1 WN, I, p. 102, my emphasis.

2 WN, II, p. 127.

3 WN, I, p. 109.

4 WN, I, p. 91.

stances which operated to raise wages,[1] and the extent to which wages were limited by the funds from which they arose,[2] and concluded that only in a progressive state of society would it be possible for wages to continue to increase over extensive periods of time. High wages, Smith insisted, benefited labourers and society whereas high profits did not.[3] "The liberal reward of labour, as it encourages the propagation, so it increases the industry of the common man."[4] Such rewards are more likely in the new trades and manufactures than the old trades or in agriculture.[5] Thus, with increasing new manufactures he optimistically predicted higher wages, (though as I have already stressed his wages theories, like his theories of rent, were numerous and often contradictory).

Smith's argument for "liberal" wages was based frequently on this effect on productivity.[6]

> A plentiful subsistence increases the bodily strength of the labourers, and the comfortable hope of bettering his condition, and of ending his days perhaps in ease and plenty, animates him to exert that strength to the utmost. Where

---

1 WN, I, p. 77.

2 WN, I, p. 77.

3 WN, I, p. 109.

4 WN, I, p. 91.

5 WN, I, pp. 128, 150.

6 WN, I, pp. 91, 88.

> wages are high, accordingly, we shall always find the workman more active, diligent, and expeditious, than where they are low; in England, for example, than in Scotland; in the neighbourhood of great towns, than in remote country places.[1]

Yet the ethical grounds for a "liberal" wage were never omitted by Smith from his discussions of possible future property relations.

> Is this improvement in the circumstances of the lower ranks of the people to be regarded as an advantage or as an inconveniency to the society? The answer seems at first sight abundantly plain. Servants, labourers and workmen of different kinds, make up the far greater part of every great political society. But what improves the circumstances of the greater part can never be regarded as an inconveniency to the whole. No society can surely be flourishing and happy, of which the far greater part of the members are poor and miserable. It is but equity, besides, that they who feed, clothe and lodge the whole body of the people, should have such a share of the produce of their own labour to be themselves tolerably well fed, clothed and lodged.[2]

Having described Smith's proposals for future agriculture, industry and for land, capital and labour, we must now consider the more general question of the goal he envisaged for future property. Did he simply advocate cheapness and plenty and the greatest increase in the material wealth of the nation, or did he propose some other more ultimate goal?

---

1 WN, I, p. 91.

2 WN, I, p. 88.

III

The various statements on future property relations presented by the members of the Scottish Historical School show a general preoccupation with improvement of men (intellectually, morally, and physically) as their desired goal of future market relations and of government policy.[1] They stressed that this goal should supersede the better known end of maximising national or individual wealth. In many ways these improvements of individuals and maximisation of wealth were correlative goals, and to achieve one was to promote the other. But on those issues where there was a conflict or a choice between opulence and human improvement these authors each chose the latter alternative. Consider their policies for training, diversions, defence, consumption and welfare.

The similar proposals of Ferguson, Millar and Smith advocating extensive subsidies for education to combat the dehumanising effects of the division of labour has already been discussed in an earlier chapter.[2] It forms the best example of the way in which each of them distinguished the enormous productive benefits of the division of labour from its erosion of individuals' mental,

---

1 Ferguson, History, p. 125. Millar, p. 175.

2 See chapter VII "Alienation of Property: Effect on Individuals", last 3 sections. And see WN, II, pp. 302-3 and Lectures, p. 255.

moral and physical capabilities and of the social fabric. For each of these authors many proposals for the future were the same: extensive education and "public diversions" such as exhibitions of art, drama, music and dance, subsidised by government funds; the introduction of mechanisation and new agricultural methods; and the creation of government inspection for factory conditions and introduction of legislation to prohibit certain kinds of child labour.[1] These proposals, while by no means original or especially unusual, were part of the Scottish School's advocacy of reform and welfare legislation and symptomatic of their priorities. Publicly subsidised training was the key to this aspect of general human improvement because otherwise with factory inspection and more machines the dehumanisation of the labouring public would continue.

A second important point of agreement between Smith, Ferguson and Millar was that "Defence is of much more importance than opulence." Ferguson, as the founder and guiding spirit behind the "Poker Club" which agitated for the Scottish Militia, and Millar as the promoter of political rights and liberties[2] took this general dictum at least as far as Smith, in his defence of "the Navigation Acts". Yet, in Smith, Ferguson and Millar we find government defence expenditure was advocated, not simply for

---

1 See Lectures, pp. 256-7. And see Edwin Cahnan, "Adam Smith's Lectures on Justice", Economic Journal (1896), p. 330.

2 Millar, Introduction.

national protection from foreign enemies, but more importantly for the promotion it gives to the mental, moral and physical courage among the general population who are called upon to learn and engage in defence activities. The promotion of the "martial virtues" is a goal, each of the Scottish School emphasise to develop "The courage of mind" even more than the courage of the body, and more than either of these to develop individuals' sense of social responsibility.[1] This was symptomatic of the general moral improvement in social and political affairs which they hoped to foster. They each express the desire of restoring the building force of social obligations, respect and the recognition, of mutual sympathy. These had been undermined by extreme division of labour, class antagonisms and political corruptions. Thus maximum national wealth without social cohesion also led to moral degradation of the population just as maximum individual wealth did.

It was primarily the Scottish School's advocacy of consumption rather than production as the proper end of the economy which distinguished its policies from the Mercantilists[2] and Physiocrats of the period. Members of these other schools of thought had set maximisation of national produce as a foremost goal without bothering, as Smith did, to indicate that:

> Consumption is the sole end and purpose of all production; and the interest of the producer

---

1 WN, II, pp. 306-8.

2 WN, II, pp. 179-180.

> ought to be attended to, only so far as it is necessary for promoting that of the consumer.1

Smith's advocacy of consumption rather than production as the goal of economic activity stressd the consumption by productive groups rather than non-productive ones. But nonetheless he advocated greater rewards to all kinds of labourers rather than to monopolists who might reinvest for greater productivity. The national policy which advocated continual increase in national productivity and neglected consumption was, Smith said, both absurd and unjust. It was typical of Mercantilist policy2 and in the long run led to both beggar your neighbour policies internationally, and internally within the country. Smith was unequivocally opposed to any fostering of producers' interests for this resulted in sectional privilege and corrupted the community as a whole.

In his desired society, what formed the ultimate goal which Smith sought? In primitive society, and in existing commercial society Smith had demonstrated that most men had not been able, or allowed by corrupt laws to achieve or use their full property or potential, because of first natural and later class domination.

> In a rude period a man had scarce the full property of his goods ...3

---

1 WN, II, pp. 179.

2 WN, II, pp. 179-180.

3 Lectures, p. 113.

He does not yet know how fully to use them, sell them or bequeath them. Smith implies that men are also denied their full property in present society. For example,

> The patrimony of a poor man lies in the strength and dexterity o f his hands; and to hinder him from employing this strength and dexterity in what manner he thinks proper without injury to his neighbour, is a plain violation of this most sacred property.[1]

How extensive did Smith consider such cases of violations of this most sacred property? If we include apprentices and some labourers generally among those whose property rights were denied or restricted this violation of rights might affect "the vast majority" of the population.[2] Of the many disenfranchised citizens and colonists Smith made the same assessment.[3] Thus this denial of property rights or restriction of their possession or use would seem to be an important theme in Smith's thought: For example Smith says,

> To prohibit a great people, however, from making all they can of every part of their own produce or from employing their stock and industry in the ways that they judge most advantageous to themselves, is a manifest violation of the most sacred rights of mankind.[4]

In the ultimate future, Smith appears to express the hope that

---

1 WN, I, p. 136.

2 WN, I, p. 136, II, p. 302.

3 WN, II, p. 95. Lectures, pp. 69-71.

4 WN, II, p. 95.

men would be able to achieve and use all their possessions: their total property or "lives, liberties, and estates." This would certainly seem to be an important part of Smith's goals for future society, if his famous normative argument can be accepted as a reflection of his own desires.1 It was in this sense of the individuals' achievement of their "full property", potential and natural rights that Smith seems to have hoped for general social improvement.

Several of Smith's interpreters have acknowledged that Smith believed in human improvement more than increased national wealth.2 As shown in an earlier chapter he argued that men's "desire of being what ought to be approved of", was men's strongest motivation. It was a more universal object of desire than greed for property or the lust for power. In fact, he implied that the desire for wealth and position, in part, stemmed

---

1 "Is this improvement in the circumstances of the lower ranks of the people to be regarded as an advantage or as an inconveniency to the society." WN, I, p. 88. "But what improves the circumstances of the greater part can never be regarded as an inconvenciency to the whole." Ibid., p. 88. "It is but equity, besides, that they who feed, clothe and lodge the whole society should be themselves tolerably well fed, clothed and lodged." "The property which every man has in his own labour, as it is the original foundation of all other property, so it is the most sacred and inviolable." WN, I, p. 136.

2 George Stigler, Five Lectures on Economic Problems (London, 1952), p. 4. "This desire for better men rather than larger national incomes was a main theme of the Classical economists." And see MacFie, The Individual and Society, op. cit., p. 520. And Small, op. cit., p. 80. And Dugald Stewart, "Account", p. liv.

from "a desire of being what ought to be approved of."[1]

Yet, simultaneously this desire for self-improvement morally was coupled with another universal drive:

> The comfortable hope of bettering his condition, and of ending his days perhaps in ease and plenty, animates him to exert that strength to the utmost.[2]

This drive appears to have been set in men by Nature, and he implies that it will certainly continue in the future to inspire men. As MacFie among other has noticed, Smith combined the desires for a future material, an educational, and a moral level of dignified human existence.

> More definitely, he believed in growth, in civilisation, though again he never analyses its different forms systematically. But, in a scattered way, we learn that he believed in growing wealth along with fair dealing and greater equality in rewards, and broadening civilisation through education.[3]

Material and moral requirements for future property combined in Smith's proposals in a variety of ways, as Mark Blaug has shown in "Welfare Indices in the Wealth of Nations"[4] and as J.M.A. Gee has shown in "Adam Smith's Social Welfare Function".[5] Smith

---

1 TMS, pp. 170-1, 236.

2 WN, I, p. 91.

3 MacFie, op. cit., p. 122.

4 Mark Blaug, "Welfare Indices in the Wealth of Nations", Southern Economic Journal, XXVI (1959), pp. 150-153.

5 WN, II, p. 399.

recognised that the "acceptable standard of each man's material possessions was steadily increasing throughout all the ages of man so that in his own time custom would not permit labourers "to work without a linen shirt." Smith was careful to define "necessities":

> Necessities [include] not only the commodities which are indispensibly necessary for the support of life, but whatever the custom of the country renders it indecent for creditable people, even of the lowest order, to be without.[1]

And again, in his statement of a subsistence minimum wage we can find another suggestion of his combining moral with material criterion. There is a natural wages limit:

> Below which it seems impossible to reduce, for any considerable time, the ordinary wage even of the lowest species of labour.[2]

This is the natural wage level which maintains the labourer and enables him "to bring up a family." According to this presumption wages may rise sensibly above this minimum rate and that for long periods. And this would occur, because of the great demand for labourers, a competition of masters who bid against one another in order to get workmen "and this voluntarily breaks through the natural combination of masters not to raise wages."[3] Yet Smith adds a curious corollary to his discussion of high wages in the progressive state, that suggests no ultimate conditions of satisfied property relations would ever be fully achieved.

---

1 WN, II, pp. 399.

2 WN, I, p. 76

3 WN, I, p. 77

> It deserves to be remarked, perhaps, that it is in the progressive state, while the society is advancing to the further acquisition, rather than when it has acquired its full complement or riches, that the condition of the labouring poor, of the great body of the people, seems to be the happiest and the most comfortable. It is hard in the stationary and miserable in the declining state. The progressive state is in reality the cheerful and the hearty state to all the different orders of society.[1]

Smith's ultimate society could have no static form; it must continue to evolve.

The physical and material level of progress called for by Smith required "cheapness and plenty", of the general public's commodities. The strength of Smith's adherence to this policy led Schumpeter to say: "A. Smith ... carried the cheapness-and-plenty doctrine to victory."[2] Smith meant by this "cheapness in terms of effort rather than in terms of money."[3] He explained the full meaning of this doctrine when he analysed the effect of the improved wages he was urging for the labourers:

> The liberal reward of labour, therefore, as it is the necessary effect, so it is the natural symptom of increasing national wealth.[4]

---

1 WN, I, pp. 90-1.

2 Schumpeter, op. cit., p. 235.

3 Schumpeter, ibid., p. 235.

4 WN, I, p. 82.

5 His population theory was sometimes misinterpreted as an advocacy of workers' poverty.

The influence and popularity of the earlier works of Mandeville and the later misinterpreted message of Malthus[1] proclaimed loudly the strength of the adherents to the contrary arguments - that vast general poverty for the many and vast luxury for the few were necessary for social cohesion and progress of the working classes themselves.

As shown in an earlier chapter Smith held conflicting views on equality. Smith admitted that some distinction of ranks was necessary not only for moral emulation but to give a spur to the economic progress of improvement. But he disagreed with the view that meagre wages and great inequality were socially beneficial or economically productive. On the contrary, he earnestly desired a greater degree of equality morally, legally, politically, and in economic and social relations. Beyond necessary property for survival Smith believed all men needed property which was simply "useful or agreeable". As MacFie has observed:

> Smith, we have noted, always went beyond "self-preservation"; we strive for the "conveniences" as well as the "necessaries" for the "agreeable" as well as the "useful".[2]

Again, Smith is here combining the material and moral standards of increased future wage levels men should strive for. As Stigler puts it:

---

1 His population theory was sometimes misinterpreted as an advocacy of workers' poverty.

2 MacFie, <u>op. cit.</u>, p. 128.

> The struggle of men for larger incomes was good because in the process they learned independence, self-reliance, self-discipline.[1]

The real point of this is that future high levels of wages which Smith advocated, were both materially and morally beneficial. Thus ultimately his proposals for future property could be justified by the extent to which they improved men, regardless of whether they quantitatively increased the nation's riches, or the individual's material possessions. According to Albion Small, Smith showed:

> The division of labour makes room for activities which have increasingly remote relations to the productive process, and sets free types of action which enrich life, whether or not they have a direct influence on the process of producing wealth.[2]

These minimum levels of material reward Smith described were less determined by market forces, physical needs of men or psychological drives within each man, than by moral standards of "dignity", which Smith believed ought to be established. The connections between this achievement of a morally dignified and a materially satisfactory level of rewards were Smith's implicit and explicit arguments for a just return for labour.

---

1 Stigler, op. cit., p. 9.

2 Small, op. cit., p. 86.

IV

Did Smith have a theory or only a desire for a "just return" for labour? Rudolf Kaulla in his book The Theory of the Just Price suggests that Smith did indeed have a theory of "just return".

> This average price was for Adam Smith the "natural" price: from the philosophic point of view, it corresponded to the idea of justice because it was deduced from the principles of natural law, while from the economic point of view it was the ideal because it assured all engaged in production through their labour, capital, or land, an ordinary or average gain.
>
> In practice, Adam Smith's "natural price" is identical with the justum pretium of Scholasticism. But its theoretic basis is entirely different, and there is a corresponding difference in the method prescribed for its attainment.[1]

Nevertheless, Kaulla concludes,

> Adam Smith regarded his book on the "Wealth of Nations" as a contribution to the philosophy of natural law. His whole theory of prices corresponding to the value of the object, and hence right and just, and the economic system by which he proposed to ensure the practical establishment of such prices, do really form an integral part of this philosophy.[2]

Schumpeter, Meek and others have argued that Smith's use of the labour theory of value was as an analytical tool for examining

---

1 Rudolf Kaulla, The Theory of the Just Price (London, 1940), p. 50.

2 Kaulla, ibid., p. 50.

economic reality and in that capacity it was quite separate from Smith's moral critique of labour's rights or wrongs.1 However, if we consider Smith's labour theory of value not "as a tool of analysis" but "as a profession of faith or as argument in social ethics",2 what do we find? First, both Schumpeter and Meek would agree that Smith's labour theory of value and his beliefs in labourer's just reward were associated conclusions drawn from his general "vision of the economic process".3

Smith's language suggests this. For instance, Smith's ethical argument for labourer's just reward is stated as follows:

> The produce of labour constitutes the natural recompense or wages of labour.4
>
> It is the labourer who raises the crop and the landowner, having appropriated the land, demands a share of it ... Profit makes a second deduction from the "produce of labour".5

Whereas, in virtually identical language we find Smith's description of the "original labour theory of value used for analytical purposes:

---

1 See Schumpeter, op. cit., p. 311. Meek, Studies in the Labour Theory of Value, op. cit., pp. 123-9.

2 Schumpeter, ibid., p. 311.

3 Meek, op. cit., p. 128. Schumpeter, ibid., p. 41.

4 WN, I, p. 72.

5 WN, I, p. 73.

> Labour was the first price, the original purchase-money that was paid for all things.1
>
> In the original state of things, which proceeds both the appropriation of land and the accumulation of stock, the whole produce of labour belongs to the labourer. He has neither landlord not master to share with him.2

A dispute has existed since the Wealth of Nations was first published as to whether this conception of labourer's rightful reward for his efforts held true only for those primitive times or held to some extent also in more advanced times as well.3 Paul Douglas argues that it sometimes did hold for modern society, whereas Schumpeter argues that it did not. The critical issue involved is stated by Paul Douglas in Adam Smith 1776-1926.

> A natural conclusion from such contentions as these [Smith's contentions that "the whole produce of labour belongs to the labourer"] would naturally seen to be that if labour produces

---

1 WN, I, p. 35.

2 WN, I, p. 72.

3 For example Paul Douglas, Adam Smith 1776-1926, op. cit., pp. 88-9 presents one side of this argument whereas Schumpeter, op. cit., p. 310, presents the other. Their two conflicting points of view are shown by the following extracts from their discussions. First Douglas: "It is sometimes said, as by Waslor, that the labour-cost theory was only intended for an explanation of value in a primitive society, and that Smith designed the labour-command theory as an explanation of how values were set in more advanced societies. This is only partially true. The labour-cost theory was applied to the primitive stage, but it was also applied at times to more modern communities as well." Whereas Schumpeter insisted, op. cit., p. 310, "But A. Smith limits this theory to "that early and rude state of society which precedes both the accumulation of stock and the appropriation of land."

> all value and if rent and interest are but deductions representing no concrete service, it should follow ethically that labour ought to receive all and that wages should be the only share in distribution.[1]

While Smith's exploitation theory of wages and rent together might point to the logic of Douglas's argument presented above, Smith's differential theory of rent, and his supply and demand theory of wages would point to a totally different conclusion.[2] Nevertheless Smith somehow left the impression that a man deserved to be rewarded in accordance with the amount of labour he expended. At times it seemed that he was justifying some profits and rent as wages of supervision, rather than fully justifying rent, and interest and profit as proper rewards themselves.

According to Smith's Theory of Moral Sentiments it was man's dignity or self respect that required that he receive his "just rewards". At least a minimum level of reward for his labour, is "what the dignity of his own character requires."

---

1 Douglas, Adam Smith 1776-1926, op. cit., p. 97.

2 The strength of Paul Douglas's case concerning Smith's use of labour-cost theory of value at times to describe existing society, rests on his exhaustive list of Smith's references for the two measures of value; labour-cost vs. labour-command. He shows that the labour-cost and the labour-command theories were frequently used on the same pages and even in the same sentences as one another. In addition he shows that they were frequently used in the same context as if they were equivalents. Note expecially, the simultaneous and/or proximate uses of these two theories on pages WN I, pp. 32-3, as cited by Douglas or WN I, pp. 34-6. "The real price ..." vs. "Its value to those who possess ..." In many cases Douglas notes Smith's phrases stating the first value theory is followed by "or what amounts to the same thing ..." which introduces the other theory of value.

> The kernel of the Lockean theory of property, with all its radical and equalitarian implications, was contained in the theory of value which Adam Smith bequeathed to the school of classical economists.1

Small,2, Douglas,3, and Schumpeter4 concur in this opinion. Schumpeter said for example of Smith's implication of labourer's unfair reward:

> It foreshadowed, in fact, all the exploitation and bargaining power theories of wages that the nineteenth century was to produce, and also suggested the idea that labour is 'residual claimant'.5

---

1 Schlatter, op. cit., p. 184. Schlatter repeats this at several points, esp. p. 182.

2 Small, op. cit., pp. 110, 111. Small for example states that Smith and Marx "seem to have held nearly identical views of labour as the ultimate measure of right to wealth. How shall we account for the evolution of the classical political economy and Marxian socialism from so nearly identical conceptions of the relations of labour to wealth." p. 110.

3 Douglas, op. cit., p. 77.

4 Schumpeter echoes Schlatter's comment exactly by saying: "There is plenty of this in the Wealth of Nations, much of it, inspired by Locke. "The produce of labour constitutes the natural recompense of wages of labour." Schumpeter, op. cit., pp. 310-11. Schumpeter again states of Smith's labour time theory of value, "No doubt is possible but that this passage is the root of Ricardo's and Marx's labour-quantity theories of value." Ibid., p. 310. And when Schumpeter is describing Marx's "preconceptions about the relations between capital and labour", he says: "A very likely source is the Wealth of Nations. A. Smith's ideas on the relative position of capital and labour were bound to appeal to him [Marx] especially as they linked up with a definition of rent and profits - as "deductions", from the produce of labour that is strongly suggestive of an exploitation theory." Ibid., p. 389. See also especially p. 268.

5 Schumpeter, ibid., p. 268-9. Schumpeter on p. 185 takes the attitude that Smith's advocacy of labourer's rights and criticisms of employers' wrongs were "all important parts of the show", along

Finally, Smith's moral attitude to labourer's rights led a number of economists and historians of economic thought to:

> Agree that the classical school, beginning with the assumption that labour was the creator of property was unable to construct an economic theory which was both consistent and did not lead to the conclusion that the man who profited without working was necessarily robbing the workman.1

The conclusion from the foregoing discussion of Smith's labour-cost theory, therefore, would seem to be that in future property relations, he seems to hope the rate of the labourer's reward would be determined, to a greater extent than in his own time, by the labour-cost theory of value.2 Furthermore, Smith seems to hope that labourers would be less completely dominated by masters and landlords in contracts and in general working

---

with his laissez-faire arguments and together: "His political principles and recipes themselves (including ideology - revealing value judgements) were no doubt what mattered most to himself and to his readers ..."

1 Schlatter, op.cit., p. 185.

2 WN I, p. 136. Labour "is the most sacred and inviolable" property. And WN I, p. 82. "Liberal reward of labour, therefore, as it is the necessary effect, so it is the natural symptom of increasing national wealth." And WN I, p. 88. "But what improves the circumstances of the greater part [of society] can never be regarded as an inconveniency to the whole." See also Small, op.cit., p. 133.

conditions.[1] Smith was arguing for an alteration of present property relations in terms of a moral, social, and political conception of how men and property ought to be.[2] As Stigler says,

> The argument is essentially that respect for private property is necessary to get men to work and save. The argument was not a dogmatic defence of the existing institutions of private property. Adam Smith stated that "the property which every man had in his own labour ... is the most sacred and inviolable," so the statutes requiring long apprenticeship were a violation of property rights.[3]

Smith was indeed arguing from the standpoint of someone seeking to uphold "the most sacred rights of mankind", of all kinds. It was because he considered many existing insititutions of private property were a "violation of property rights", that most strongly

---

1 WN I, pp. 72-76, esp. p. 74. The masters "force ... compliance with their terms. The masters, being fewer in number, can combine much more easily; and the law, besides, authorises, or at least does not prohibit their combinations, while it prohibits those of the workmen. We have no acts of Parliament against combining to lower the price of work; but many against combining to raise it. In all such disputes the masters can hold out much longer. A landlord, a farmer, a master manufacturer, or merchant, though they did not employ a single workman, could generally live a year or two upon the stocks which they have already acquired. Many workmen could not subsist a week, few could subsist a month, and scarce any a year without employment. In the long-run the workman may be as necessary to his master as his master is to him, but the necessity is not so immediate." Smith's desire was an end to discriminatory laws in favour of employers' combinations.

2 WN I, p. 136. WN II, p. 95. WN I, p. 88-9. Lectures, pp. 68-72.

3 Stigler, op.cit., p. 9.

allied Smith's ethical prescriptions for a "just return" and "equity" and a greater equality of advantages, with his practical policies for the market and government.

Although, as we have shown, Smith was in favour of greater future equality, or rights, advantages, and rewards, he nevertheless desired the continuance of material differentials between members of the same society. These differential rewards express a propensity in men to regard the dignity of a man's station or rank as being directly in line with his material possessions or reward.1 In his Theory of Moral Sentiments Smith, however, had described most luxurious wealth which men strived for, as "trinkets of frivolous utility." Yet, although the hope of luxury, to gain respect and happiness was "a great deception", it was nonetheless useful in providing men with a driving motivation for positive acts and communal assistance. Therefore, Smith argued that the differential of high and low material rewards, (and even more important the general distinction of ranks) should be kept, though with greater general equality and less corruption, oppression and injustice.

His general presupposition seems to be that the affluence of the lowest and meanest of society is and should be less than that of the most respected member. At times Smith appears to echo exactly his great master Hutcheson's assertion that:

---

1 See ch. 4. "Property in Smith's System of Moral Philosophy."

> The value of commodities is raised by the dignity of station ... and the dignity and expense of their stations must be supported by the higher price of their goods and services.1

Smith frequently appears in agreement with this relation of dignity to affluence. Yet, Smith's emphasis demonstrates his careful delineation of his own position from that of Hutcheson. For instance, even in such similar passages to Hutcheson's as Smith's following one, we find it is "rank" not "affluence" which Smith felt was most important for social dignity.

> We trust our health to the physician; our fortune, and sometimes our life and reputation, to the lawyer and attorney. Such confidence could not safely be reposed in people of a very mean or low condition. Their reward must be such, therefore, as may give them that rank in the society which so important a trust requires.2

However, Douglas has examined this relation of "Stations" to Property in Smith's work and notes that although:

> Smith implies that people would not patronize professional men who did not live upon a standard considerably above that of the rest of the community.3

Nevertheless:

> Smith believed ... that in those occupations which had the great prizes, the average rate of remuneration was lower than in others.4

---

1 System, Vol. II, p. 55.

2 WN I, p. 118. My emphasis.

3 Douglas, op.cit., p. 84.

4 Douglas, ibid., p. 84.

Hence men's reason for entering these professions was the "dignity" that these "great prizes" or "honourable professions" accorded their members.1 Smith also reminds us of those honourable occupations which men accept and perform with little or no material reward; and in this category he includes posts from the crown's ministers, and judges to the lowest magistrates or public functionary.2 Differential rewards for those persons of greater dignity were therefore responsible for the inequality of material rewards during any particular age and the historical rise in material standards of living as men strove to achieve dignified conditions. These two aspects of dignity were intimately related to each other because in any primitive age those material rewards which men of dignity received in partial compensation for their study and effort became the rewards which all other members of the society would themselves seek and in a future age would gradually obtain in accordance with the "progress of improvement."

Thus in the final analysis we find that Smith did believe that those who deserved great respect usually would be in future, and should be, rewarded more highly than the "lowest and most despised member". But the difference in reward, in the future,

---

1 WN I, p. 119. Smith makes this clear in the case of lawyers: "How extravagant soever the fees of counsellors at law may sometimes appear, their real retribution is never equal to [their exertions in learning and practising this trade]."

2 WN I, p. 112. "Honour is a great part of the reward of all honourable professions."

Smith thought, ought to be limited by several explicit criteria. First, "a subsistence wage minimum."[1] Second, a level of material rewards "consistent with common humanity".[2] Third, a level of general abundant industrial productivity such that would "give the labourers an advantage, and enable them to raise their wages considerably above this rate; evidently the lowest which is consistent with common humanity."

V

Some of the future property developments Smith desired differed from those which he expected to occur. His works never presented a systematic analysis of these differing projections and prescriptions. Nor did he ever attempt to resolve the different futures towards which they pointed.[3] These alternative futures present major problems for interpreting his thoughts which have been touched on already. For example, Smith's conflicting theories of wages and rent, and to a lesser extent profit, project very different future property relations from each other. His

---

1 WN I, p. 76. "At least sufficient to maintain him." Se also Small, op.cit., p. 133. "The beginnings of the classical subsistence minimum theory of wages, as contained in ch. VIII of the Wealth of Nations."

2 WN II, pp. 399-400 and see Small, ibid., p. 77.

3 Viner, "ASLF", pp. 214-5. Viner has analysed several of these discrepancies between his desired harmony of social interests and expectations of conflict in self interests of various groups, classes and individuals.

exploitation theory of rent, profit, and wages if considered together might suggest a pessimistic future whereas his supply and demand theory of wages and productive increments theory of profits would suggest a more optimistic future. But more important, Smith recognised the possibly disastrous consequences of population explosions,[1] prolonged famines[2] and inept and corrupt governments,[3] and the independent influences these might exert over future property relations.

In general he was sure there would never be an entirely free market in Britain, or internationally. It was utopian to hope for one.[4] Furthermore he never believed individuals would be fully conscious of and act in accordance with their true self interest, although government must help them strive towards that end. He expected indifferent landlords, and the collusions of merchants always to make it impossible to remove all influence of propertied interests from the acts and departments of government and from the personnel who make and administrate law.[5] Thus he hoped, but

---

1 Smith went a long way towards enunciating the population argument that Malthus was to make famous. See, WN I, pp. 89, 82, 163.

2 WN I, p. 82, WN II, pp. 32-33.

3 WN II, p. 33, pp. 478, 490.

4 WN I, p. 519.

5 WN I, p. 519. "The mean rapacity, the monopolistic spirit of merchants and manufacturers ... thought it cannot perhaps be corrected." And WN I, p. 493 and WN I, p. 519. "The violence and injustice of the rulers of mankind is an ancient evil, for which,

was not fully sure, the corn laws would be repealed because of the harm they could wreak on the entire society; though he expected the landlords who controlled Parliament to fight to the end to defend their property priveleges.

Finally, to some extent, Smith, like Malthus and Ricardo, believed the labouring population increased in relation to their subsistence and hence would perhaps be incapable of substantial improvements in their welfare.1 Nevertheless, though he suggested all these pessimistic possibilities for the future his general prognostications are justly considered optimistic.

In this chapter I have attempted to analyse what Smith felt future property would be and should be. He expected a greater advance in industry than in agriculture; in cities than in rural areas with great resources. He expected the progressive state of rising wages ad decreasing profits to continue. Yet regardless of the removal of the Corn Laws he expected rents continually to

---

I am afraid, the nature of human affairs can scarce admit of a remedy."

1 WN I, p. 89. "Every species of animals naturally multiplies in proportion to the means of subsistence, and no species can ever multiply beyond it. But in civilised society it is only among inferior ranks of people that the scantiness of subsistence can set limits to the further multiplication of the human species; and it can do so in no other way than by destroying a great part of the children which their fruitful marriages produce."

"The liberal reward of labour, by enabling them to provide better for their children, and consequently to bring up a greater number, naturally tends to widen and extend those limits. It deserves to be remarked that it necessarily does this as nearly as possible in the proportion which the demand for labour requires."

rise, and with them some prices as well, especially of agricultural produce. In general Smith expected wages to rise. But he also believed that for healthy social relations labourers required a reasonable prosperity and a just return for their efforts regardless of what level of wages the future market might provide for them.

Smith desired a progressive society with steadily advancing conditions of the economy. He desired low but reasonable prices, profits and rents, and a moderate fixed rate of interest. Although he recognised that the general rate of wages must be determined by the conditions of the market, he desired a "liberal" wage both to provide incentive and to ensure social stability. All of these together he hoped would make possible an increasing equality of advantages and cheapness and plenty in all necessary, useful and agreeable commodities. Finally these future property relations he desired were but a means to the moral, sensual, intellectual, and physical betterment of individuals.

Smith believed that economics was not only pedagogically subsidiary to the general field of "moral philosophy", but wealth was subsidiary to, and primarily necessary for the improvement of individual's moral sentiments, self-reliance, and self-discipline.

The following chapter on the objectives of government which Smith advocated, will attempt to discover what policies he desired for the achievement of these future property relations I have summarised in this chapter.

# CHAPTER X

## THE OBJECTIVES OF GOVERNMENT

This chapter is divided into two parts: the first deals with Smith's proposals of government policies for different kinds of property; the second examines the political goals he prescribed for the future state. I intend to show that Smith believed the future state should in certain ways be activist, not laissez-faire: that he prescribed some form of government activity into most areas of private property: and he prohibited government no activity if it could be shown to benefit public welfare. And because of Smith's view of the natural propensities of individuals and classes to self interest, the state, even in the most distant future, would have to be in certain ways activist and selectively interventionist. Moreover, Smith believed that government, not the free market, was the social force capable of creating moral improvement in corrupt property relations and corrupt individuals. Thus in certain of his references laissez-faire seems a utopian dream of Smith's, not a practical systematic policy which he expected to be fully enacted. Laissez-faire was by no means a general policy that can be drawn from Smith's various particular policies for future government action.

### I

In 1926, the 150th anniversary of the Wealth of Nations was celebrated by many articles and a renewed interest in the reassessment of Smith. At the University of Chicago in a series of lectures, two papers especially analysed Smith's political thought. The foremost assessment of Smith's philosophy and goal of government was by G. R. Morrow in "Adam Smith: Moralist and Philosopher."1

Morrow suggested that the primary end of government for Smith was the promotion of individuals' moral improvement and general welfare. The other paper, by Jacob Viner entitled "Adam Smith and Laissez Faire", remains the best and most comprehensive examination of Smith's policy prescriptions for future government. Viner sought to qualify Smith's reputation for exclusively "laissez-faire" government policies.

In the years after these reinterpretations of Smith's belief in laissez-faire and in a government whose end was supposedly materialistic these aspects of Smith's politics were neglected. There were articles published such as C. A. Cooke's on "Adam Smith and Jurisprudence,"2 which re-examined the well known subordinate relation of Smith's political economy to the larger field of "Jurisprudence." And following this there were other articles such as W. C. Dunne's on "Adam Smith and Edmund Burke Complementary Contemporaries"3 that looked at Smith's political policies in their historical context and sketched Smith's similar

---

1 Glen R. Morrow "Adam Smith: Moralist and Philosopher" op.cit., pp. 321-343.

2 C. A. Cooke. "Adam Smith and Jurisprudence" Law Quarterly Review LI (1935) pp. 326-332.

3 W. C. Dunne, "Adam Smith and Edmund Burke' Complementary Contemporaries" Southern Economic Journal, VII, (1941) 330-346.

views to those of his contemporaries. But it was not until the 1950's that two books really took up the strands from Viner's and Morrow's articles. The first was Lionel Robbins' The Theory of Economic Policy in the English Classical Political Economy which attempted to prove the existence of a single "Classical Theory of Policy" for which Smith's Wealth of Nations was the first comprehensive exposition. Robbins' implicit method was to compare Viner's reinterpretation of Smith's policies with the policies of Smith's successors. This book sparked considerable controversy about whether there was or was not any such single classical policy (however defined), and who did and who did not propound it.1 The other book implicitly attacked G. R. Morrow's view that the goal of government and individuals was moral improvement. This book, Polity and Economy, by Joseph Cropsey, attempted to prove that the goal of human activity throughout Smith's works was self preservation and self interest. Except for one or two

---

1 There is considerable disagreement as to whether there was any clear, consistent, or comprehensive "classical policy". Whether this classical theory of policy is interpreted in Lord Robbins' sense as "The agenda or non-agenda of the state" or in Elie Halevy's more generalised rule of thumb, as the classical "message of individualism," there are a number of critics including Bitterman op.cit., pp. 717-8 who argue that Smith's system "contained no implications of specific standards or policies." Frank H. Knight, in his "Theory of Economic Policy and the History of Doctrine" Ethics Vol. 63 p. 287 has concluded that the classical economists did not really have a theory of policy at all. See also Warren J. Samuels The Classical Theory of Economic Policy op.cit., p. 211. S. G. Checkland "The Prescriptions of the Classical Economists" Economica Vol. 20 (1953) and W. D. Grampp in "The Politics of the Classical Economists" in his Economic Policy. op.cit. for other views.

passages Cropsey asserted that Smith believed in minimal government whose single goal should be to permit maximum self interest to its citizens in their free market interactions.

This chapter is an attempt to relate Smith's practical policies to his ultimate ends of government. Instead of beginning with his general goals and prescriptions for the proper scope of government I will begin with his range of policies. Only after we have fully examined Smith's comprehensive proposals for state acts, institutions and influence, can we appraise justly the meaning of his famous generalisation that,

> According to the system of natural liberty, the sovereign has only three duties to attend to: three duties of great importance, indeed, but plain and intelligible to common understandings; first, the duty of protecting the society from the violence and invasion of other independent societies; secondly, the duty of protecting, as far as possible, every member of the society from the injustice of oppression of every other member of it, or the duty of establishing an exact administration of justice; and, thirdly, the duty of erecting and maintaining certain public works and certain public institutions, which it can never be for the interest of any individual, or small number of individuals, to erect and maintain; because the profit could never repay the expense to any individual or small number of individuals, though it may frequently do much more than repay it to a great society.[1]

This list of government activities included far more tasks, (by Smith's definition of them), than would at first appear warranted by such a restricted view of government. Nevertheless, we also

---

1 WN II, pp. 208-9.

find that Smith by no means adhered rigidly or even loosely to this famous generalisation when actually confronted with areas of the economy, or of social conflict, or social improvement which he wished government to regulate or influence. Many authors including Viner and Macfie have mentioned both these points.1

Of government's "duty of protecting, as far as possible, every member of the society from the injustice or oppression of every other member of it,"2 Viner has said, "if broadly interpreted, would assign to government the task of a major reconstruction of the economic order, since Smith, as has been shown, recited many phases of it in which injustice and oppression prevailed."3

Putting aside for the present the question of the scope of future government action, we may begin by asserting that Smith unquestionably believed some form of future government intervention in the market would be necessary. It should be for the public benefit and so the expenses of that government should be paid for by the public.

---

1 Viner, "AS and LF" pp. 223, 227-8 Macfie Individual and Society op.cit., p. 131 Albion Small, Adam Smith and Modern Sociology. op.cit., p. 215.

2 WN II, pp. 208-9.

3 Viner, "AS and LF", p. 223.

Some Government intervention would consist of tax and other interventions would be paid for by tax.1 Thus tax is central to Smith's interventions of government into the market. Smith set four maxims for taxation. Taxes should be: (1) proportionally equal to income; (2) clear and certain; (3) exacted at convenient times; (4) minimally disruptive of the economy.2 These four maxims of taxation we shall find are indicative of Smith's aims of future government policies in general.3

Smith advocates some form of government policy, whether of control, intervention, supervision or influence, in every area of property: in agriculture, industry, in movables and immovables,

---

1 Adam Smith was neither an advocate of "all tax" nor of "all debt". The controversy over this issue is essentially as follows. Smith usually tended to prefer tax to debt or sinking funds because taxes paid off expenses quickly, efficiently and cheaply. Smith recognised that heavy debts must be incurred at the beginning of wars and so in some instances he admitted the need for extraordinary National Debts. However his criticism was that many such debts were contracted one after the other at the outset or even before a war, and these heavy debts could never be repaid in time of peace except by destroying the value of the currency by "making all the sixpences, shillings." Robert Walpole's Sinking Fund arrangements for permanent National Debt repayments met with Smith's approval largely because Walpole 'Kept out of war.' See J. Shield Nicholson "Economics of Imperialism" Economic Journal XX (1910) pp. 155-171, and "Adam Smith on Public Debts." Economic Journal XXX (1921) pp. 1-12.

2 WN XX. pp. 350-1.

3 See Nathan Rosenberg, "Some Institutional Aspects of the Wealth of Nations" Journal of Political Economy, Vol. 68 (1960) pp. 557-70. On the aims of state compulsion Rosenberg makes a strong argument for seeing the entire Wealth of Nations as a proposal for exact aims for institutions, rather than as an argument for "Laissez Faire". See also Charles Ryle Fay, "Adam Smith and the Dynamic State" Economic Journal XL (1930) pp. 24-34.

in rent, profit, and wages, and more specifically in capital, interest, land, and even the price of corn.

II

Smith advocated a land plan for control of long range usage and social productivity.

> Such a system of administration might ... serve to introduce into the common management of land such a plan or policy, as might contribute a good deal to the general improvement and good cultivation of the country.[1]

This administrative plan was to be enforced by tax incentives and disincentives to make landlords and farmers comply.[2] He urged the government to remove primogeniture and entail which restricted private ownership of land so that the public generally be given a chance of buying and improving the nations lands. The aim of this land plan, suggested taxes, and reform of entails was not only maximum productivity, but to ensure maximum public consumption and to spread the ownership and cultivation of land to these small-holders who would improve it and develop it as a productive industry rather than as a unit of ownership for social status and meagre revenues. If the existing landowners' monopoly in land and corn continued because of their control over Parliament, then Smith was in favour of government control of corn

---

1 WN II, pp. 357-8.

2 WN II, pp. 357-60.

prices, bread prices and some land prices,[1] for as long as the monopoly continued, especially in times of general scarcity.[2] Smith did not say how the same landowners who controlled Parliament sufficiently to keep the corn laws that prohibited foreign imports, could be directed to control corn prices against themselves. He does say that the self interest of the corn dealers which led them to export grain in time of internal famine to keep prices high, must be stopped.[3] Smith then goes on to outline how a liberal system of free exportation and importation of grain among all nations would operate.[4] The advantages of Smith's land plan would act in concert with this free trade in corn to encourage improvements and productivity and would tie the interests of the sovereign to improvements in land as well as the landlords. This plan Smith argues would be largely self regulating once in operation: and would "readily suit itself to the actual situation of things, and would be equally just and equitable in all these different changes." Smith was in favour of a general land tax with proportional relief for the improvers. He was emphatically against a corn tax, or fixed production tax or

---

1 WN II, p. 159. See also Viner, "ASLF" p. 224 for evaluation.

2 WN II, pp. 47-8.

3 WN II, p. 47.

4 WN II, pp. 47-52.

any tax that discourages improvements and productivity.[1] His general "unalterable" land tax must also be accompanied by a complete reassessment of all the rateable values of land which had not changed since their original assessment.[2] The abolition of corn laws, entails, primogeniture, and tithes,[3] he recommended because of not only their unproductive character, but their very unequal effect on different classes of the public. And in all these proposals for government plans, reforms, and influence in private agricultural property whether land or produce, we find the same justification used by Smith. Such government influence in agricultural property "would be equally just and equable" and provide maximum productivity. Smith recommended two further government acts to ensure the success of his Land plan: compulsory registration of all mortgages[4] and laws such as those in the colonies which prohibited agricultural progress by checking the engrossing of land.[5]

Smith urged the sale of crown land to those small-holders who would improve it productively. This too was an effort to place more lands and agricultural produce in public hands. Yet it is

---

1 WN II pp. 35-9.

2 WN II p. 377.

3 WN II p. 362-4.

4 WN II pp. 391-2. Viner, "ASLF", pp. 227-8.

5 WN II pp. 83-4.

the inefficiency and lack of public benefits in either produce or revenues, that Smith complains of with the crown lands,1 not that this land is held by the state. If the State was an efficient forester or farmer (as was the case in certain states in Germany at this time, but with which Smith was not familiar) there is every indication that Smith was perfectly prepared, as Jacob Viner has argued, to welcome government control of certain lands.2 In all cases of extensive new lands created in the marshes, along rivers, or along sea coastline, Smith was in favour of the existing practice of government control of the sale or ownership of these lands rather than automatic appropriation by those whose lands bordered these new acquisitions.3 He was most thoroughly in favour of the retention of crown lands for public parks and recreation centres.4 Thus in these cases of public lands, as in the case of private lands, Smith adhered to the same principal of maximum public benefit, rather that retention of private holdings, when deciding government policy.

---

1 WN II p. 349.

2 Viner "ASLF" pp. 226-7.

3 Lectures pp. 107-127.

4 WN II p. 349.

III

Smith's future government policy for manufacturing industry[1] like that for agriculture, suggests a coordinated plan of state measures for improvement. Unlike agriculture where preferential encouragements "really and in the end discourage their own favourite species of industry," in manufacturers such preference does at least "promote" factories and produce.[2] A free market in which capital could move to whichever industry or area was profitable, would usually be more advantageous than any special government encouragements, yet Smith made it clear that it was wiser for government encouragements, yet Smith made it clear that it was wiser for government to err on the side of preferences for manufactures than for agriculture. Since according to Smith it was utopian to hope for an absolutely free market this suggestion of a policy preference for manufactures over agriculture provides a guideline for assessing his more detailed prescriptions for government acts.

Smith's proposals for free trade applied especially to manufactures because they constituted the principal support of

---

1 In previous chapters I have already touched on Smith's suggestions for government intervention in various aspects of industry and specifically the altering of present corrupt government military contracts, monopolies, bounties, tariffs, and import prohibitions.

2 WN II p. 208.

foreign trade[1] and they required a more extensive market than agricultural goods.[2] In countless cases Smith put the argument for abolishing the existing government preferences, monopolies, bounties, tariffs and import and export prohibitions especially with regard to manufactures.[3] However, Smith's argument regarding government control regulation and influence on manufacturing industry was far more extensive and more subtle than the familiar laissez-faire doctrine might lead us to believe. For example, manufacturers' overwhelming dependence on coal led Smith in the interest of promoting equality to say[4] "If a bounty could in any case be reasonable, it might perhaps be so upon the transportation of coals from these parts of the country in which they abound to these in which they are wanted." And Smith favoured a moderate tax on foreign manufactures which would permit domestic workmen "a considerable advantage in the home market."[5] Far from believing the effects of free trade were universally

---

1 I have already mentioned his criticism of the restrictions upon Irish and Colonial American manufactures and trade of their manufactures. Such attacks are typical of his general view of removing British manufacturing restrictions and prohibitions on their exports and imports. WN II 201

2 WN II p. 203.

3 WN II pp. 413-414.

4 WN II p. 404.

5 WN II p. 413-414. "It is scarce possible to devise a tax which could produce any considerable revenue to the sovereign, and at the same time occasion so little inconvenience to anybody." WN II p 172

beneficial, Smith considered the cases of those manufacturing industries which would suffer as a result of free trade:

> The silk, perhaps is the manufacture which would suffer the most by this freedom of trade, and after it the linen, though the latter much less than the former.1

Most manufactures such as tanned leather, and hardware "are annually exported to other European countries without any bounty," and hence neither needed, nor were likely to get, much government assistance. But Smith advised a tax on wool for both revenue and to provide an advantage for British manufacturers.2 So we are led to the conclusion that Smith's advocacy of free trade for most manufactures was based on its moral superiority over restraint, but largely on its practical benefits to some industries and relatively slight suffering to others. Yet where it did harm some industries _considerably_ these manufactures were still to be protected by some Government aid.

Smith recognised the benefit to some manufactures of some prohibitions and regulation of imports:

> By means of such regulations [restraint upon particular imports] a particular manufacture may sometimes be acquired sooner than it could have been otherwise, and after a certain time may be

---

1 _WN_ I p. 492 "It is scarce possible to devise a tax which could produce any considerable revenue to the sovereign, and at the same time occasion so little inconvenience to anybody." WN II p 172

2 _WN_ II p. 172.

> made at home as cheap or cheaper than in the foreign country.[1]

However he went on to stress that "It will by no means follow that the sum total of [the society's] industry or its revenue can ever be augmented by such regulation."[2]

Nevertheless, in all new manufactures Smith was prepared to grant temporary monopolies in the form of patents,[3] and copyrights. Smith was even prepared in the case of new manufacturing and trading companies to grant monopolies abroad:

> When a company of merchants undertake, at their own risk and expense, to establish a new trade with some remote and barbarous nation, it may not be unreasonable to incorporate them into a joint stock company, and to grant them, in case of their success, a monopoly for a certain number of years. It is the easiest and most natural way in which the state can recompense them for hazarding a dangerous and expensive experiment, of which the public is afterwards to reap the benefit.[4]

And in addition to these special cases of his justification for manufacturers' monopolies, patents, or other priveleges, Smith was adamant that humanity required that those cases where free trade was to be enforced on companies and individuals it should be "only by slow gradations, and with a good deal of reserve and

---

1 WN I p. 479.

2 WN I p. 479.

3 WN II p. 278.

4 WN II p. 277-8.

circumspection." His over-riding concern was to avoid the flooding of the home market with cheaper foreign goods "as to deprive all at once many thousands of our people of their ordinary employment and means of subsistence." Thus, though Smith was certainly in favour of introducing more freedom of trade, especially into manufacturing industries, he recognised that it was not a universal blessing, and sought through government aid to ameliorate some of its distributed sufferings.

While it is true that Smith sought few areas for government manufactures or government monopolies or state companies, the broad description of public works he gave, we shall find, by no means ruled out future government corporations. He seems only to have retained the stipulation that in them government must make a net revenue surplus, just as would a private company. He sanctioned the government management of the post office if it could be done with financial success. Smith never seems to have even considered private manufacture of coins or paper currency, and we are left with the interesting conclusion of Jacob Viner that:

> He in general disapproves of government ventures into business, but solely on the ground that the government is a poor trader and a poor manager ...
> The modern advocate of laissez-faire who objects to government participation in business on the ground that it is an encroachment upon a field reserved by nature for private enterprise cannot find support for this argument in the Wealth of Nations.[1]

---

1 Viner, "ASLF" pp. 226-7.

The greatest commercial enterprise of Smith's time was supplying government. The production, storage and transport of supplies for the army and navy engaged more labour and capital than any other industry. And that enterprise which the state so financed, it also regulated, inspected and partially controlled. Smith recognised the vast influence of government military contracts on the whole range of agriculture and manufacture from sheep to guns. And he implied that this vast government influence on the market must continue. He considered the Navigation Acts which perpetuated these various contracts for military stores and manufactures and trade to be "perhaps, the wisest of all the commercial regulations of England."[1] Thus, although he wished for the removal of the corruption, bribery, and many of the extensive monopolies among the manufacturers thriving on government military contracts, he was by no means advocating that the government leave the market free from the extraordinarily important influence of military contracts.[2] In addition to military restrictions upon foreign produce and foreign shipping, Smith supported bounties on manufactures necessary for defence, which would not otherwise be produced at home.[3]

---

1 _WN_ I p. 487.

2 Namier _Structure_ pp. 20, 234.

3 _WN_ II p. 28.

Defence expenditure, and navigation acts and other laws for national defence, do not lead to the greatest commercial opulence or freedom of trade. However, Smith emphatically stated the order of his priorities when he concluded that "defence, however, is of much more importance than opulence."

Therefore the general government policy Smith advocated with regard to manufactures was by no means simply the famous laissez faire doctrine. In the case of the new manufactures, patents, or extremely necessary goods for defence Smith was fully prepared to continue or to create monopolies, bounties, and other protectionist arrangements.

IV

Smith recommended various forms of direct government regulation of manufacturing industries, and other more indirect and remote forms of government influence on them. The direct government controls were exemplified by the formal charter. The registration of a company with the government, strictly limited the special priveleges which were to be granted and renewed by the state. As Viner says:

> The corporation was treated in the 18th century as an evil, sometimes as a necessary evil, but then to be specially chartered, with whatever privileges it was to be permitted to exercise to be specifically stated in the charter, to

> run only for a limited time, and to be renewable at the pleasure of the elected representatives of the people.[1]

Other direct government regulations Smith recommended were quite varied. They included State inspection of factories, for safety and fire hazards, soundness of walls, drainage, and even to ensure proper lighting.[2] He warned against the dangers of fraud and negligence and to counter these he urged government to inspect and certify various products as genuine and not harmful, including foods, drugs, and chemicals. Smith urged also the more persuasive government regulation of manufactures in the form of quality certificates. Such "stamps upon linen and woollen cloth gives the purchaser much greater security than any statute of apprenticeship."[3] Of a purchaser Smith says "He generally looks at these quality certificates", and "The sterling mark upon plate." Smith implies that these are valuable government assurances to the public of the safety or quality of manufactured goods.[4]

To prevent fraud in the form of short weight Smith urged fixed weights and measures. Likewise, the registration of all manufacturing companies (besides a formal charter of privileges

---

1 Viner, Long View and the Short, op.cit., pp. 123-4.

2 WN I pp. 344-345.

3 WN I p. 136.

4 WN I p. 136.

and term of existence) should include a list of the owners and directors, their profits for tax assessments and the company's complete assets. Though such information concerning immovable capital was difficult to conceal, movables such as stocks and loans and mortgages were easy to keep secret and usually were. But nevertheless he insisted that open disclosure and registration of as much information about a company as possible should be sought by Government, not for abusive personal inquisition of directors, but to ensure honesty in public dealings and accuracy of tax assessments.

Smith advised other more indirect influences of government in the sphere of manufactures. Smith desired a multiplicity of producers such that conspiracies or effective monopolies or collusions could not fix prices, wages, or profits. Government must encourage this variety of business interest to ensure competition. This influence of government was, he recognised, far more difficult, to achieve and could never be fully accomplished by legal enactments alone. Merchants would always meet in their social gatherings and always contrive ways of gaining effective monopolies against the public.

> It is impossible indeed to prevent meetings, by any law which could be executed, or would be consistent with liberty and justice. But though the law cannot hinder people of the same trade from sometimes assembling together, it ought to do nothing to facilitate such assemblies; much less to render them necessary.1

---

1 WN I p. 144. And see Robbins p. 25, for discussion.

Other indirect influences by government on manufactures included education, oral legislation and "the strict administration of justice;" all of which will be dealt with later in this chapter concerning public institutions and public works.

V

Smith advocated Government supervision of the industrial labour force by several regulations. These related to cash wages, apprenticeship restrictions, child labour, forced labour, enforced education, setting tests or qualifications for responsible positions, government regulation of wages or the price of labourers subsistence, and finally taxes on the wages of government officials. Together, these government policies Smith describes in scattered passages, amount to a plan of improved labour conditions wages, and increased practical education for general social well being.

Smith was sure Government in general should not regulate wages, for legal regulation of most wages would destroy individuals ingenuity and initiative. Besides, if all workers "were to receive equal wages there would be no emulation."[1] But Smith's basic reason for objecting to government regulation of wages was that masters who controlled government would legislate a low maximum wage as they had in the past.[2]

---

1 WN I pp. 158-9.

2 WN I pp. 158-9.

> Whenever the legislature attempts to regulate the differences between the masters and the workmen, its counsellors are always the masters. When the regulation, therefore, is in favour of the workmen, it is always just and equitable; but it is sometimes otherwise when in favour of the masters.1

Smith recognised the right and duty of Government to regulate the price of corn and of bread in times of distress (so long as the landlord's monopoly of corn prices and Parliamentary Corn Laws prohibited imports.) "Where there is an exclusive corporation it may perhaps be proper to regulate the price of the first necessary of life."2 He was recognising the government's duty to regulate the price of that which formed the subsistence of the labourer and that commodity on which the major portion of his wages were spent. This was in effect equal to or identical in effect to a government subsidy to, and thus a partial regulation of wages.

While Smith recognised the difficulties of his times presented by the shortage of small coin and the prevalence of payment in "truck",3 or "kind", or paper vouchers or notes of

---

1 WN I p. 158-9.

2 WN I p. 159. See Viner, "ASLF" p. 244 for observations on this.

3 The eighth statute of George II and the eighth of George III which set certain wages by government decree and permitted the payment of wages in truck, were thus a step backward from Queen Ann's statute 2, c, 18 which enforced money payments in the woollen, linen, cotton, and iron manufactures, George II c8, though it extended money payments to the manufacture of gloves, boots, shoes and other leather wares actually was no advance because it prohibited truck payments only when made without the

credit, he nevertheless insisted that wages be paid in money.

> Thus the laws which obliges the masters in several different trades to pay their workers in money and not in goods, is quite just and equitable. It only obliges them to pay the value in money which they pretended to pay, but did not alwasys really pay in goods. This law is in favour of the workmen; ... 1

Smith insists that the statute of apprenticeship must be altered or abolished.2 The institution of long apprenticeship does not ensure good workmenship, or make the young industrious, it simply provides free labour for the master which Smith says is unjust and ultimately unproductive. Both master's profits and wages of skilled tradesmen would fall if the apprenticeship restrictions were abolished, but the public would benefit by cheaper produce. Thus government should implement new labour legislation so that a worker from the beginning,

> wrought as a journeyman, being paid in proportion to the little work which he could execute, and paying in his turn for the materials which might sometimes spoil through awkwardness and inexperience. His education would generally in this way be more effectual, and always less tedious and expensive.3

---

request and consent of the labourers. Workmen however could often be intimidated into making such agreements to ensure they were paid at all.

1 WN I p. 159.

2 WN I p. 136.

3 WN I pp. 137-8.

In a similar vein Smith argued that governments generally should abolish slavery and all forms of indenture. In his Lectures he says that Government should institute other labour legislation to prohibit child labour at early ages, and for long hours, especially in mines and factories.1

Finally, he considered the effects of taxes on various wages and concluded that "a direct tax upon the wages of labour can have no other effect than to raise them somewhat higher than the tax."2 In manufactures, such a tax would fall on the consumer. In agriculture the tax would fall upon landlords in decreased rents from tenant farmers who first had to pay the tax. Yet the more severe consequences of taxes upon wages, and the prime reason Smith was against these "absurd and destructive" taxes, was that

> If direct taxes upon the wages of labour have not always occasioned a proportionable rise in those wages, it is because they have generally occasioned a considerable fall in the demand for labour. The declension of industry, the decrease of employment for the poor, the diminution of the annual produce of the land and labour of the country, have generally been the effects of such taxes.3

For this reason, though some wages might be higher because of these taxes, Smith nevertheless vehemently opposed them. Only the wages of those in government administration who generally "can in

---

1 Lectures pp. 256-7. See also Edwin Cannon, "Adam Smith's Lectures on Justice" op.cit., p. 320.

2 WN II p. 393.

3 WN II p. 394.

most cases very well bear to be taxed", did he recommend being thus burdened. Such taxes upon political office holders, he says are always very popular.

In conclusion, Smith's proposals for government legislation for labourers in manufacturing industries amounts to a consistent plan for improved working conditions, improved wages and practical education for moral and social improvement.

Smith was less interested in the conditions of agricultural labourers although he recognised their wages were often three and five times worse than those in manufactures. The cheapness and availability of material subsistence was perhaps one reason he worried less over their condition. But primarily, it was their necessarily varied tasks which kept farm labourers from the stultification of factory employment. This apparent lack of concern with farm labourers' poverty and conditions is also suggested in his passing comments on their forced labour on the roads which he says was not really a hardship nor cruelly exacted as in France. He neglected to comment on the justice of "forced labour" and "service" exacted from all country labourers for laird, church, town, mill etc. Though this was perhaps an omission of oversight, it nonetheless may be added to his more famous oversight in neglecting an analysis of poor law legislation, which also concerned primarily rural labour.1

---

1 WN I p. 152. Smith's treatment of the poor laws is interrelated with his discussion of the Settlement laws WN I p. 151-8. His argument is that the removal of the poor is a violation of Natural liberty WN I p. 157. Finally, Smith forcibly argues that

Smith's concern with the poor laws was almost always linked with the settlement restrictions. Laborers, he said, should be free to move to the new manufacturing areas without being prevented by municipal or county legislation which objected to new labourers falling onto the poor register in the new parish. Thus, here again, Smith's interest in the shifts of the labouring population was with their possible employment in manufactures not primarily in agriculture. This was but another instance of his lesser interest in agriculture's future than manufactures. He was sure agricultural labourers would continue to earn less, achieve less division of labour,[1] and acquire less education for well paid skills. He seems to imply that whatever steps government might take, these disparities between country and urban labour would continue, so that government funds and personnel should be primarily devoted to industrial labour improvements.[2]

## VI

I turn from Smith's legislation for labour to his suggestions for state control and influence over capital. Money capital, Smith divided into two parts; profit and interest. Smith advocated control of interest rather than profit which is but a

---

the Laws of Settlement that prevent the movement of the poor ought to be repealed. WN I p. 493.

1 WN I pp. 9-10.

2 WN II pp. 208, 195, 203.

"moderate compensation, for the risk and trouble of employing the stock." Interest, however, like rent is "a neat produce which remains after completely compensating the whole risk and trouble of employing the stock." Smith therefore argued for the justice, first of fixing the interest rate at the current level of 5% and then second, justifying certain increased "tax upon the interest of money."[1] In his argument justifying the maintenance of the fixed rate of interest Smith says essentially that government has a responsibility to society to ensure that funds are lent to moral and thrifty people, not profligate.

> The legal rate, it is to be observed, though it ought to be somewhat above, ought not to be much above the lowest market rate. If the legal rate of interest in Great Britain, for example, was fixed so high as eight or ten percent, the greater part of the money which was to be lent, would be lent to prodigals and projectors, who alone would be willing to give this high interest. Sober people, who will give for the use of money no more than a part of what they are likely to make by the use of it, would not venture into the competition. A great part of the capital of the country would thus be kept out of the hands which were most likely to make a profitable and advantageous use of it, and thrown into those which were most likely to waste and destroy it. Where the legal rate of interest, on the contrary, is fixed but a very little above the lowest market rate, sober people are universally preferred, as borrowers, to prodigals and projectors.[2]

---

1 WN II p. 374.

2 WN I p. 379.

Here again we find an example of Smith's attempt to foster moral behaviour and social improvement by governmental regulation of certain property relations, in this case the rate of interest on capital.

Smith implied that interest was in theory a good and acceptable subject of taxation[1] for it did not aid or diminish profit. But Smith then concluded that such a just and reasonable tax could not be fully enacted. This was because capital owners were corrupt, secretive and lacked patriotism and would quickly take their money from any country where a burdensome tax on interest prevailed. To prevent secrecy and keep funds in the country, only excessively moderate taxes on the interest of capital have been prevalent. Such minimal taxes as nations have enacted upon interest are, Smith says, of "very loose and therefore more or less arbitrary estimation."

Smith's evident displeasure at so minimal a tax[2] on the interest on capital especially in manufactures led him to say: "If the greater part of the lands of England are not rated to the land-tax at half their value, the greater part of the stock of England is, perhaps, scarce rated at the fiftieth part of its actual value."[3] The only substantial taxes on the stock of

---

1 WN II p. 374.

2 WN II p. 376.

3 WN II p. 377.

manufacturers were upon dealers, hawkers, pedlars, and shops which all ultimately fell on consumers and hence pressed no burden on the owners of stock.1

Smith summarizes the aims of all property tax by saying:

> While property remains in the possession of the same person, whatever permanent taxes may have been imposed upon it, they have never been intended to diminish or take away any part of its capital value, but only some part of the revenue arising from it. But when property changes hands, when it is transmitted either from the dead to the living, such taxes have frequently been imposed upon it as necessarily take away some part of its capital value.2

There follows a lengthy analysis by Smith of the different modes of transferring property: from the dead to the living, from the living to the living, secretly, or publicly and in writing. Smith deals extensively with the benefits that arise from public registration of companies and government charters and he dwells on the evils of secret registration of companies and secrecy of their assets, income and names of directors. As elaborated in the foregoing pages he desired maximum public knowledge about companies and ocrporations and strict government regulation where necessary. In essence Smith's argument is that government should keep a close check on companies through public registration of all transfers of sizeable properties whether movables or immovables, land or

---

1 _WN_ II pp. 377-85.

2 _WN_ II p. 386.

capital, and require accurate assessments for tax or stamp duties directly proportional to value. Where this assessment was difficult because of secrecy Smith implied that the government, instead of being more lax, should be more vigilant. Its vigilance should never amount to a personal inquisition and it should never attempt to drive capital from the country by its strict codes and inspections. However, Smith seems utterly opposed to a continuance in Great Britain of those minimal duties which were not really proportioned to the value of any property. Such unjust duties allowed "an eighteen penny or half a crown stamp being sufficient upon a bond for the largest sum of money."[1] Although Smith was in favour of taxes upon property which were far heavier than those which existed in his time and which would be more equitable than the flagrantly arbitrary and unjustly lenient taxes on stock and land and interest and rent of his time; he nonetheless did not wish "the capital value" of these forms of property to be diminished, for government if it ate into the productive capital of industries was unlikely to spend it on anything but more unproductive retainers.[2] Although Smith investigates the kinds and effects of various taxes upon capital and interest, in many countries and in different ages he leaves the reader uncertain how far taxes upon these in future would be

---

1 WN II p. 388.

2 WN II p. 391.

more successful or just or equal than in his own time. Secrecy and lack of patriotism would always make the holders of stock difficult to tax or to politically control.

VII

Smith's general unifying theme of all these various government policies for different kinds of property is best demonstrated by his argument for proportional and progressive taxes. Smith's first maxim of taxation it will be remembered was that it be equal, proportionally upon the three constituent classes of the society.1

Smith desired an equality of advantages and opportunities as shown by his justification of a bounty for the transport of coal to make its price equal throughout the country.2 He subtly differentiated this call for equality of advantages from a call for complete equality of income. Advantages were distributed by the laws and customs and economic system.

---

1 "The subjects of every state ought to contribute towards the support of the government, as nearly as possible, in proportion to their respective abilities; that is, in proportion to the revenue which they respectively enjoy under the protection of the state ... In the observation or neglect of this maxim consists what is called the equality or inequality of taxation." WN II p. 350. Lionel Robbins has argued that Smith in laying down the rule that the just tax was proportionate to ability to pay - or roughly to income, made this the chief cannon of all the classical economists with regard to tax. Robbins Theory of Policy op.cit., p. 66.

2 WN II p. 404.

Smith believed income ought to be derived from labour, or risk. Thus unequal incomes if they were derived from unequal effort were just whereas unequal advantages derived by some classes from unequal and corrupt laws were unjust. But, Smith desired a degree of greater general equality of incomes for both social peace and prosperity and for the moral dignity of the poor and to limit the immortality of the rich. This would be partially achieved by equalizing those legal and political advantages which had in the past been so unequally distributed. Earlier Chapters have shown that Smith believed government should ensure a greater proportional equality in incomes and advantages (in his apprenticeship views, corn, bread, and some land price regulation, and in monopoly reform legislation. And without doubt this was true in his policy on education.)

However, Smith's attitude concerning the contribution of different classes to government and different classes benefit from government expenditure was not simple proportional equality. For example, Smith says concerning tax:

> It is not very unreasonble that the rich should contribute to the public expense, not only in proportion to their revenue, but something more than in that proportion.1

We find a similar attitude expressed in Smith's often restated approval of luxury taxes and disapproval of taxes on necessities, or wages or on the labouring classes general expen-

---

1 WN II p. 368.

diture. He supports heavier highway tolls upon luxury carriages than upon freight wagons, so that "the indolence and vanity of the rich is made to contribute in a very easy manner to the relief of the poor."1 "The gains of monopolies, whenever they can be come at [are] certainly of all subjects the most proper" for taxation.2 He urged partly for health reasons and partly as a moral and class reform the heavy taxation of spirituous liquors and a reduction in the tax on "the wholesome and invigorating liquors of beer and ale,"3 the drink of the common people. Likewise, though he applauds house rents as the just subject for tax because their burden falls almost as exactly proportionally on the different classes, he is even more in favour of the less proportional tax on Ground rents which burden the monopolising landlords alone. "Ground rents are a still more proper subject of taxation than the rent of houses."4

VIII

What was the range of Future Government action which Smith proposed? In contrast to Schlatter I suggest Smith may have been heavily in debt to Hume in his effort to put more power in the

---

1 WN II p. 246.

2 WN II p. 424.

3 WN II p. 422.

4 WN II p. 370.

hands of the state.[1] For this to be true of Smith who is reputed to be the archotypal "laissez faire" economist, is more than paradoxical. Smith certainly did not go as far as Hume[2] in giving property rights or property control explicitly to the state, yet he entirely agreed that the government was "the guardian of the general welfare," and that the authority of "justice" must be embodied in all property laws and contractual relations. And finally, Smith, by stating no area of property relations where government action or interference would not be permitted if general welfare called for it, implied his agreement with Hume that "all questions of property are subordinate to the authority of the civil laws." Yet Smith did not agree to Hume's total utilitarian justification for government activities. Smith says:

> To hinder ... the farmer from sending his goods at all times to the best market, is evidently to sacrifice the ordinary laws of justice to an idea of public utility, to a sort of reasons of state; an act of legislative authority which ought to be exercised only, which can be pardoned only in cases of the most urgent necessity.[3]

Hume and Smith were arguing for similar forms of government activity on a very broad range of subjects. Smith would justify

---

1 Schaltter, Private Property op.cit., pp. 242-3.

2 David Hume said "Government is the guardian of the general welfare all the questions of property are subordinate to the civil laws." Cited by Schlatter ibid. pp. 242-3.

3 WN II p. 48. See discussion by Viner, "ASLF" pp. 224-5.

such acts as protections and promotions of natural rights, whereas Hume would argue for their social utility. The two forms of argument were, however, very close and often intermingled in the use of proposals for state responsibility over the public's general welfare.1 Smith provides a good example of the extent of future government's tasks when he says:

> The civil magistrate is entrusted with the power not only of preserving the public peace by restraining injustice, but of promoting the prosperity of the commonwealth, by establishing good discipline, and by discouraging every sort of vice and impropriety; he may prescribe rules, therefore, which not only prohibit mutual injuries among fellow citizens, but command mutual good offices to a certain degree. When the sovereign commands what is merely indifferent, and that antecedent to his orders, might have been omitted without any blame, it becomes not only blameable but punishable to disobey him. When he commands, therefore, what, antecedent to any such order, could not have been omitted without the greatest blame, it surely becomes more punishable to be wanting in obedience. Of all the duties of a lawgiver, however, this, perhaps, is that which it requires the greatest delicacy and reserve to execute with propriety and judgement. To neglect it altogether exposes the commonwealth to many gross disorders and shocking enormities, and to push it too far is descruction of all liberty, security and justice.2

---

1 See H. Myint "Welfare Significance of Productive Labour: A reinterpretation of the Classical Doctrine" Review of Economic Studies XI (1943) pp. 20-30. And see Schaltter, op.cit., p. 242.

2 TMS p. 116.

In describing the actions government was to promote Smith was no longer merely correcting wrongs or making people obey the law so that they do not wrong their neighbours. These actions, he suggests, propose to alter the morals of society through institutions, public works, and acts that sponsor the sentiment of moral obligation.1 These actions are not government benevolence nor are they ordinary acts of justice, such as prevention of harm through enforced obedience to the laws.2 These promotive actions of government cannot be encompassed by a "laissez-faire" theory of government.

Smith's repeated references to "perfect justice" suggest his concern with the improvement of the existing standards of justice in line with a more perfect standard. This "perfect justice" is obviously not merely the with-holding from doing harm to others, keeping contracts, obeying the law and keeping to the written rule. If contractual obedience were all that justice

---

1 Smith proposed for instance to "correct whatever was unsocial or disagreeably rigorous in the morals of all the little sects into which the country was divided." WN II pp. 317-8. And see the discussion of state legislation to improve morals generally in Macfie, Individual In Society, op.cit., p. 120.

2 TMS p. 127. "As society cannot subsist unless the laws of justice are tolerably well observed." See also TMA p. 125. "Society may subsist, though not in the most comfortable state without beneficence, but the prevalence of injustice must utterly destroy it.

meant to Smith he would scarcely have denigrated "mere justice" of obedience to laws, which is the only prevalent example of "justice" required by the free market. Throughout the Theory of Moral Sentiments Smith appears to contrast "perfect justice" to "mere justice,"

> Though the breach of justice ... exposes to punishment, the observance of the rules of the virtue seem scarce to deserve any reward ... Mere justice is upon most occasions, but a negative virtue ... It only hinders us from hurting our neighbour ... We may often fulfill all the rules of justice by sitting still and doing nothing.1

Smith contrasts this implicitly with the man of perfect justice who is at all times governed by the impartial spectator.2 These commands which Smith says a government may give to promote "good offices" and the morality of the people would probably be dictated by just such a higher social justice.3

In his provisions for public works and public institutions which are beyond the individual purse, Smith repeatedly assigns to the government a duty of promoting general welfare other than

---

1 TMS pp. 117-120.

2 TMS p120, WN, I. p. 75.

3 TMS p. 206. Smith distinguishes justice and benevolence but they are both recommended to us by our "benevolent affections" unlike prudence. TMS p. 385.

simply for defence and to administer justice.[1] If the means to do so are within the power of government, but not within the power of individuals, he clearly indicated that the state had a duty to regulate currency, prevent fire, protect public health and engage in numerous activities that promote moral and intellectual improvement of society for their own sake.

Jacob Viner has said:

> In many instances Smith supported government restrictions on private initiative where neither justice nor defence was involved and where the sole aim was to improve the direction which private initiative gave to the investment of capital, the course of commerce, and the employment of labour.[2]

His justification for each public works or public institution frequently completely ignore his original criterion that these projects should be impossible for individuals to erect or maintain profitably. Both roads and canals he said could be profitably built by private companies of individuals, but he approves their being built, operated and regulated by government. The state should provide "good roads, bridges, navigable canals,

---

1 Charles Ryle Fay, "Adam Smith and the Dynamic State" op.cit., pp. 25-34, also C. A. Cooke, "Adam Smith and Jurisprudence" op.cit., pp. 326-332, also H. Myint. "Welfare Significance of Productive Labour: A Reinterpretation of the Classical Doctrine" op.cit., pp. 20-30. And see Gee, "Adam Smith's Social Welfare Function" op.cit., pp. 283-299. Gee shows that social welfare was not exclusively measured in material terms by Smith, but always stressed moral and political aims.

2 Viner "ASLF" p. 228.

harbours, and other public works."[1] "Each scheme defraying its own expenses" is Smith's criterion for justifying these government projects.[2] He indicates that he would permit public companies for banking, insurance, and "works of art and general utility" as for example "bringing water for the supply of a great city."[3]

Concerning more legislation (in addition to prohibition of child labour, fixing of interest rates, taxes on spirituous liquors and luxuries which we have already mentioned) Smith accepted poor relief as a public function. He insisted upon state subsidies for education of the public in moral behaviour, martial spirit, and family planning.

Robbins has rightly concluded from Smith's remarks on diseases that "had he known any available technique he would have favoured health legislation."[4] Smith says for example that:

---

1 WN II p. 246.

2 Macfie, Individual and Society op.cit., p. 133, has said of Smith's broad scope of public works "You will notice how comprehensive this rubric can be (projects beyond individual purses). It could include all the triumphs or extravagances of modern planning, from new towns or electrical and irrigation achievements to Kenya ground-nuts or Gold Coast chickens as yet unhatched." Jacob Viner reminds us "ASLF" pp. 227-8, "It is quite probable that Smith overlooked some current activities of government to which he would have given his approval if they had been brought to his attention," On Smith's many proposals for various public works see Viner's discussion, pp. 226-32 and Lionel Robbins discussion p. 38 on "The content of Smith's agenda."

3 WN p. 279.

4 Robbins op.cit., p. 38.

> It would deserve its most serious attention to prevent a leprosy or any other loathsome and offensive disease, though neither mortal nor dangerous from spreading itself ... [1]

Jacob Viner has concluded from this that it may be reasonably inferred "that he would even more strongly support public action taken to prevent the spread of dangerous diseases and thus would include public hygiene among the proper functions of government."[2]

## IX

What adequate conclusions about the scope of future government can be drawn from Smith's many proposals for government action where neither defence, justice, nor impossibility of individual profit is concerned.[3] First, I would suggest that the usual order of priorities attributed to Smith regarding private before public interest must be reversed to gain anything like a realistic assessment of his whole view of future government. For example, Smith seems to express this presumption in his famous statement that "Defence is of much more importance than opulence." We see it also in his argument justifying prohibiting exports of corn in time of famine; and of the justice of "reasons of state" interventions in private business in times of urgency to promote social welfare. This priority of public over

---

1 WN II p. 308.

2 Viner AS & LF p. 228.

3 Viner "ASLF" p. 225.

private interest he also suggests in his advocacy of regulations of paper money banking which,

> May, no doubt, be considered as in some respect a violation of natural liberty. But those exertions of the natural liberty of a few individuals, which might endanger the security of the whole society, are, and ought to be restrained by the laws of all governments' of the most free, as well as of the most despotical. The obligations of building party walls, in order to prevent the communication of fire, is a violation of natural liberty, exactly of the same kind with regulations of the banking trade which are here proposed.[1]

The second conclusion to be suggested by Smith's great variety of proposals for government acts to improve and intervene in individuals' affairs, is that Smith's future government tended more to the activist, and in some ways even the interventionist pattern than to laissez-faire. Several recent authors besides Robbins, Viner, and Samuels have examined the range of Smith's government policies and remarked upon the extraordinarily activist character the State was to be given. In assessing Smith's total conception of future public works Albion Small in his Adam Smith and Modern Sociology[2] asserts that "Smith had in mind a range of public works which would tend towards the socialistic rather than the laissez-faire extreme." Smith's whole range of government

---

1 WN I pp. 344-345.

2 Albion Small, Adam Smith and Modern Sociology op.cit., p. 215.

planning, which I analysed incorporating Smith's conception of a land plan for agricultural improvement and productivity, a fixed interest rate, tax incentives for manufacturers, and import taxes on foreign goods all reinforce the argument for considering Smith's future government to be most definitely activist rather than laissez-faire. A. L. Macfie has made a similar assertion to Small's with regard to Smith's range of planning: namely that Smith "might win the surprised admiration of socialist, even Marxist planners ..."[1] Jacob Viner's book The Long View and the Short expressed in a far more implicit fashion much this same view by his famous list of exceptions to trusting in the natural harmony of interest alone, scattered throughout various passages of the Wealth of Nations. These defects Viner concludes "would suffice to provide ammunition for several socialist orations."[2] Lionel Robbins was led to conclude that: "without a firm framework of law and order, harmonious relations between individuals are unlikely to come into being." The pursuit of self-interest, unrestrained by government or other suitable institutions, guarantees nothing except chaos. Neither harmony nor these institutions are "natural" in the sense that they arise inevitably. Indeed Robbins went even so far as to say that the invisible hand "is the hand of the law-giver." "Government is the hand which

---

1 Macfie, Individual In Society, op.cit., p. 131.

2 Viner, "AS & LF" p. 215.

withdraws from the sphere of the pursuit of self-interest those possibilities which do not harmonise with the public good."[1]

The third conclusion to be drawn from Smith's extensive tasks for future government is that Smith's system of political theory represented an attempt to integrate freedom of the individual (personally, politically, and economically) with strong and clear and unbiased controls upon that same individual by government and other social institutions.[2] Indeed, the freedoms of the individual in whatever political and economic liberty he possessed were largely a result of, and only could continue in existence because of an active and strong, uncorrupt, and unbiased state authority.[3]

> Only the strong power of legislation and the courts can here, precariously, prevent invasions of the rights and due freedoms of individuals. There is no reason to doubt Smith's support for them.[4]

These necessary checks upon freedom, as well as the range of state action which Smith desires, and his general presumption that

---

1 Robbins, op.cit., p. 56.

2 Macfie indicates this when he says "The strategic factor, however, is not so much the freedom of the individual, which has received too unqualified attention since 1776, as the limitations on freedom which Smith always added were necessary, if freedom to pursue self interest were to be moralized." Macfie, op.cit., p. 118.

3 Robbins, op.cit., p. 26. Samuels op. cit. Introduction, and his two chapters on "The Economic Role of the State."

4 Macfie, op.cit., p. 119.

the interest of the public must come before private individuals opulence, all tend to contradict those who view Smith simply as a "laissez-faire" economist. These interpreters assume that Smith did not intend the state to interfere in the market. He makes it quite clear that it must control, regulate and influence the various selfish interests of those who compose the market if it is to survive and prosper. Proponents of laissez faire often claim that Smith believed government should clear out of all the more intimate areas of personal life - but as Macfie rightly points out Smith "was certainly prepared for state control of interests which we feel are more intimate than economic ones."1 Those who wish to prove Smith's belief in laissez-faire government imply that Smith desired only the minimum of government organisation and activity to handle the proverbial functions of "night watchman." Yet, as we have shown in the cases of public works and public institutions, Smith sets no limits on government activities as far as any area of the market which it may not enter and interfere with if the public can be shown to benefit from such acts.

X

Viner, Cropsey and Robbins all acknowledge Smith's requirement for a certain amount of government intervention in the market in the near future. However, although they qualify the view of

---

1 Macfie, ibid p. 120.

Smith as a proponent of laissez-faire or minimal government they all imply that Smith's desire was for an eventual reduction of government interventionist acts in the market as soon as the market becomes able to regulate itself. Robbins says:

> And it was the central contention of the classical economists that, when the market conformed to the conditions which they postulated then interference with its working was harmful and self frustrating.1

And Viner, Cropsey and Samuels make much the same point.2 They suggest that although in the immediate future the state is necessary to coerce obedience to the market requirements for honesty and harmony of interest, in the distant future the "non-legal forces of social control"3 will take over many of the inteventionist activities and socializing influences of the state. Thus their broad conception of Smith's policy for the state in the distant future is similar to the proponents of the "minimal government" interpretation of Smith's views.4

It is true that Smith hoped for the natural improvement of individuals and especially for harmony of their self interest in the market with their social interest in justice, morality and

---

1 Robbins, op.cit., p. 57.

2 Viner, "ASLF" pp. 219, 232. And see Cropsey, op.cit., pp. 80-90 and Samuels, op.cit. The Market - Plus - Framework. pp. 1-15.

3 Samuels ibid. Ch. 2. "The Non Legal Forces of Social Control" pp. 21-97.

4 Viner "ASLF" p. 219. Robbins, op.cit., p. 57.

dignity. And it is also true that Smith believed education would enable men to comprehend their true interest and so act more rationally in the market. But his expectation was not that the natural propensities of individuals and classes to look after their own self interests would or should cease. Therefore a primary question for appraising Smith's conception of future markets and future governments seems to be the following: Would the natural propensities to social disharmony resulting from conflicting self interest between individuals and between classes permit future government to cease its regulation of and intervention into the market at even the most distant time? This is the question Viner, Cropsey, Robbins and Samuels do not seem to have asked.

Lionel Robbins notes that "harmony" in the system of the classical economists "was very strictly limited" and that there were dangers to that harmony which "were not inconsiderable."[1] But he nonetheless later argues that once the market had been set on course, state intervention to control excessive self interest of an individual or group, or corruption or collusion, "was harmful and self frustrating." Jacob Viner in section IV of his "Adam Smith and Laissez Faire," entitled "Flaws in the Natural Order", indicated some of these natural propensities which Smith described in different groups which cause them to pursue their

---

1 Robbins <u>Theory of Policy</u> op.cit., p. 25.

self-interest in ways and at times when it is definitely destructive of social improvement or harmony or even of public health. But Viner uses this list of flaws to,

> demonstrate beyond dispute the wide divergence between the perfectly harmonious, completely beneficient natural order of the Theory of Moral Sentiments and the partial and limited harmony in the economic order of the Wealth of Nations.1

Although he had suggested his recognition that these flaws were a permanent aspect of Smith's commercial society, Viner nevertheless implies that - once government has corrected the corruptions and injustices, and monopolies, import/export restrictions and various other laws - the market will improve and could be left greater freedom than at present to govern itself. Until the free market had been created, government must be the temporary instrument for harmonizing social tensions. In his conclusion, Viner says of Smith:

> He saw, nevertheless, that it was necessary in the absence of a better instrument, to rely upon government ...2

Lionel Robbins suggests the same idea when he implies that much of the far distant policy would consist of "the inaction" or "non-agenda" of the state. Once the market had been "so conditioned as to conform to [Smith's and the other Classical economists'] idea

---

1 Viner, "ASLF", p. 214.

2 Viner, "ASLF", p. 232.

of what was self acting, then it was not merely superfluous but positively pernicious to attempt to use other coercive influences."1

In contrast to these suggestions that the interventions of the state were only temporarily necessary until the free market came into existence, I would advance the view that Smith believed government was always to be relied upon to intervene in the market to prevent the selfish propensities of individuals and classes from causing injustice or social conflict. Government should erect a new structure of many "perpetual regulations" to make clear the fundamental laws and economic regulations desired by the state. And in addition to these Smith seems to have expected the steady growth of certain areas of government's responsibility.

First, in agriculture and industry Smith makes a strong argument for rational and coordinated "plans" to ensure the steady development of production and the speedy, efficient, and somewhat more equitable distribution of rewards. These plans, as described earlier, were to coordinate the systems of tax incentive and restriction to ensure the improved use of land and resources. Far from desiring government to remove its influence from the agricultural and industrial development and from their market relations Smith says concerning his land plan of general land taxation:

---

1 Robbins, Theory of Policy op.cit., p. 57.

> It would, therefore, be much more proper to be established as a perpetual and unalterable regulation, or what is called a fundamental law of the commonwealth, than any tax which was always to be levied according to a certain valuation.1

Smith did not intend these "perpetual" regulations to be minimal and arbitrary taxes and arrangements, or to be "unalterable" because they did not interfere in the market. On the contrary, his "plan" was "a system of administration" to be "managed as to give ... some encouragement to the improvement of land" and the industry. The plan would be "a fundamental law of the commonwealth" because it would encourage perpetual improvement by control over the market.2

The second indication by Smith that strong interventionist government must persist even in the most distant future (besides his description of these perpetual and unalterable" government laws) is that the need for government to protect property would not disappear. When did Smith ever say the antagonisms between labourers and employers would cease? The natural propensity of classes was to look after their own self interest. This self interest directly conflicted. When would master and workmen cease to have a conflict of interest with respect to wages? Did Smith

---

1 WN II p. 359.

2 WN II pp. 357-8. "Such a system of administration" as this plan for land might remove "any degree of uncertainty ... and ... introduce into the common management of land such a plan or policy, as might contribute a good deal to the general improvement and good cultivation of the country."

describe a time when the weakness in bargaining power of labourers would not ordinarily give the advantage in any dispute to employers?[1] The interests of merchants and manufacturers is in high profits which are disadvantageous to labourers and to the general public.[2] Smith was well aware that social gatherings of people of the same trade seldom met but that "the conversation ends in a conspiracy against the public or in some contrivance to raise prices." Although he says, "It is impossible indeed to prevent such meetings"[3], he nevertheless, does not advoctate a laissez-faire market in which these conspiracies and price rises remain unchecked. Government can and should intervene to prevent the damaging effects of these conspiracies from undermining the market.

Not only do merchants and manufacturers have an interest opposed to labourers and the general public[4] but an interest opposed to farmers and landlords.[5] Similarly Smith described the interest of landlords as opposed to all other classes. When would this conflict cease? Certainly not as rents steadily increased both with the progress of the economy, and with the exhaustion of

---

1 WN I pp. 74-6.

2 WN I pp. 110, 278, 519. II p. 81.

3 WN I p. 144.

4 WN I p. 278.

5 WN I pp. 142-3.

the better lands. Smith was well aware that self interested landlords had instituted and perpetuated the "corn laws" which protected them from competition with imported foreign corn. Unless the corn laws were repealed, Smith, like Ricardo, predicted a "stagnant state" where high rents would cease to permit investment from obtaining a reasonable profit and so would lay off labourers and cause general stagnation and possible poverty. Even the abolition of the corn laws would not remove this antagonistic interest of the landlord to other classes, nor prevent the steady rise in his rents. It merely slowed the drift towards possible stagnation. Smith's suggestion, that so long as a monopoly in land existed, in time of dearth or emergency the state should be able to control grain, bread, and land prices. Thus he indicates a state function that would persist even in the most distant future since Smith expected land to continue to be monopolistically owned. In that distant future when Britain was an old country Smith gives indications that the situation might be similar to other old countries where "rent and profit eat up wages and the two superior orders of people oppress the inferior one."[1] The natural propensities of individuals to conflicts of self interest would always persist as would conflicts between classes.

---

1 WN II p. 76.

In any future period individuals conflicts of interest would always require the vigilance and occasional action of the state. When would the corn merchant's "excess of avarice" cease? When would it not be true that "The merchant exporter sometimes finds it to his interest, when dearth prevails both at home and abroad," "very much to aggravate the calamities of the dearth" at home by exporting corn. Acknowledging such natural propensities to self interest, Smith recommended that the state must in future ages be able to intervene in the market to prevent such acts of self interest from harming the public.

Self interest might also dictate the advantages of fraud, short weight, and other corruptions of harmonious property relations. A free market of private self interested individuals will always be unable to prevent fraud, Smith argues, and only such a coercive power as the state can certify foods, drugs and the quality of goods. With the increase of produce and population he expected, such regulatory agencies of government, he suggests, will, and ought to, increase their scope and importance.

In a third area Smith suggests a future strengthening not weakening of government. Smith prognosticated the physical, mental, and moral corruption of workers engaged in extremely detailed tasks. This demoralisation caused by extreme division of labour would steadily increase as the tasks of labourers steadily became more and more subdivided. Schumpeter has pointed out that for Smith division of labour was almost the sole cause of progress. Therefore, every increase in industrial progress would be accomplished by an increase in the demoralisation of the workers.

> But in every improved and civilised society this is the state into which the labouring poor, that is the great body of the people, must necessarily fall, unless government takes some pains to prevent it.1

Since the division of labour will, Smith implies, expand throughout industry, governments in the advanced countries would be forced to employ ever greater funds, and personnel in developing means to prevent these demoralising effects of division of labour.

Another consequence from Smith's theory of division of labour as the motor of progress, was that goverment powers must grow with division of labour among state authorities. Government, like industry, would expand and experience increased activity as tasks of a legislative nature were divided from executive or judical functions. Smith had already acknowledged his debt to Montesquieu in crediting Britain's successful government to its division of powers. These powers were, Smith suggested, increased in their efficiency (at least theoretically) by their division of labour. His history of justice, courts, legislatures, and armies all suggest this division of labour as the key cause of the improvement and strengthening of each branch of the state. Where does Smith ever suggest that this process of continual division of

---

1 WN II p. 303.

labour in government activities would cease? With the new tasks he assigned to government such as the prevention of the spread of harmful or loathsome diseases, and the setting of qualifications for entrance into any general profession, Smith implies that state departments will in future increase and subdivide even in the most distant period.

Aside from state institutions and state activities which would increase Smith suggested many state subsidied institutions which would steadily expand. A public responsibility Smith devoted a great deal of discussion to was education.

In his various proposals for government subsidies and support for different forms of schools, training and exams we find his clearest expression of his activist state, promoting intellectual and moral improvement, greater equality, and greater productivity simultaneously. Though Smith derided the "cobweb science" of the universities of his day he prescribed for both the "education of the people of some rank and fortune" and "of the mass of the people." Though he seems to recommend state subsidies for private schools rather than a system of state schools he is nevertheless quite adamant that:

> The government should provide the populace with the maximum of literary education which they can absorb, for the reason of their capacity.[1]

---

1 WN V III 2. Cannan p. 736.

He also said that future government must provide encouragement for "the frequency and gaiety of public diversions" and for training in "painting...poetry...music...dancing and all sorts of dramatic representations and exhibitions."1 Availability of these activities for the mass of the people was totally unknown in Smith's Britain.2

Smith relied on education "to humanize" the entire population, to correct especially the "moral decadence" of the factory workers and the physical, mental, judical, martial and sympathetic demoralisation "so justly lamented." But most of all Smith expected education to give men self respect and obedience to law as well as to foster social dignity.3

It was, of course not by government subsidies to education alone that Smith expected the masses and the rich to be inspired to the "temperate judgement and mildness of manners, that alone can tolerate the responsibilities of freedom." It was rather by his entire range of government policies and institutions that he hoped to influence moral behaviour. That this was Smith's clear

---

1 WN II p. 318.

2 See Macfie op.cit., p. 120 and Cropsey op.cit., p. 85. These measures were recommended by Smith to alter the unsocial morality of sects and individuals.

3 WN II p. 309. "The State, however derives no inconsiderable advantage from their instruction ... An instructed and intelligent people besides are more decent and orderly that an ignorant and stupid one. They feel themselves, each individually, more respectable, and more likely to obtain the respect of their lawful superiors, and they are therefore more disposed to respect those superiors."

intention is made plain in many of his general comments in the Theory of Moral Sentiments such as his comparison of government's intentions with the aims of the deity:

> to promote the happiness of mankind as the general prevalence of wisdom and virtue. All government is but an imperfect remedy for the deficiency of these.[1]

Though government in most cases should not force individuals to private benevolence (for this dictation will destroy their self command) it can and should force them to perform "public duties."[2] Yet more important than these was Smith's explicit desire that government should attempt to improve the morals of the population[3] through various forms of public training and public diversions and the curbing of the influence of sects.[4] Likewise we find that Smith, in order to foster general moral behaviour, recommended a system of tuition, exams and periods of probation for all tasks of public responsibility from druggist to judge. He even urged state sponsored examination for general fields of employment to assure capability but more important, moral

---

1 TMS p. 269.

2 TMS "Of Duty" pp. 229-242.

3 See WN II pp. 317, 318. And see Macfie, Individual in Society. op.cit., p. 120.

4 "There are two very easy and effectual remedies by whose joint operation the state might; without violence, correct whatever was unsociable or disagreeably rigorous in the morals of all the little sects into which the country was divided." WN II, p. 317.

certitude, and to prevent fraud.1

The wholesale delegation to the state of the task of improving men and property relations was as typical of Smith as his laissez-faire announcements. Individual freedom and Governmet control were not really separable policies in Smith's thought, they were inseparable aspects of the same policy; the promotion of and protection of individuals' rights.

Jacob Viner suggests that Smith would have been surprised at his own extensive list of tasks assigned to government.2 In contrast to Viner, I would contend that Smith may well have been aware of the scope of government activity he was proposing. As shown by Edwin Cannan and H. B. Vanderblue3 and implied by Sir John Sinclair,4 Smith wrote and revised the sections of the Wealth of Nations on government and administration after the first edition in 1776. These new sections were written during his term as a government administrator of Scottish Customs and Collector of

---

1 WN II p. 318. "... by instituting some sort of probation ... to be undergone by every person before he was to be permitted to exercise any liberal profession or before he could be received as a candidate for any honourable office of trust or profit. If the state imposed upon this order of men the necessity of learning, it would have no occasion to give itself any trouble about providing them with proper teachers."

2 Viner, "ASLF", pp. 218-19.

3 Edwin Cannan WN Introduction. And H. B. Vanderblue, "An Incident in the Life of Adam Smith Commissioner of His Majesty's Customs." op.cit., pp. 305-8.

4 Sir John Sinclair, Correspondence, op. cit., 1, p. 389. And in Rae, Life p. 332.

the Salt Tax. Vanderblue's article shows that it was this practical government experience in his last years which led Smith to write some of the passages not thought of as the core of his political thought.1

The most significant additions were to his chapter on the "Expenses of the Sovereign" which, it will be recalled, is the foremost political chapter of the entire book. An entirely new chapter on the "Conclusion to the Mercantile System" was written by Smith during this period as a government official and added to the work.2 There were also descriptions of technical details of administration that Smith altered as for example his additions to the chapters on "Drawbacks" and "Bounties" that considered the Treasury's mode of financing its interventions in the economy. If Cannan's and Vanderblue's evidence is correct that these important sections on politics were added after the first edition and during his period of practical government activity then it is quite reasonable to assume that this concentration on the scope of government, and the tasks, expenses and efficiency of state administration were not casual reflections as Viner implies, but considered revisions. Taken together these additions suggest a considerable deepening of Smith's political enquiry in his last years and suggest that he may well have been aware of the scope of government activity he was proposing.

---

1 Vanderblue, op.cit., p. 305.

2 Vanderblue, ibid pp. 305-6.

## XI

Considering the existing experience Smith describes of corrupt government legislatures, courts and administration is it surprising that he should have prescribed as many new tasks to government as he did? It is vital for an accurate assessment of the character of future government he desired to recall Smith's comparison of the good government of Venice and Amsterdam with the poor government of Britain to show that if government were honest and competent he would permit giving it greater powers and responsibilities over the economy.

> The orderly, vigilant and parsimonious administration of such aristocracies as those of Venice and Amsterdam, is extremely proper, it appears from experience, for the management of a mercantile project of this kind. But whether such a government as that of England; which, whatever may be its virtues, has never been famous for good economy; which, in time of peace, has generally conducted itself with the slothful and negligent profusion that is perhaps natural to monarchies; and in time of war has constantly acted with all the thoughtless extravagance that democracies are apt to fall into; could be safely trusted with the management of such a project, must at least be a good deal more doubtful.[1]

Smith's famous attacks on kings, ministers and politicians as "the greatest spendthrifts in the society" caused Jacob Viner to conclude that it was the low calibre of existing government

---

1 WN II p. 342.

administration that led Smith to make his many attacks on government, and led him to question governments' greater competence than individuals to solve problems of the economy.

> The standards of honesty and competence of the governments of his day with which Smith was acquainted were unbelievably low, moreover, not only in comparison with what they are today in England, Germany, and the Scandinavian countries but apparently even in comparison with earlier periods in English political history. Smith had encountered few instances in which government was rendering intelligent and efficient service to the public welfare outside the fields of protection and justice. The English government of his day was in the hands of an aristocratic clique, the place-jobbing, corrupt, cynical, and class biased flower of the British gentry ... 1

Smith, by his repeated insistence on democratically elected, republican, responsible, removable representatives in government2 and by his criticism of property interests which controlled and influenced existing parliament3 can be seen to desire a major political reform.4

---

1 Viner "ASLF", p. 221. And see WN I p. 494, 519.

2 Lectures, pp. 68, 70, 72. WN I p. 494, 519.

3 See Ch. VIII on Existing Government in Smith's time especially Conclusion. And see WN I pp. 494, 519. WN II pp. 137-40, 484.

4 By Smith's repeated criticisms of existing politics and his many extensive proposals for tax and financial reform he left no doubt that he desired a major reform of many aspects of government. However, Smith did not set out a programme for the reform of sufferage and representation in Parliament. He had noted the injustice of existing representation and the tiny minority who actually had a vote. And he had noted that only the

The wealthy corrupt politicians and statesmen of his time Smith contrasts with those who adhere to:

> The science of the legislator whose deliberations ought to be governed by general principles which are always the same, ... 1

In the best future state Smith apparently hoped these would be the legislators. Though in part this was, Smith admits a utopian hope, he nonetheless believed that in each country eventually the "natural aristocracy" would emerge and prevail, and through them the ordinary people would be represented. Smith suggests this natural aristocracy should be composed at least partly of members of the lower classes because they had less vast property interest to protect and would be probably more unbiased

---

most exalted "ranks" of society really controlled the government. But Smith did not write his long promised work on government and in his final days he ordered all his manuscripts in preparation for it to be destroyed.

Although Smith would have agreed with a good many of the political sentiments advanced by Millar in pamphlets there is no evidence that he wrote any such tracts of his own. Millar had several pamphlets of which The Need for Parliamentary Reform (Millar pp. 390-94) is the most explicit. Millar presented a strong attack on the increase of the royal perogative and of ministerial power, and on the patronage system. His many letters echo this attack. Millar at one point of this pamlphlet summarizes his attack in such terms that Smith suggested at many points in his works (Millar p. 392) "A great majority of the Commons being, in the present state of the representation, returned by the interest of a small number of individuals, a dissolution of Parliament, as far as related to that House, was not, in reality, an appeal to the nation at large, but in a great measure, an appeal to such of the nobility and gentry as had acquired the direction of rotten boroughs, or of certain political districts."

1 WN I p. 490.

and just.[1] Smith concludes that "kings are the servants of the people."

> This doctrine dictates that the people should not charge a delegate but should have some share in the management of affairs through the leading men, the natural aristocracy of every country.[2]

In summary, this chapter has attempted to examine Smith's government policies for each form of future property relations and to reappraise the total scope of future government activites he desired. I have shown he advocated some form of government regulation or influence in every kind of future property relation: including land, corn, rent, interest, labour, necessities, and luxuries. Furthermore, an examination of the list of public works and public institutions and general influences government should exert reveals that Smith believed the state to be the prime factor in the creation of market harmony and in the moral improvement of men. This extensive range and depth of the responsibilities he

---

1 High government positions were often filled by men educated in the lower middle ranks, but in government they acted to protect the interests of those in the highest rank not those in the lower ranks from which they themselves may have arisen. TMS. p. 78. In the future Smith hoped that the natural aristocracy that arose from these middle and lower classes would not act solely in the interest of the rich. For he says when government legislates in favour of the lower classes it is always acting justly but is sometimes otherwise when it legislates in favour of the rich. WN I pp. 277-8.

2 Cited by Dunne, "Adam Smith and Edmund Burke" op.cit. p. 342. Dunne cites Smith, Wealth of Nations p. 586. Everyman ed. I cannot find the passage, but TMS p. 74 refers to this same doctrine.

delegated future government suggests his advocacy not of a pure laissez-faire state, but of a strong and activist one.

Strong government would always be relied upon to intervene in the market to prevent the selfish propensities of individuals and classes from causing injustice or social conflict. There was no forseeable time in which he expected state regulations and restrictions to cease to be justified to promote new industry, patents, copyrights, or defence industries. Smith appears to have believed that some of government's interventionist activities and most of its welfare activities would steadily increase.

This is not to say that Smith did not wish for an increased freedom of trade internationally and internally than that which existed in his times. But, there were severe limits to the freedom he was anxious to promote. State regulation of various market practices was the only means by which the market could safely be allowed any freedom. New government regulations were recommended by Smith to give government a greater control over the erratic, corrupt, and self interested members of the market.

Smith did not anticipate the achievement either of pure laissez-faire government or totally interventionist government. In terms of 18th century thought these polarities probably had little meaning. To which form of govern ment, laissez-faire or interventionist did Smith incline, is not however, purely a question of individual readers' predispositions. In neither the near nor the distant future did Smith envisage a laissez-faire government, or a government which did not intervene in the market. And he explicitly denies any expectation of achieving in Britain anything approaching a totally free market. In the absence of a free market it is highly questionable to what extent the "invisible hand", understood as the self regulating mechanism of the market, could be said to exist; unless like Robbins, we accept the curious postulate that the invisible hand "is the hand of the law-giver,"1 the hand of interventionist state government.

But, on the other hand, although Smith at times was an advocate of an activist and interventionist government he did not set forth a clear systematic or unambiguous form for that government. Smith was definitely not a socialist defined as a proponent of the state ownership of the means of production. He was not a socialist if that is defined as one who advocates distribution of income to each according to his work (at least not comprehensively across class lines.) But at times Smith did adhere to certain elements of socialist state principles if these are defined loosely as state intervention in the market and social relations for social improvement, general welfare and some equalitarianism.

Smith did advocate the coordination of state programmes for rational "plans" in agriculture and manufacturing. And he advocated some government intervention from any area of the economy where it could reasonably be claimed to aid public welfare.

---

1 Robbins, op.cit., p. 56.

Government had the duty to tax not only proportionally to income "but something more than in that proportion" to make the extravagances of the rich pay for aid to the poor. Finally, Smith specifically recognised government's responsibilities to include "the promotion of good offices" or moral behaviour among men through laws, institutions and its general influence. Although these are policies which most present day governments in capitalist nations perform, to some degree or another; Smith's conception of future government action and intervention do not exactly correspond to any twentieth century "form of government." His conception reflects the peculiar hopes and inconsistencies of an 18th century Scottish Moral Philosopher, not the absolutist forms of government of thinkers who preceded him, nor the systematic and functional conception of government which was to follow him. A few absolute principles and a good deal of functional analysis of government acts and taxes were included in his political conception, but they weren't automatically or exclusively adhered to as a system of political theory.

# CONCLUSION

Smith was a remarkably eclectic thinker. In his attempt at a comprehensive study of society, he drew together the disciplines and principles of traditional and modern enquiry. Few other works provide so many examples of the conflicting currents of thought flowing through the 18th century as are found in Smith's Wealth of Nations. Strong arguments for the protection of men's natural rights share the same page with modern economic analysis. Certain of his various theories have been argued to epitomise positive empiricism, while others exemplify the foremost moral philosophy of his age. Clearly, the property theory of such a complex and varied thinker could be expected to relate to other fields besides the laws of "realty and personality" of his own time. In fact, in some ways his property theory could be argued to relate to most of the economic, political, social and moral subjects he writes upon.

The purpose of this book has therefore been specifically directed at examining what Smith's theory of property was, what it meant, and what were the main logical implications which followed from it. Because Smith's property theory was central to his entire social and economic and political thought, it provides a key to understanding the ambiguities in the rest of his social analysis.

Smith and the Scottish Historical School based their analysis of society on property; considered, historically, conjecturally, morally and empirically. Their studies centred upon "the change in the nature of property" throughout history. They concluded that changes in property marked "the progress of civilization." Their interest was not only in factual evidence of changes in production but in discovering the effects of these changes on men and society.

Smith's main point of his Glasgow lectures was, he says himself, to investigate whether the effects of market commercial society were good or bad for individuals and government. I have sought to show that this normative end was Smith's primary concern not only in his _Lectures_ but in the _Wealth of Nations_ and in his entire theory of property.

Modern analysts of the _Wealth of Nations_ have often disregarded this normative end which was foremost for Smith, and have concentrated instead on the positive analysis (of wages, rents, profits and prices,) Smith himself considered secondary to his main argument that individualistic market property relations are beneficial to men and government _if_ proper protection is given to society generally from the excessive selfishness and corruption of some individuals.

Smith's ultimate goal was a moral improvement of men, not the increase in national or individual's opulence. Albion Small in his _Adam Smith and Modern Sociology_ has concluded that "Adam Smith's whole scheme of thinking ... might be explained as follows: The destiny of mankind is to work out a certain moral achievement.[1] This assertion is given weight by the views of Glenn R. Morrow, A. L. Macfie and Joseph Cropsey that Smith's critique on behalf of morality, justice and excellence belies his suggestion that opulence of nations and individuals was his primary end as signified by the full title of his major work.[2] George Stigler concludes that better men rather than increased income was the policy of the entire "Classical School" following from Smith's lead.[3]

This achievement of better men, justice and morality was not an empty abstract ideal for Smith: not simply "a utopia or oceana". To a degree, it had been the practical accomplishment of historical stages of progress, up to and including his commercial age. And ultimately this improvement of men and laws would provide a reasonable objective for future government policy proposals. Schumpeter makes the important judgement that Smith's advocacy of future policies in government and property were what interested him and his readers most, and that these were what accounted for the Wealth of Nations' lasting success. Yet, even more important, Schumpeter argues that Smith "made his analysis serve" those normative ends he advocated.[4] Though Schumpeter

---

1 Albion Small, Adam Smith and Modern Sociology, op.cit. p. 81.

2 An Inquiry into the Nature and Causes of the Wealth of Nations.

3 Stigler, Five Lectures op.cit., pp. 4-9.

4 Schumpeter, op.cit., p. 186.

would probably argue that Smith's economic analysis served his policy proposals, I have argued that Smith's analysis also frequently served to support his more ultimate normative goal - the improvement of men and government. His analysis helped to argue his case not only for free trade and maximum productivity, but also for the increase in justice and morality.

Each property stage of the four in his historical sketch is analysed in terms of its effect on men's behaviour, social cohesion, and form of government. Each tax he considered also from this vantage point for future society. Did it create improved, social, moral and political relations? The normative argument of the Wealth of Nations is that commerce and exchange introduced regular habits and behaviour and good government, "This though it has been the least observed is by far the most important of all their effects."[1]

II

For Smith, it is the individual's paramount desire for the approval of other men which motivates him to virtuous acts and to property accumulation. And this approval which men desire springs from their ability to sympathise with the situation or acts of one another. Although Smith gave numerous indications that self-interest was men's rational motive for their acquisition of wealth

---

1 WN I p. 433.

their more fundamental desire was to receive sympathy from other men for their material as well as their moral situation. That is, men sought to acquire approval by the acquisition of wealth. Thus I argued that sympathy rather than self interest was the basis of property in Smith's system of moral philosophy.

Next, it has been shown here that Smith held two unresolved and conflicting views of the source of property rights: first, labour was the cause of property and the measure of its value; and, secondly, social conventions and traditions of ownership by established laws were the proper justification of property and source of its origin.1 Smith implies that claims based upon either of these justifications of property rights, were capable of receiving the approval or positive sympathy of the public depending upon the circumstances of the case. Labour and convention are intermingled in Smith's thought as explanations of property claims to such an extent that both justly can be argued to be the source of rights at different historic periods. Yet, what is more important, they provide alternative justifications of present and future property rights.

From these crucial ambiguities about what can be shown to be Smith's fundamental theory of property, follow logically his indecisions about constituent forms of property in wages, rent and

---

1 Whether the second is a "theory" has been questioned in Ch. III.

profit. Smith had several theories of wages which I have referred to:[1] his supply and demand theory, and his reserve claimant theory. I have touched on Smith's various theories of rent"[2] his supply and demand theory, his exploitation theory and his differential theory. And finally, I have taken note of his theories of profits:[3] again a supply and demand theory, an exploitation theory, and his half way houses that provide justifications of some profits as actually the wages of labour, others as payments for effort of direction and supervision, and others as payments for risk of capital invested for periods of time.

I have argued that these theories often contradicted each other. If profit was usually a "fair and reasonable reward" for risk, how could it also be exploitation? If rent was always monopoly exploitation, how could it be based on a differential between worthless and valuable lands? Could rent accord with a supply and demand theory if it was always a monopoly? Likewise if wages were governed by supply and demand only, there was no logical reason why in the short run they could not fall below subsistence minimum level. If minimal wages always resulted from exploitation of the labourers by the masters' control of contracts, could wages also simultaneously rise and fall with supply and demand for labour?

---

1 See Ch. 7 "Alienation of Property: Effect Upon Individuals" sec. II.

2 See Ch. 7, sec. II.

3 See Ch. 7, sec. II.

In each case these alternative theories present a positive and a normative conception of wages, profits and rents. In each case Smith's ambivalence regarding wages, profit and rent reflects his deeper seated indecision about the justice or rights to that property from which these three incomes are derived. That is, Smith provides very equivocal justifications of the ownership of capital, land and the proper rewards of labour. The positive theories of supply and demand do not consider the justice of rent, profit and wages, they simply state the income levels to be expected from adjustment of different variables in the economy. The normative theories Smith presents, in each case are suggestions that property relations are based on exploitation of the propertiless by the propertied classes.

His positive discussions of property were based strictly on conventions of society as the justification and origin of ownership. That is, those who by whatever means had acquired property which the state now recognised as legally theirs, were the owners and the only owners that positive theory would consider in its analysis. On the other hand, Smith's normative theories of exploitation, each related to property as justified by labour. They described income as earned by effort, or risk, whether by labourers, managers, or landowners. These normative theories of exploitation imply that rewards gained by means other than effort or risk are unjust. Other implications from this argument were that conventions of society by which individuals possessed and justified property, were class controlled social conventions and class controlled governments who made the laws which upheld these conventions.

Smith was ambivalent in combining these positive and normative discussions of rewards. For example, he was led to analyse the many cases in which profits of master manufacturers and landlords were in fact "real wages" for actual labour they performed alongside their men, or efforts of directing their business. A similar equation of labourers risk with that of investors and landlord improvers was also implied to justify increased profits. Yet, Smith's more general suggestion remained, that most rent and interest and many profits involved no labour or effort of direction, and often little risk and so were unjust rewards. This impression was given added weight by Smith's various tax proposals which in case after case suggested that unearned income, or that derived without labour or risk, was a more proper subject for taxation than earned income. It was only their record of successful secrecy, corruption and removal of capital from countries with burdensome taxes which made Smith pause for a moment in levelling heavy burdens upon those who had such unearned incomes. In these discussions of an optional tax policy and optional distribution of wealth or incomes, Smith comes as close as he ever does to attempting an integration of his positive and normative property analysis.

III

Smith and the other members of the Scottish Historical School were influenced by John Locke's two distinct conceptions of property's origin: from labour, and from social conventions and civil laws. Yet Smith and the Scottish School fundamentally changed the scope of Locke's traditional inquiry into property. They divided history into progressive stages of property and productive development. And their method, although partly conjectural, was also characterised by empirical evidence about the various historical stages of property and production. Former historians had established facts and series of factual events. Smith and others of the Scottish School showed that there was a material basis of each historic period and that this made periods primarily distinguishable according to their mode of property, production, or mode of subsistence. Furthermore, they presumed an historic progression from primitive modes of property relations to advanced property which they termed the process of civilization.

Whereas the whole of the Scottish Historical School showed that property forms were the distinguishing characteristic of different historic periods, Smith was the first member of that School to set forth a clear scheme of the way these property forms evolved in a series of stages. And he was the one who attempted to set out a materialist explanation for the motive force of historic change and development from one property stage to the next. Smith created a motor for historic development: the material needs and drives of men. As expressed within various periods these material needs and drives caused developing forms of property, production, distribution and modes of subsistence. That is, unlike Ferguson, Smith established a scheme of material progress and stages of social development not only to distinguish historic periods from one another, but to establish the pressure of material needs and of production advance as the motive force of social development and the civilisation of man.

In setting out this scheme Smith was more conjectural and less factually historic than Ferguson. But just because of this clearer set of stages and clearer picture of the motive force of development, Smith's was less an exposition of the actual property of various societies (as was Ferguson's and Millar's treatment) and more an argument for seeing all of history in these material terms of property progression from barbarism to civilization.

## IV

The question "what is Smith's theory of property," is thus capable of no simple or single answer. He recognised four historic stages or periods of property development, and two separate origins of property justifications for property claims. Yet the two justifications are not distinguishable by being the products of different historic stages, one totally primitive and before government, the other civil, as in Locke's thought.

Although labour was the first justification of property it did not cease to be a justification when the first social conventions or civil laws were introduced into herding tribes or primitive agricultural communities. The labour theory and the conventional theory exist simultaneously and are intermingled as sources of property's origin and justification of rights and ownership in each of the three different stages of historical progress after the state and its laws of property came into being. Thus whether in societies or barbarous herdsmen, feudal farmers or modern industrial labourers, some property rights have been argued to originate in a man's labour and some from civil laws and conventions. Smith demonstrates this clearly in his detailed analysis of different kinds of property rights in his Chapter of his Lectures entitled "Private Law". In Chapter V of this present book I dealt in detail with Smith's assertion that "Property is acquired if five ways." These included occupation, accession, prescription, succession and voluntary transference. Although all these five methods of acquiring property were justified by existing codes of "private law" Smith persisted in recognising property rights derived from labour of industrial workers, craftsmen, colonists, inventors and authors. Smith suggests that property rights derived from individuals' labour should be guaranteed by the state to apprentices and colonists regardless of the existing conventions and laws.

Smith justifies the government's adjudication of property rights of newly found, or silted or reclaimed lands; of new corporations or companies, or prices in times of monopoly or famine, or national emergency. On the other hand, Smith criticises many acts of government which fixed property rights by laws creating new monopolies, bounties, protections, or justifying existing ones. Therefore, we find the state is advised to confer some property rights according to Smith, but not others. Likewise we find that labour of an individual confers some property rights to a just share of what it produces, but not necessarily to the whole of that produce. Furthermore, although Smith's labour-cost theory of value at times suggests some equality of property rewards, it is clear from a closer observation that equal labour justifies equal property rights only among labourers; not equal property rewards between labourers and masters.[1]

Finally because the protection of property was the reason for the creation and continuance of the state, conventional property rights have usually predominated over those rights derived from individual labour. Yet Smith does not argue that this is either just, or of greatest social benefit, as might Hume, or Bentham and other utilitarians. Smith, on the contrary, never commits himself wholly either to natural property rights of labourers, or to the

---

1 See Jacob Viner's commentary on Cannan in his <u>The Long View and the Short</u>, where he says, Cannan is mistaken in believing Smith went beyond this understanding of "equal rewards."

property justification from conventional rights for "social utility" or "reasons of state." His one possible integration of them was that property distribution ought to fulfill the general expectations of men, that they will continue in possession of those things which they have long enjoyed. This conception of property rights might also hold for the general expectation of men to enjoy the fruits of their labour.[1]

V

Smith believed that the historical progression of property stages was reflected in improved production and distribution, defence and justice. Mainly because of increased division of labour each stage brought about the progress not only of material production but of "property and manners", "the progress of civilisation". Thus Smith's argument seems to have been that increases in the division of labour had caused the progress, of good habits, greater industriousness, improved skills, and finally good government. If the division of labour could infinitely increase then logically production and wealth and "civilization" could continue to develop indefinitely as well.

But Smith's argument was not solely based on this positive logic. His actual argument was that <u>only</u> if the harmful effects of gross selfishness, corruption, injustice, class conflict and

---

1 See conclusion to Ch. III, "Locke's Property Doctrine".

industrialism's demoralisation of workers, were ameliorated or removed, could the future improvement of civilisation or individuals be assured.

Smith's observation of industry led him to describe the effects of detail tasks on the majority of workers, as alienation - the estrangement from their own human capabilities, physically, mentally and morally. Workers were also estranged from the ability to sympathise with others, that fundamental human attribute according to Smith for any and all moral sentiments and social intercourse. But although he criticised workers selfishness he especially attacked the selfishness of monopolising merchants, landlords and those who used government for their own ends and benefits.

Their awareness of the contrast between these benefits and corruptions of market society was the Scottish Historical School's most original contribution. It is in these contradictions that we must search for an answer to Smith's original question: of the effects of the commercial spirit on the temper and manners of the people and government.

There were three vital self contradictions of existing commercial society which Smith describes. The increased productivity and wealth of modern commerce was always accompanied by continual class tensions such that it was in the very character of commercial classes to oppose each other regardless of new wealth, or new laws. Second, the regularisation of habits and the increased skills caused by the advanced division of labour had simultaneously been accompanied by the estrangement of the vast majority of detail workers from their physical, mental and moral selves. And third, we find that the development of good structures of government through the division of labour which facilitated a separation of executive, legislative and justicial functions of the state, was in some cases entirely undermined by rampant corruption, and ubiquitous propertied-class control of politics.

## VI

These three central contradictions of market society are, I have argued, based on three dilemmas in Smith's conception of the nature of property. These were as follows. Labour was, or was not the basic form of property, its original and continuing justification for ownership and rewards. Second, property ought, or ought not to be the key differential between men of various social ranks and moral standing. And finally Smith poses the question of whether government's chief reason for being, was to protect existing property rights of the ruling class or to promote and protect the property right of all citizens.

Smith remained slightly ambiguous in his explanation for each of these vital self contradictions of existing society. But his general conclusions seem to have been as follows. Labour deserves a just reward. Men's rights to property in that which they have laboured upon, and rights to contractual justice, demanded that there be an attempt made by government to promote equity in labourers wages when disputes arose, or in times of need. Furthermore, the state should, as a general practice or policy, promote labourers' (the vast majority's) knowledge of their own interests and promote their opportunities for the acquisition of property especially in savings accounts in banks or savings institutions.

Smith believed that men sought property ultimately to obtain dignity or honour. Degrees of wealth would always be an index of social hierarchy, and to a moderate extent, it was right that this be so. Although this tendency provided a useful device for directing men to moral behaviour and social intercourse and industriousness, it was in fact a great deception since the beggar could possess the same happiness as the king. Thus, though men should be supplied with a dignified level of property as reward for their labour, and it was proper that they should strive for greater property, to increase their social estimation among their fellows, true dignity, he asserted, came only from virtuous behaviour. For this end, market society did help to make the vast majority's behaviour more regular and industrious, and law abiding. Among the hardworking poor, commerce led them along an identical path to prosperity and to virtue, specifically because the poor would never be capable of that great wealth which led the rich to feel contemptuous, to act immorally, and to be above the law.

## VII

At the foundation of Smith's property theory was a contradiction. This was his belief on the one hand that the origin of property is labour, and hence every man has his first and fundamental property in himself and his own labour; and on the other that the labourers in commercial society are the "propertyless." Smith never really resolved this issue. Any deeper seated explanation must rest upon Smith's indecision as to whether property was a normative right or a positive fact. But the basic issue was simply whether labour was property or not. Labour was the 'original property', according to Smith's conception of men's birthright. But according to his positive economic analysis, labour did not rise and fall in value as other property. Instead it was the goods and property objects which labour created which had changed in value, not labour itself. However, labour was equivalent to other property in that it was an exchangeable commodity. Thus in theory labour was both a source of rights and of real substance.

But in factual observations of his times Smith always conceived labour as "a sacrifice", "a giving up of a man's ease", effort, pleasure and time. It was "a toil, a trouble and an expense", "a giving up of his real desired interest". In short, labour, men's fundamental property, was at times alien to the labourer. Here was the root cause of alienation - in Smith's concept of labour itself. The basis of property alienation in exchange of labour was also the basis of human alienation in Smith's conception of labour as a sacrifice. Labour, although it was man's primary property, only had a value for men when it was being alienated or sacrificed for actual property goods.

Another source of alienation is found in Smith's basic description of moral relations. One principle of Smith's theory is that individuals all confront each other as spectators. Although individuals have the ability to sympathise or imagine the feelings of others they only sympathise with others on the basis of viewing the external behaviour of others. There is no direct relation between men's internal selves.

Smith believed that men adopt the role of "impartial spectator" to judge the conduct of other men and eventually adopt the role of impartial spectator to judge their own acts. Only from this self imposed alien's viewpoint which we adopt do we come to know and feel with others, or to know our own virtue and feel happy with ourselves.

However, Smith showed that men tended to sympathise more with those who possessed wealth or high position rather than with the sick, the poor or the virtuous. Also he stated that the vast majority of the public were, because of the detrimental effects of advanced division of labour, steadily loosing their capacity to enter into the ordinary sentiments of their fellows. It was thus that Smith illucidated a view of alienated relations of individuals as normal in commercial society.

Smith's argument was not that the sale or the division of labour should cease, but that considerable government attention was necessary to subsidise education to restore men's faculties and ability to sympathise. Thus wage labour, so long as it was expended or sacrificed with the labourer's consent, to obtain that which he desired more than his ease, was a proper "alienation" or sale.

Likewise, Smith was not against individuals adopting the external rules of morals and justice they saw in society around themselves. On the contrary this was an unavoidable part of social life and learning. The dangerous individual was he who did not sympathise with, or involve himself in other's judgments and opinions and so did not feel bound to keep the moral codes or obey the law.

In both the learning of sympathy, and learning obedience to the mechanism of the "free market", Smith envisaged a model of society in which occur repeated "confrontations of individuals" as "observed by spectators". Men confront each other as strangers or aliens and then as impartial observers or impartial consumers. In Hobbes and Locke these collisions or confrontations took place in a "state of nature" which was so unsafe that individuals were forced to form government. In Smith, who denied the factual character of a "state of nature," these random confrontations were part of his abstract theory of the way men were socialised. In his abstract conjectures Smith reached a similar conclusion to Hobbes and Locke, that in their confrontations men gradually tend to appreciate the need for law and government and some sort of protection from the greed and selfishness of others. Says Smith, governments make judicial decisions in response to similar random conflicts of individuals or groups. Economic markets for all kinds of property result from the same interactive conflicts and gradual sharing of interests.

Yet, alongside this abstract conception of indivuduals' socialization, Smith's historical approach described the organic growth from tribal family societies to modern classes and states. And he recognised that actual confrontations were, in practical affairs, especially those to do with property, strongly influenced by the conditions of that particular society and especially the historic economic relations of groups confronting one another.

In his factual descriptions Smith shows that existing society was not composed of atomistic individuals randomly colliding. Commercial society was composed of economic "classes". The "dominant classes" taking part in these confrontations and those who almost invariably triumphed were "the propertied rich". These were not collisions between equals but between "propertied" superiors and "propertiless" inferiors. Such collisions did not remove, but reinforced the prevailing distribution of wealth.

## VIII

In conclusion, the chapter on Smith's political experience and the chapter on the "Objectives of Government" have discussed Smith's political thought and the scope of government action which he prescribed. It was shown that Smith looked at politics in conjectural, historical, moral and legalistic terms and tended to blend these approaches in each of his works. Although he never coherently integrated them into the consistent history of jurisprudence which he promised to create in the first edition of the Theory of Moral Sentiments, nonetheless, there are some conclusions we can draw.

Smith believed government was simultaneously a natural and social creation. Although states were based on natural rights, their forms were the contrivances of ruling classes to control others. And thus the best government would attempt a contrived harmony of interests among sects, classes, individuals and in external international arrangements. On the other hand, Smith was a firm believer in the enlargement of the franchise, and equality of political and judical rights. But because he was convinced of the need to continue some "distinction of ranks," to ensure the moral "emulation" of the qualities of excellence in the virtuous man, he muddled, to some extent, the question of the degree of economic and social equality to be sought through legislation.

On the importance of politics in Smith's thought as a whole I would tend to agree with Harold Laski that "Few discussions of the sphere of government have been so productive as that in which Adam Smith gave a new basis to economic science."[1] But the question of the actual scope or objectives of government which Smith set forth are more difficult to evaluate.

---

1 Laski, Political Though in England From Locke to Bentham. op.cit., p. 9.

He most definitely was not advocating simply a laissez-faire government that would permit the monopolists and self interested businessmen a free rein over their own and the nations affairs. Government, in both the near and the most distant future at times must be activist. At times Government will always be required to intervene in the market. The state must always, not only provide defence, justice and essential public works, but must promote social welfare, and "equity". This promotional aspect of Smith's prescriptions for future government is given greater weight by Smith's tax proposals that called for the rich to be taxed more than proportionally to the poor in order to finance new benefits for the poorer classes. These benefits would include new public institutions and public works and new subsidies to education, health, and encouragements to public entertainments, arts and diversions.

By adding up all the activities Smith prescribed for future government we find that the state should in his view regulate or influence, to some extent or other, every broad area of property such as land, capital or labour. Moreover, although he disapproved of certain government controls on particular private activities, he did not specifically prohibit the state from taking action in any general area of property, if intervention or regulation could be reasonably argued to benefit the public.

Although Smith said government has always protected those social "ranks" who have propertied interests, his argument throughout his works was that the state ought to promote the property rights of all citizens. The tension between these two viewpoints was at the heart of his ambiguities concerning the scope and purpose of government.

# APPENDIX

## THE INFLUENCE UPON SMITH OF THE PHYSIOCRATS, MONTESQUIEU, MANDEVILLE AND LORD KAMES

In this thesis I dealt with the influence of Locke, Hutcheson and Hume upon Smith, and the general climate of thought among the members of the Scottish Historical School. Other sources of influence upon Smith have been studied in numerous works. The Physiocrats, Montesquieu, Mandeville and Lord Kames are the authors whose works are most frequently studied as sources of influence upon Smith. I will here list some of the more important works and their particular concerns in the study of Smith's predecessors.

The influence of the Physiocrats upon Smith's thought in the Wealth of Nations was thought to be vitally important until the end of the nineteenth century. Leslie Stephen was typical of most writers upon Smith in claiming their influence to be a most obvious source of his thought, especially concerning capital, productive and unproductive labour, distribution etc. Since 1896 this view has almost completely changed. Edwin Cannan's discovery of Smith's "lost" Lectures on Justice, Police Revenue and Arms in 1896 and the realization that Smith held his views concerning most subjects discussed in the Wealth of Nations long before travelling to France, and meeting or, even (according to the evidence) reading the Physiocrats, has forced critical opinion to question the degree of influence upon Smith attributable to the Physiocrats. Cannan has said in describing the relation of the Glasgow Lectures to the Wealth of Nations that "the dissertation on the division of labour, money, prices and the causes of the differences of wages in different employments, evidently existed very nearly in their present form before Smith went to France, and the scheme of distribution was wholly absent. It is plain that Smith acquired the necessity of the scheme of distribution from the Physiocrats."1

However, in 1937 W. R. Scott discovered Smith's Draft of the Wealth of Nations which he claims was written in 1763, so that Smith would secure the tutoring job that would take him to France. The text of this Draft and its date demonstrated that Cannan was probably wrong in even describing the Physiocrats as the source of Smith's theories of distribution, capital and of productive and unproductive labourers. These theories of Smith's are, as Scott shows, at times almost word for word the same in the Draft as they were to be in the final Wealth of Nations. On page 321 of Scott's book Adam Smith as Student and Professor, he claims that during 1763, although Smith knew the works of French philosophers, it is "highly improbable that he was acquainted with any work of the Physiocrats during this period. He was fully conversant with the chief sources from which they reached the general standpoint which they, in large measure, shared with him."

---

1 Lectures, p. XXXI

The controversy on the Physiocrats' influence still goes on nevertheless. For an appraisal of the current debate see Jacob Viner's "Guide to the Life of Adam Smith" where discussion still centres on Smith's use of the term "capitals".

The influence of Montesquieu's Spirit of the Laws upon Smith was first conjectured upon by Millar in a conversaton with Dugald Stewart. Millar believed that Montesquieu was the Bacon of the new social science, Smith the Newton. Montesquieu did indeed have the most profound influence upon Smith. It is probably just to say that Montesquieu's history of the development of law strongly influenced Smith in his general conception of the progressive stages in the history of production, property and manners. But it was more the influence of method, and broad historical approach rather than influence upon Smith's theory of property. Montesquieu did certainly influence Smith's conception of the different powers within the state - legislative - judicial - administrative - and their separate institutional heirarchy and allegiances. Yet Smith was perhaps more prone than Montesquieu to discount the real "separation" of these powers of government. Smith recognised that in England the separation was often more apparent than real, since the same group of landowners and a few merchants controlled all three branches of government. It was thus Smith's stronger interest in property which gave his social thought, and especially his conception of different political states, a quite new focus from that of Montesquieu. Perhaps it is for this reason, or because Montesquieu's influence upon Smith is so well known, that several authors, including Schlatter in his Private Property, and Lorimer in "The Social and Economic Philosophy of Adam Smith", have hardly mentioned Montesquieu's influence on Smith at all.

The influence of Bernard Mandeville's Fable of the Bees on Smith, Hutcheson and Hume and those who later adopted Smith's market psychology has often been mentioned, and has been the subject of considerable examination. Selby Bigg, Mandeville's biographer in his lengthy introduction considers specifically this issue, as does A. L. MacFie in his Individual In Society, pp. 43-4, 113-116, and Gladys Bryson in Man and Society, in the chapter on the social theory of the Scottish thinkers. Bryson, like several other authors, contrasts the influence of Mandeville on Smith's psychological assumptions with the influence of Hutcheson and Hume on the moral and philosophic assumptions. As shown by George Sabine, Leslie Stephen, Eric Roll and other authors of Histories of Political, Economic and Social thought, this influence of Mandeville extended not only to Smith's general view of human behaviour as it is sometimes thought, but to his conception of individual's conflicts and their harmony in the market. It, also showed itself in Smith's view of the purpose and policies of government. Lorimer's dissertation has a section dealing with Mandeville's system of thought, which includes a summary of the various similarities between his thought and

Smith's. Nathan Rosenberg's article "Mandeville and Laissez-Faire"[1] provides an excellent basis for further study of the foundation of Smith and Mandeville's agreement. Several recent authors have stressed the most important fact that Smith was among the few to take Mandeville's work seriously and not to dwell on Mandeville's unpopular view of general morals.

The influence upon Smith of Lord Kames (Henry Home), a famous lawyer, judge and agricultural and industrial improver in 18th century Scotland, has been the subject of some attention. Kames, in addition to his other activities was also an author who is still taken seriously in Scottish Jurisprudence. Kames' influence upon Smith's thought on property matters was briefly touched on in John Ramsay's Scotland and Scotsmen in the 18th Century.[2] Kames not only secured Smith his first lecturing position in Edinburgh[3] but was the older mentor for several members of the Scottish Historical School including Hume, Ferguson and Smith among others. Though David Daiches criticises Kames for being an intellectual lightweight in his book The Paradox of Scottish Culture, Bryson makes frequent mention of Kames' range of interests and influence by his theories and energetic promotion of

---

1 Nathan Rosenberg, "Mandeville and Laissez-Faire" Journal of the History of Ideas (1963).

2 John Ramsay, Scotland and Scotsmen in the Eighteenth Century, op.cit., Ch. III on "Lord Kames" and Ch. VI "Professors and Clergymen".

3 Rae, Life, pp. 30-31.

new industrial and agricultural methods. Smith's relation to Kames was for the most part one of gratitude and respect, as is shown by all the written testimonials describing him as "learned author" and "generous friend." Yet Smith also knew Kames' drawbacks as is shown by a chance comment to Boswell, a mutual friend which the letter recorded[1] and which has become the title of the most complete work on Kames, "'The Most Arrogant Man in the World': "The Life and Writings of Henry Home, Lord Kames".[2]

In spite of this comment Smith nonetheless was influenced by Kames' breadth of knowledge about actual property improvements. It is also reasonable to argue that Smith appears to have drawn from Kames both his conception of "propreity" and his distinct view of "justice" as a separate virtue with its special "necessity", in contrast to Hume's and Hutcheson's view of justice as but one of other virtues.

---

1 Rae, Life p. 341.

2 I. S. Ross "'The Most Arrogant Man in the World': The Life and Writings of Henry Home, Lord Kames." Dissertation submitted for the degree of Doctor of Philosophy at the University of Texas, Austin, Texas, 1960.

# BIBLIOGRAPHY

This Bibliography is divided into five parts. The first gives a complete list of Smith's works, and indicates the editions used in this book. The second section gives a list of the main works of some of Smith's predecessors and contemporaries which have been important to this study. The third section gives a catalogue of the books on Smith which I have found most useful. Fourth, I list the periodical literature on Smith which has been relevant to the issues considered in this work. The fifth section is a general bibliography of the other works cited.

# I
# WORKS OF ADAM SMITH


Draft - "An Early Draft of Part of the Wealth of Nations" ed W.R. Scott in W.R. Scott, Adam Smith as Student and Professor (Glasgow, 1937)

Lectures - Jurisprudence or notes from the Lectures on Justice, Police, Revenue and Arms Delivered in the University of Glasgow by Adam Smith in Edwin Cannan ed., Lectures on Justice, Police, Revenue and Arms delivered ... reported by a student in 1763 (Oxford, 1896)

- Lectures on Rhetoric and Belles Letters Delivered in the University of Glasgow by Adam Smith reported by a student in 1762-3 ed. John M. Lothian (London, 1963)

EPS - Essays on Philosophical Subjects, 1795 (Basil, 1799)

TMS - The Theory of Moral Sentiments: or An Essay Towards an Analysis of the Principles by which Men Naturally judge concerning the Conduct and Character, First of Their Neighbours, and afterwards of Themselves. Twelfth ed. in one volume (London, 1907) To which is added, "A Dissertation On the Origin Of Languages."

WN - An Inquiry into the Nature and Causes of the Wealth of Nations, ed. Edwin Cannan Sixth Ed. (in two volumes) London, 1950 (reprinted in the University Paperback series London, 1961.)

AR - "Adam Smith on the American Revolution: An Unpublished Memorial," ed, G.H. Guttridge, American Historical Review XXXVIII (1932-3) pp. 714-20

- "A Letter to William Stratham concerning the Death of David Hume, Nov. 9, 1776, "Scots Magazine January 1777 (edition cited: in David Hume, Essays Moral, Political and Literary ed. T.H. Green and T.H. Grose Vo. 1 London 1912)

- "A Dictionary of the English Language, by Samuel Johnson," Edinburgh Review January 1755 Appendix (anonymous)

- "A Letter to the Authors of the Edinburgh Review," Edinburgh Review July 1755 (anonymous)

Works - The Works of Adam Smith, ed. Dugald Stewart, 5 vols. (London, 1811-12)

II

The Works (referred to in this dissertation) of John Locke and Smith's Contemporaries in 18th Century Scotland

John Locke, An Essay Concerning Human Understanding, 2 vols. ed. A.C. Fraser (New York, 1959) (first ed. 1690)

John Locke, Essays on the Law of Nature ed. Wolfgang Von Leyden, (Oxford, 1954)

John Locke, Collected Works, London 1714 Including Some Considerations of the Lowering of Interest and Raising the Value of Money, and Further Considerations Concerning Raising the Value of Money and other papers on money. Considerations of Further Considerations are used for citations because all the papers in the volumes are numbered separately

John Locke, Two Treatises of Government, ed. Peter Laslett (Cambridge, 1963) (Hereafter cited as Two Treatises)

John Locke, The Works of John Locke, 10 vols. (Aalen, Germany, 1963) Photoduplicated reprint of the 1823 ed. (Scientia Verlag.)

Francis Hutcheson, Introduction to Moral Philosophy (Glasgow, 1747)

Francis Hutcheson, A System of Moral Philosophy, 2 vols. ed. William Leechmen (Glasgow, 1755)

David Hume, Enquiry Concerning Human Understanding and Concerning The Principles of Morals., ed. L. A. Selby-Biggs, Second ed. (Oxford, 1927) (First Part originally published 1748; second part 1751)

David Hume, Essary, Moral, Political and Literary. ed. T.H. Green and T. H. Gross (London 1912) (First part originally published 1741-2; second part 1752)

David Hume, The Letters of David Hume 2 vols. ed. T.V.T. Greig (Oxford, 1932)

David Hume, History of England from the Invasion of Julius Ceasar to the Revolution in 1688, (Edinburgh, 1773) ed. was the edition used by Smith the edition I have used is the 10 vol. (London 1810-11)

David Hume, Political Discourses in Essays, Political and Literary ed. T. H. Green and T. H. Gross (London, 1912) (Originally published 1752 in second part of Essays)

David Hume, Treatise of Human Nature (1793 ed) ed. L. A. Selby-Biggs, (Oxford, 1960)

Adam Ferguson, An Essay on the History of Civil Society, ed. Duncan Forbes (Edinburgh, 1966) originally published, Edinburgh 1766) (cited as History)

Adam Ferguson, Reflections Previous to the Establishment of A Militia, (London, 1756)

John Millar, The Origin of the Distinction of Ranks; or an Enquiry into the Circumstances which Give Rise to Influence and Authority in the Different Members of Society, (1771 Third ed. corrected and enlarged in William C. Lehmann, John Millar of Glasgow. op.cit., (Millar's writings in this work cited as Millar)

John Millar, An Historical View of the English Government; From the Settlement of the Saxons in Britain to the Accession of the House of Stewart, 1787; later revised and expanded and published as An Historical View of the English Government; From the Settlement of the Saxons in Britain to the Revolution in 1688; to which are Subjoined some Dissertations Connected with the History of the Government from the Revolution to the present time, 1803; of which portions are reprinted in William C. Lehmann, John Millar of Glasgow. op.cit., (Millar's writings in this work cited as Millar)

William Robertson, The History of America in Works 12 vols (London, 1812) vol. VII

William Robertson, The History of the Reign of Emperor Charles the Fifth With a View of the Progress of Society in Europe From the Supression of the Roman Empire, to the Beginning of the Sixteenth Century. 2 vols. (London 1857-67)

William Robertson, History of Scotland during the Reigns of Queen Mary and King James VI till his Accession to the Crown of England With a Review of the Scottish History Previous to That Period. (Edinburgh, 1840)

## III

## Books dealing with Adam Smith and his Thought


Mark Blaug, Economic Theory in Retrospect. (London, 1964)

James Bonar, Moral Sense (London and New York, 1930)

James Bonar, A Catalogue of the Library of Adam Smith Second ed. London, 1932 (cited as Catalogue)

James Bonar, Philosophy and Political Economy In some of their Historical Relations (London, 1927)

Gladys Bryson, Man and Society, The Scottish Inquiry of the 18th Century. (Princeton, 1945)

Edwin Cannan ed., Wealth of Nations By Adam Smith Sixth ed. (London, 1961)

Edwin Cannan ed., Lectures on Justice, Police, Revenue and Arms by Adam Smith (Oxford, 1896)

J. M. Clark (and others), Adam Smith 1776-1926 (Chicago, 1928) [The most important articles in this book also appeared in the Journal of Political Economy; they are listed here under their author's names and references are given to that journal.]

Joseph Cropsey, Polity and Economy: An Interpretation of the Principles of Adam Smith, (The Hague, 1956)

T. E. Cliffe Leslie, Essays in Political and Moral Philosophy. (London, 1881)

David Daiches, The Paradox of Scottish Culture: The Eighteenth Century Experience (Oxford, 1964)

J. A. Farrer, Adam Smith, (London, 1881)

Charles Ryle Fay, Adam Smith and the Scotland of His Day (Cambridge, 1956)

B. Franklin and F. Cordasco, A Bibliographical Checklist; An International Record of Critical Writings and Scholarship Relating to Adam Smith and Smithian Theory 1876-1950 (New York, 1965)

William D. Gramp, Economic Liberalism Vol II The Classical View (New York, 1965)

T. W. Hutcheson, "Positive" Economics and Policy Objectives (London, 1964)

Rudolph Kaulla, The Theory of the Just Price (London, 1940)

W. C. Lehmann, John Millar of Glasgow 1735-1801 His Life and Thought and his Contribution to Sociological Analysis (Cambridge, 1960) (Millar's writings in this work cited as Millar)

J. M. Lothian ed., Lectures on Rhetoric and Belles Lettres by Adam Smith, (London 1963)

James Lorimar, "The Economic and Social Philosophy of Adam Smith" Submitted for the degree of Ph.D. in the University of London 1966

Karl Marx, Capital 3 vols. (Moscow, 1961)

A. L. Macfie, Individual in Society, Papers on Adam Smith (London, 1967)

Adam Smith, Wealth of Nations, ed. James McCulloch, (London, 1843) James McCulloch has a lengthy Introduction

Ronald L. Meek, Studies in the Labour Theory of Value, (London, 1956)

Glenn R. Morrow, The Ethical and Economic Theories of Adam Smith (Cornell University Studies in Philosophy, No. 13) (New York, 1923) cited as Theories

Ethel Muir, The Ethical System of Adam Smith (Halifax, 1898)

John Rae, Life of Adam Smith, ed. Jacob Viner (New York, 1965) (cited as Life) Jacob Viner has a "Guide to John Rae's Life of Adam Smith" in this 1965 ed. (cited as "Guide")

David Ricardo, Principles of Political Economy and Taxation Vol. I in Works 10 Vols ed. Piero Sraffa and M. H. Dobb (Cambridge, 1962)

Joseph Schumpeter, History of Economic Analysis, ed. Elizabeth Boody Schumpeter (London, 1963)

W. R. Scott, Adam Smith as Student and Professor (Glasgow, 1937)

W. R. Scott, Studies Relating to Adam Smith during the Past Fifty Years ed. A. L. Macfie from Proceedings of the British Academy Volume XXVI London

Albion Small, Adam Smith and Modern Sociology (Chicago, 1907)

Albion Small, Origins of Sociology (New York, 1924)

Duggald Stewart "Account of the Life and Writings of Adam Smith" from the Transactions of the Royal Society of Edinburgh, read by Mr. Stewart January 21 and March 18, 1793. Stewart's "Account" was appended to Adam Smith: Essays on Philosophical Subjects, 1979 and has since been included in many works of Smith's as a biographical introduction

C. H. Taylor, A History of Economic Thought (New York, 1960)

W. L. Taylor, Francis Hutcheson and David Hume as Predecessors of Adam Smith (Duke University Press at Durham, N. Carolina, 1965) pp. 1-180

T. Yansihara ed., A Full and Detailed Catalogue of Books which Belonged to Adam Smith now in the Possession of the University of Tokyo (Tokyo, 1951)

Douglas Young and others Edinburgh in the Age of Reason, (Edinburgh, 1967)

## Articles on Adam Smith and his Thought


J. F. Bell, "Adam Smith, Clubman", Scottish Journal of Political Economy VII (1960) pp. 113-115

Henry J. Bitterman, "Smith's Empiricism and the Law of Nature", Journal of Political Economy XLVIII (1940) pp. 487-520; 703-34

V. W. Bladen, "Adam Smith on Productive and Unproductive Labour; A Theory of Full Development", Canadian Journal of Economics and Political Science 26 (1960) pp. 625-630

V. W. Bladen, "Adam Smith on Value," in Essays in Political Economy in Honour of E. I. Urwick ed. N. A. Innis (Toronto, 1938)

Mark Blaug, "Welfare Indicies in the Wealth of Nations", Southern Economic Journal XXVI (1959) pp. 150-153

James Bonar, "The Theory of Moral Sentiments by Adam Smith, 1759", Journal of Philosophic Studies. I (1926) pp. 333-53

Gladys Bryson, "Sociology and Moral Philosophy", Sociological Review Vol. 24 (1932) pp. 26-36

William F. Campbell, "Adam Smith's Theory of Justice, Prudence and Beneficence" American Economic Review, LVII (1967) pp. 571-576. Extract from Dissertation "Prudence, Justice and Beneficience as the Foundation of Adam Smith's Normative Economics" Submitted to the University of Virginia

Edwin Cannan, "Adam Smith's Lectures on Justice", Economic Journal Vol. (1896) p. 330

S. G. Checkland, "Prescriptions of the Classical Economists", Economics XX (1953) pp. 61-72

Arthur H. Cole, "Puzzles of the Wealth of Nations", Canadian Journal of Economics and Political Science 24 (1958) pp. 1-8

C. A. Cooke, "Adam Smith and Jurisprudence", Law Quarterly Review LI (1935) pp. 326-332

Herbert J. Davenport, "Ethics of the Wealth of Nations: Review of Ethical and Economic Theories of Adam Smith" With reply by G. R. Morrow, Philosophical Review 34 (1925) pp. 599-611

S. Davis, "Adam Smith and the Human Stomach", Quarterly Journal of Economics LXVIII (1954) pp. 275-286

W. C. Dunn, "Adam Smith and Edmund Burke; Complementary Contemporaries" Southern Economic Journal, VII (1941) pp. 330-46

Charles Ryle Fay, "Adam Smith and the Dynamic State", Economic Journal XL (1930) pp. 24-34

Duncan Forbes, "Scientific Whiggism: Adam Smith and John Millar", Cambridge Journal VII (1954) pp. 643-670

J.M.A. Gee, "Adam Smith's Social Welfare Function", Scottish Journal of Political Economy 15 (1968) pp. 283-99

William D. Gramp, "Adam Smith and the Economic Man", Journal of Political Economy LVI (1948) pp. 315-336

G. H. Guttridge, "Adam Smith and The American Revolution: An Unpublished Memorial" American Historical Review, XXXVIII (1932-3) pp. 714-720

F. Holender, "Some Technological Relationships in the Wealth of Nations and in Ricardo's Principles". Canadian Journal of Political Science Vol. 32 (1966) pp. 184-201

J. Laird, "The Social Philosophy of Smith's Wealth of Nations", Journal of Philosophical Studies II (1927) pp. 1-22

A. L. Macfie, "Adam Smith's Moral Sentiments as foundation for his Wealth of Nations", Oxford Economic Papers II (1959) pp. 12-26

A. L. Macfie, "Adam Smith's Theory of Moral Sentiments", Scottish Journal of Political Economy. VIII (1961) pp. 12-27

A. L. Macfie, "The Scottish Tradition in Economic Thought", Scottish Journal Of Political Economy II (1955) pp.81-103

Ronald L. Meek, "Adam Smith and the Classical Concept of Profit". Scottish Jounal of Political Economy I (1954) pp. 138-53

Ronald L. Meek, "The Scottish Contribution to Marxist Sociology", in John Seville ed. Democracy and the Labour Movement (London, 1954) ch. 3. Reprinted in Ronald L. Meek, Economics and Ideology and Other Essays: Studies in the Development of Economic Thought (London, 1967)

G. R. Morrow, "The Significance of the Doctrine of Sympathy in David Hume and Adam Smith". Philosophical Review XXXII (1923)

G. R. Morrow, "Adam Smith: Moralist and Philosopher", Journal of Political Economy XXXV (1927) p 321-42

Milton M. Myers, "Division of Labour as a Principle of Social Cohesion", Canadian Journal of Economics and Political Science XXXIII No. 3, Aug. (1967) p. 432

H. Myint, "Welfare Significance of Productive Labour: A Reinterpretation of the Classical Doctrine", Review of Economic Studies XI (1943) pp. 20-30

Royal Pascall, "Property and Society - The Scottish Historical School of the 18th Century", Modern Quarterly (London) Vol I (1938) pp. 167-178

H.M. Robertson and W.L. Taylor, "Adam Smith's Approach to the Theory of Value", Economic Journal LXVII (1957) pp. 181-198

Nathan Rosenberg, "Adam Smith, Consumer Tastes and Economic Growth", Journal of Political Economy 66 (1968) pp. 361-74

Nathan Rosenberg, "Adam Smith on the Division of Labour: Two Views of One?", Economica 30 (1963) pp. 23-32

Nathan Rosenberg, "Some Institutional Aspects of the Wealth of Nations" Journal of Political Economy vol 68 (1960) pp. 557-70

G. Rosenbluth, "A Note on Labour, Wages and Rent in Smith's Thoery of Value", Canadian Journal of Economics and Political Science Vol 35 No. 2 (1969) pp. 308-314

Albert Salomon, "Adam Smith as Sociologist", Social Research, XII (1945) pp. 22-42

W. R. Scott, "Adam Smith at Downing Street. 1766-1767" Economic History Review VI (1936) pp. 79-89

W. R. Scott, "Adam Smith and the City of Glasgow", Proceedings of the Royal Philosophical Society of Edinburgh LII (1923) pp. 138-148

W. R. Scott, "Adam Smith and the Glasgow Merchants", Economic Journal XLIV (1934) pp. 506-8

Andrew Skinner, "Economics and History - The Scottish Enlightenment", Scottish Journal of Political Economy XII (1965) pp. 1-22

Andrew Skinner, "Natural History in the Age of Adam Smith", Political Studies XV (1967) pp. 32-48

W. L. Taylor "Eighteenth Century Scottish Political Economy. The Impact on Adam Smith and his Work, of his association with Frances Hutcheson and David Hume" South African Journal of Economics XXIV (1956) pp. 261-276

W. L. Taylor and H. M. Robertson, "Adam Smith's Approach to the theory of Value", Economic Journal (LXVIII) (1957) pp. 181-198

H. B. Vanderblue, "An Incident in the Life of Adam Smith, Commissioner of his Majesty's Customs", American Historical Review XXVII (1937) pp. 305-8

Jacob Viner, "Adam Smith and Laissez-Faire" first published in Journal of Political Economy, XXXV (1927) pp. 198-232. Though it was reprinted in Adam Smith 1776-1926 ed. John Clark (Chicago, 1928) and in Jacob Viner, The Long and the Short (Glencoe, III 1958) I cite it as "ASLF" and its original page references in JPE to distinguish this article from others in these two later works

Jacob Viner, "The Intellectual History of Laissez-Faire", Journal of Law and Economics III (1960) pp. 45-69

E. G. West, "Adam Smith's Two Views on the Division of Labour", Economica 31 (1964) pp. 23-32

E. G. West, "The Political Economy of Alienation: Karl Marx and Adam Smith" Oxford Economic Papers Vol 21 (1969) pp.1-23

V

## General Bibliography of Other Works Used


T.S. Ashton, An Economic History of England in the 18th Century (London, 1966)

T.S. Ashton, The Industrial Revolution 1760-1830 (London, 1962)

Ernest Barker, Social Contract: Locke, Hume Rousseau (London, 1960)

Ernest Beaglehole, Property, (London, 1931)

M.W. Beresford, "Commissioners of Enclosure", Economic History Review, Vol. XVI (1944) pp. 130-40

Arthur Birnie, An Economic History of Europe 1760-1939 (London, 1964)

Robert Brady, Historical Treatise of Cities and Burgs or Boroughs (London, 1711)

Alexander Campbell, Journey from Edinburgh Through North Britain, 2 vols. (London, 1802)

R.H. Campbell, Scotland Since 1707 Rise of an Industrial Society (Oxford, 1965)

Alfred F. Chalk, "Natural Law and the Rise of Economic Individualism in England", Journal of Political Economy LIX (1951) pp. 332-347

S.G. Checkland "Scottish Economic History: Recent Work", Economica 31 (1964) pp. 296-313

M. Cherno, "Locke on Property" Ethics, 61 (1959)

Maurice Cranston, John Locke: A Biography (London, 1957)

C.J. Czajkowski, The Theory of Private Property in Locke's Political Philosophy (Notre Dame, Ind. USA. 1941)

Phyllis Deane, The First Industrial Revolution (London, 1967)

Daniel Defoe, A Tour Through England and Wales, 2 vols. (London, 1948)

K.E. Digby, An Introduction to the Law of Real Property (Oxford, 1982)

John Dunn, The Political Thought of John Locke (Cambridge, 1969)

Keith Grahame Feiling, The Second Tory Party 1714-1832 (London, 1938)

H.A.L. Fisher, A History of Europe 3 vols. Vol II esp. From the Beginning of the Eighteenth Century to 1935 (London, 1962)

F.H. Giddings, The Principles of Sociology (New York, 1896)

F.H. Giddings, Studies in the Theory of Human Society, (New York, 1922)

Otto Gierke, Natural Law and the Theory of Society, trans. Ernest Barker (Boston, 1957)

J.W. Gough, John Locke's Political Philosophy, Eight Studies, (Oxford, 1950)

Malcolm Gray, The Highland Economy 1750-1850 (Edinburgh, 1957)

John C. Grey, Restraints Upon the Alienation of Property (Boston, 1895)

Hugo Grotius, De Iure Belli et Pacis, Eng. Trans. Francis W. Kelsey (Oxford, 1925) as No. 3 of "Classics of International Law"

H.J. Habakkuk, "English Landownership, 1680-1740", Economic History Review vol. X (1957) pp. 1-17

Elie Halevy, The Growth of Philosophical Radicalism (London, 1949)

Henry Hamilton, "Economic Growth in Scotland 1720-1770" Scottish Journal of Political Economy VI (1959)

Henry Hamilton, An Economic History of Scotland in the 18th Century (Oxford, 1963)

Henry Hamilton, The Industrial Revolution in Scotland (Oxford, 1936)

John Lawrence, (and Barbara Hammond), The Skilled Labourer 1760-1832 (London, 1920)

John Lawrence, (and Barbara Hammond), The Town Labourer 1760-1832 (London, 1936)

John Lawrence (and Barbara Hammond), The Village Labourer 1760-1832 (London, 1948)

James Handley, The Agricultural Revolution in Scotland (Glasgow, 1963)

C.P. Hill, British Economic and Social History 1700-1939 (London, 1966)

Thomas Hobbes, Leviathan or the Matter, Forme and Power of a Commonwealth Ecclesiastical and Civil ed. Michael Oakeshott, (Oxford, 1960)

E.J. Hobsbawm, Labouring Men; Essays in the History of Labour (London, 1976)

Eric Hobsbawm, Industry and Empire (London, 1968)

T. Johnston, History of the Working Classes in Scotland (Glasgow, 1921)

Willmore Kendall, "John Locke and the Doctrine of Majority Rule", Illinois Studies in the Social Sciences, Vol XXXVI No. 2 (Urbanna, III 1941)

Harold J. Laski, Political Thought in England from Locke to Bentham (London, 1937)

Pashell Larkin, Property in the 18th Century, with Special Reference to England and Locke (Cork, 1930)

William C. Lehmann, Adam Ferguson and the Beginnings of Modern Sociology (New York, 1930)

Staughton Lynd, Philosophical Origins of American Radicalism, (New York, 1968)

C.B. MacPherson, "Locke on Capitalist Appropriation". Western Political Quarterly VII I (Salt Lake City, Utah, USA 1951)

C.B. MacPherson, The Political Theory of Possessive Individualism (Oxford, 1962)

C.B. MacPherson, "The Social Bearing of Locke's Political Theory", Western Political Quarterly X (1954)

David MacPherson, Annals of Commerce, 4 vols. (London, 1805)

James Makinnon, The Social and Industrial History of Scotland from The Union to the Present Time (London, 1921)

Bernard Mandeville, The Fable of the Bees: Or, Private Vices, Publick Benefits, First volume 1714, containing "The Grumblin Hive: Or, Knaves turn'd Honest" first published 1705, second volume 1729 ed. F.B. Kaye, two volume, Oxford, 1924 (cited as Fable)

William Marshal, The Landed Property of England (London, 1804)

William Marshal, On the Appropriation and Enclosure of Commonable and Intermixed Lands (London, 1801)

M.W. Marwick, Scotland in Modern Times (London, 1964)

Karl Marx, The Holy Family (Moscow/London, 1956)

Karl Marx, Theories of Surplus Value (Moscow/London, 1956)

Brian Redman Mitchell and Phyllis Deane, Abstract of British Historical Statistics (Cambridge, 1962)

H. Myint, Theories of Welfare Economics (Cambridge, Mass. 1948) ch. 2

Lewis Namier, Charles Townshend His Character and Career (Cambridge, 1959)

Lewis Namier, England in the Age of the American Revolution, (London, 1930)

Lewis Namier, The Structure of Politics at the Accession of George III 2 vols (1929) (London, 1963) cited as Structure

Fritz Papenheim, The Alienation of Modern Man (New York, 1959)

William Petty, "An Essay Concerning the Multiplication of Mankind" in Several Essays in Political Arithmetic (London, 1682)

J.H. Plumb, Chatham (London, 1953)

J.H. Plumb, England in the Eighteenth Century (Harmondsworth, 1950)

J.H. Plumb, The First Four Georges (London, 1956)

J.H. Plumb, The Growth of Political Stability in England 1675-1725 (London, 1967)

J.H. Plumb, Sir Robert Walpole 2 vols (London, 1956, 1960)

Karl Polanyi, The Great Transformation (Boston, Mass. 1957)

Edward Porritt and A.G. Porritt, The Unreformed House of Commons: Parliamentary Representation Before 1832, 2 vols. (Cambridge, 1909)

John Prebble, The Highland Clearances (London, 1963)

Property Its Duties and Right: Historically, Philosophically and Religiously Regarded, Essays by Various Writers ed. Charles Gore (London, 1922)

Samuel Pufendorf, De Jure Nture, et Gentium, Eng. trans. Basil Kennet (London, 1710) (first published, Lund, 1672)

John Ramsay of Ochtertyre, Scotland and Scotsmen in the 18th Century, 2 vols. ed. Alexander Allardyce (Edinburgh, 1888)

Arthur Redford, The Economic History of England 1760-1860 (London, 1965)

David G. Ritchey, Darwin and Hegel with other Philosophical Studies (London, 1893)

Patrick William Joseph Riley, The English Ministers and Scotland 1707-1727 (London, 1964)

Eugene Rotwein, Hume's writings on Economics (Madison, Wisconsin, 1955)

George H. Sabine, History of Political Theory (London, 1963)

Richard Schlatter, Private Property: The History of an Idea (London, 1951)

W.R. Scott, Francis Hutcheson (Oxford, 1900)

Walter M. Simon "John Locke Philosophy and Political Theory", American Political Science Review 45 (1951) pp. 386-399

Peter Stein, "The General Notions of Contract and Property in Eighteenth Century Scottish Thought", Juridical Review (1963) pp. 1-13.

Peter Stein, "Legal Thought in Eighteenth Century Scotland", Juridical Review (no vol) (1957) p. 1-20

Leslie Stephen, History of English Thought in the 18th Century 2 vols. (London, 1876)

Duggald Stewart, Collected Works, 11 Vols. ed. William Hamilton (Edinburgh, 1854-60)

George Stigler, Five Lectures on Economic Problems (London, 1952)

Leo Strauss, Natural Right and History (Chicago, 1953)

O.H. Taylor, A History of Economic Thought (New York, 1960)

W.E. Tate, "The Commons' Journals as Sources of Information Concerning the Eighteenth-Century Enclosure Movement", Economic Journal, Vol. LIV (1944) pp. 75-95

W.E. Tate, "Members of Parliament and the Proceedings upon Enclosure Bills", Economic History Review XII, (1942) pp. 68-75

W.E. Tate, "Opposition to Parliamentary Encosure in Eighteenth-Century England", Agricultural History, Vol 19 (1946) pp. 137-42.

O.H. Taylor, "Economics and the Idea of Natural Law" and "Economics and the Idea of Jus Naturale", Quarterly Journal of Economics 1929 and 1930 (reprinted in O.H. Taylor, Economics and Liberalism: Collected Papers (Cambridge Mass., 1955)

Edward P. Thompson, The Making of the English Working Classes, (London, 1963)

Tracts Relating to Trade Manuscript 13. Volume of Papers filed at the British Museum.

George Macauley Trevelyan, History of England (London, 1937)

James Tyrrell, Brief Disquisition of the Laws of Nature (London, 1701)

Brian Tunstall, William Earl of Chatham, (London, 1938)

C.A. Viano, John Locke, dal Razionalismo al Illuminismo (Turin, 1960)

Jacob Viner, The Long View and the Short (Glencoe, 1958)

R.R. Watcott, English Politics in the Early Eighteenth Century (London, 1956)

Sidney and Beatrice Webb, History of Trade Unionism (London, 1950)

Basil Willey, The 18th Century Background (Harmondsworth, 1962)

A.F. Basil Williams, The Life of William Pitt, Earl of Chatham 2 vols. (London, 1915)

Charles Wilson, England's Aprenticeship 1603-1763 (London, 1966)

Sheldon Wollin, Politics and Vision (Boston, 1960)

For Product Safety Concerns and Information please contact our EU
representative GPSR@taylorandfrancis.com
Taylor & Francis Verlag GmbH, Kaufingerstraße 24, 80331 München, Germany

ɔntent.com/pod-product-compliance
Group UK Ltd.
ɔynes, MK11 3LW, UK
ʾ26
ʾB/1393
8 1 1 3 8 2 3 0 6 1 3 *